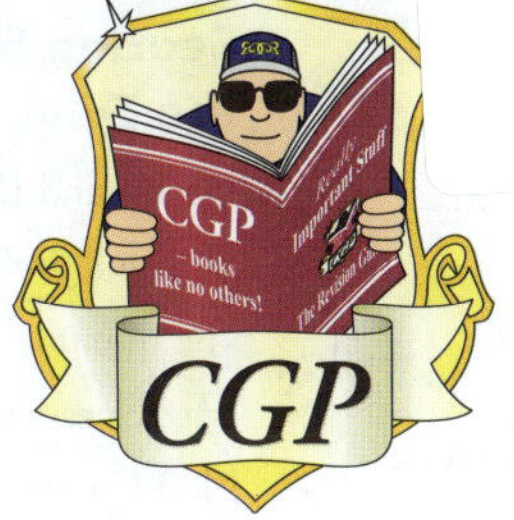

Get your facts straight with CGP!

This CGP Knowledge Organiser has one mission in life — helping you remember the key facts for Edexcel GCSE Combined Science.

We've boiled every topic down to the vital definitions, facts and diagrams, making it all easy to memorise.

There's also a matching Knowledge Retriever book that'll test you on every page. Perfect for making sure you know it all!

CGP — still the best! ☺

Our sole aim here at CGP is to produce the highest quality books — carefully written, immaculately presented and dangerously close to being funny.

Then we work our socks off to get them out to you — at the cheapest possible prices.

Contents

Section 20 — Forces and Energy

Section 21 — Electricity and Circuits

Section 22 — Magnetic Fields

Section 23 — Matter

Core Practicals

Practical Skills

This book only contains the Physics equations that you need to remember.
All other Physics equations will be given to you in the exam.

Published by CGP
From original material by Richard Parsons.
Editors: Ellen Burton, Katherine Faudemer, Emily Forsberg, Sharon Keeley-Holden, Luke Molloy, Sarah Pattison, Claire Plowman, Rachael Rogers, Charlotte Sheridan and George Wright.
Contributor: Paddy Gannon
With thanks to Emily Smith for the copyright research.
ISBN: 978 1 78908 850 2

Printed by Elanders Ltd, Newcastle upon Tyne.
Clipart from Corel®
Illustrations by: Sandy Gardner Artist, email sandy@sandygardner.co.uk

The Scientific Method

Developing Theories

Come up with hypothesis
↓
Test hypothesis
↓
Evidence is peer-reviewed
↓
If all evidence backs up hypothesis, it becomes an accepted theory.

HYPOTHESIS — a possible explanation for an observation.

PEER REVIEW — when other scientists check results and explanations before they're published.

Accepted theories can still change over time as more evidence is found, e.g. the theory of atomic structure:

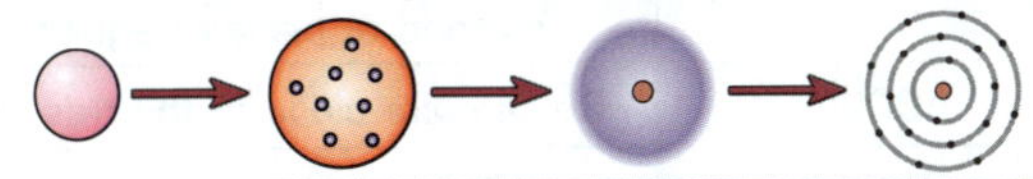

Models

REPRESENTATIONAL MODELS — a simplified description or picture of the real system, e.g. the kinetic theory model of matter:

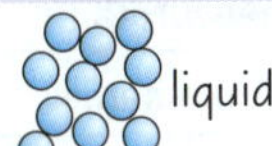

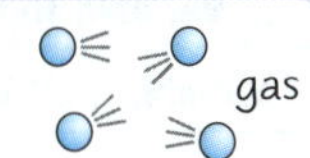

Models help scientists explain observations and make predictions.

COMPUTATIONAL MODELS — computers are used to simulate complex processes.

Issues in Science

Scientific developments can create four types of issue:

1. **Economic** — e.g. beneficial technology, like alternative energy sources, may be too expensive to use.
2. **Environmental** — e.g. new technology could harm the natural environment.
3. **Social** — decisions based on research can affect society, e.g. taxes on fossil fuels.
4. **Personal** — some decisions affect individuals, e.g. a person may not want a wind farm being built near to their home.

Media reports on scientific developments may be oversimplified, inaccurate or biased.

Hazard and Risk

HAZARD — something that could potentially cause harm.

RISK — the chance that a hazard will cause harm.

Hazards associated with science experiments include:

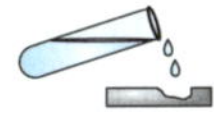

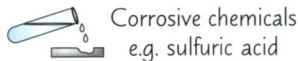

Corrosive chemicals e.g. sulfuric acid

Faulty electrical equipment

Fire from Bunsen burners

The seriousness of the harm and the likelihood of it happening both need consideration.

Designing & Performing Experiments

Collecting Data

Data should be...	
REPEATABLE	Same person gets same results after repeating experiment using the same method and equipment.
REPRODUCIBLE	Similar results can be achieved by someone else, or by using a different method or piece of equipment.
ACCURATE	Results are close to the true answer.
PRECISE	All data is close to the mean.

Reliable data is repeatable and reproducible.

Valid results are repeatable and reproducible and answer the original question.

Fair Tests

INDEPENDENT VARIABLE	Variable that you change.
DEPENDENT VARIABLE	Variable that is measured.
CONTROL VARIABLE	Variable that is kept the same.
CONTROL EXPERIMENT	An experiment kept under the same conditions as the rest of the investigation without anything being done to it.
FAIR TEST	An experiment where only the independent variable changes, whilst all other variables are kept the same.

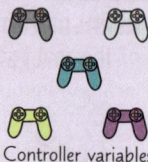

Controller variables

Control experiments are carried out when variables can't be controlled.

Four Things to Look Out For

1. **RANDOM ERRORS** — unpredictable differences caused by things like human errors in measuring.
2. **SYSTEMATIC ERRORS** — measurements that are wrong by the same amount each time.
3. **ZERO ERRORS** — systematic errors that are caused by using a piece of equipment that isn't zeroed properly.
4. **ANOMALOUS RESULTS** — results that don't fit with the rest of the data.

Anomalous results can be ignored if you know what caused them.

Processing Data

Calculate the **mean** — add together all repeat measurements and divide by number of measurements.

UNCERTAINTY — the amount by which a mean result may differ from the true value.

$$\text{uncertainty} = \frac{\text{range}}{2}$$

range: largest measurement minus smallest measurement

In any calculation, you should round the answer to the lowest number of significant figures (s.f.) given.

Presenting Data

Bar Charts

Bar charts can be used when independent variable is categoric or discrete.

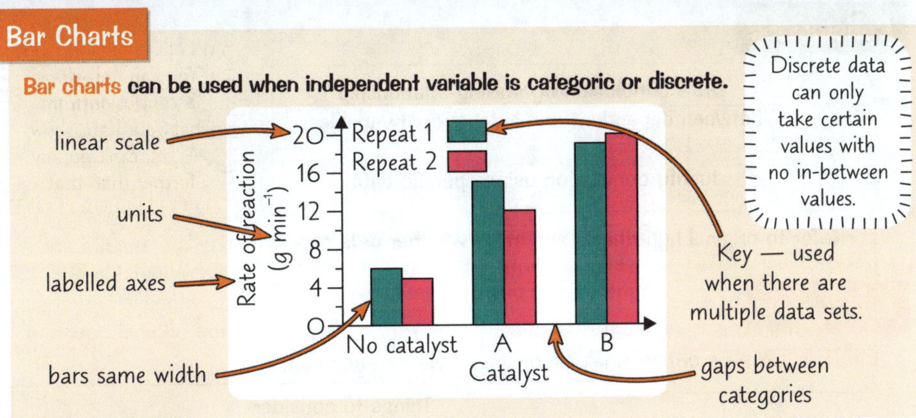

Plotting Graphs

Graphs can be used when both variables are continuous.

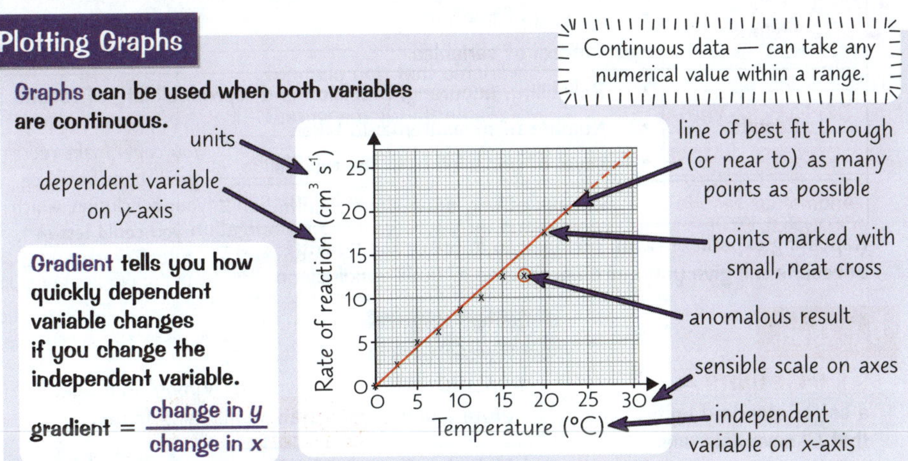

Gradient tells you how quickly dependent variable changes if you change the independent variable.

$$\text{gradient} = \frac{\text{change in } y}{\text{change in } x}$$

Three Types of Correlation Between Variables

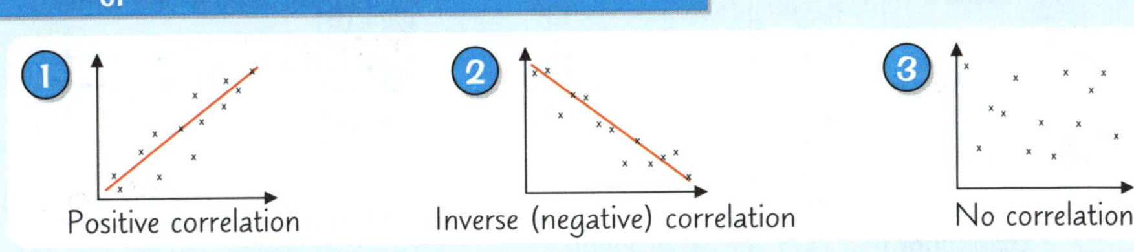

1. Positive correlation
2. Inverse (negative) correlation
3. No correlation

Possible reasons for a correlation:

Chance — correlation might be a fluke.

Third variable — another factor links the two variables.

Cause — if every other variable that could affect the result is controlled, you can conclude that changing one variable causes the change in the other.

Conclusions, Evaluations and Units

Conclusions

Draw conclusion by stating relationship between dependent and independent variables.

↓

Justify conclusion using specific data.

↓

Refer to original hypothesis and state whether data supports it.

You can only draw a conclusion from what your data shows — you can't go any further than that.

Evaluations

EVALUATION — a critical analysis of the whole investigation.

	Things to consider
Method	• Validity of method • Control of variables
Results	• Reliability, accuracy, precision and reproducibility of results • Number of measurements taken • Level of uncertainty in the results
Anomalous results	• Causes of any anomalous results

Repeating experiment with changes to improve the quality of results will give you more confidence in your conclusions.

You could make more predictions based on your conclusion, which you could test in future experiments.

S.I. Units

S.I. BASE UNITS — a set of standard units that all scientists use.

Quantity	S.I. Unit
mass	kilogram (kg)
length	metre (m)
time	second (s)
temperature	kelvin (K)
current	ampere (A)
amount of a substance	mole (mol)

Scaling Units

SCALING PREFIX — a word or symbol that goes before a unit to indicate a multiplying factor.

Multiple of unit	Prefix
10^{12}	tera (T)
10^{9}	giga (G)
10^{6}	mega (M)
1000	kilo (k)
0.1	deci (d)
0.01	centi (c)
0.001	milli (m)
10^{-6}	micro (μ)
10^{-9}	nano (n)
10^{-12}	pico (p)

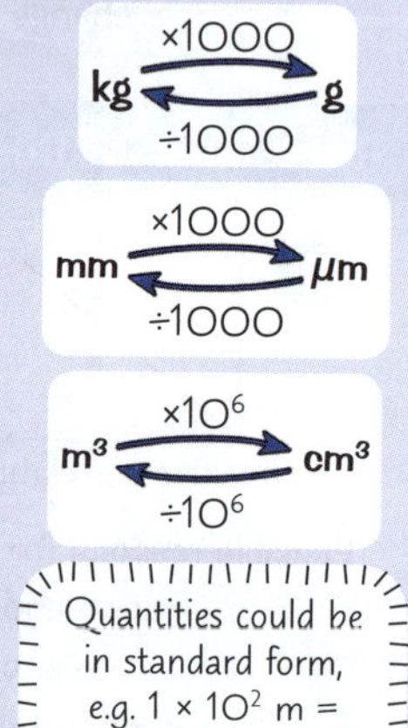

Quantities could be in standard form, e.g. 1×10^2 m = 100 m.

Cells

Eukaryotic Cells

ANIMAL CELL

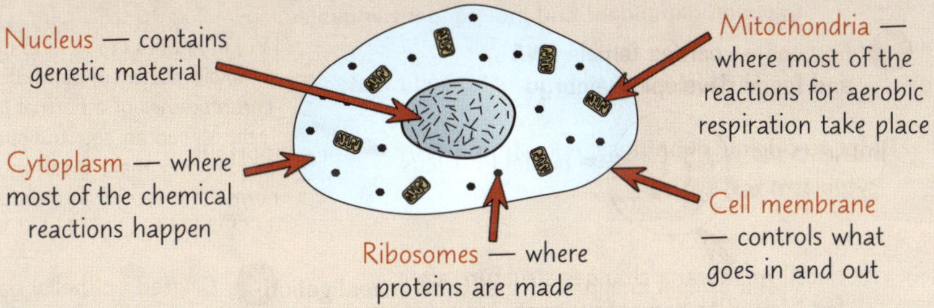

Nucleus — contains genetic material
Mitochondria — where most of the reactions for aerobic respiration take place
Cytoplasm — where most of the chemical reactions happen
Cell membrane — controls what goes in and out
Ribosomes — where proteins are made

Plant cells have the subcellular structures labelled above, as well as the ones labelled here.

PLANT CELL

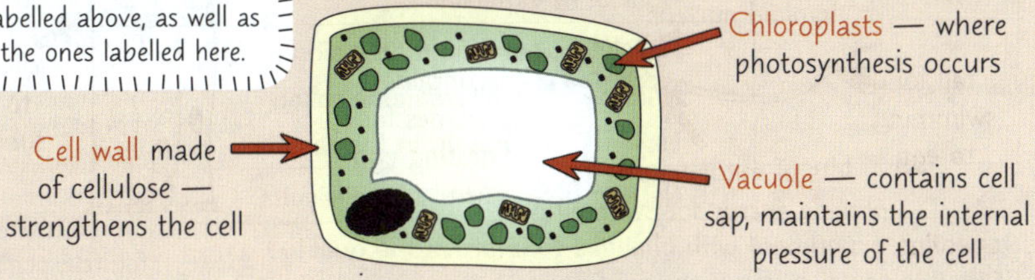

Chloroplasts — where photosynthesis occurs
Cell wall made of cellulose — strengthens the cell
Vacuole — contains cell sap, maintains the internal pressure of the cell

Prokaryotic Cells

BACTERIAL CELL

Cell membrane
Ribosome
Chromosomal DNA — controls cell's activities and replication
Plasmid DNA — can be passed between bacteria
Flagellum — for movement

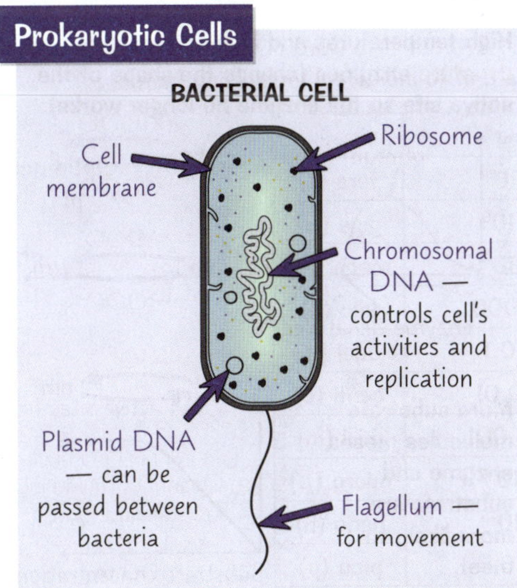

Microscopy

Electron microscopes were invented later than **light** microscopes.

They have a higher **magnification** and **resolution** than light microscopes.

This means they let us see smaller things in more detail, so we can understand subcellular structures better now.

Specialised Cells and Enzymes

Three Specialised Cells

SPECIALISED CELL — a cell that has a structure adapted to its function.

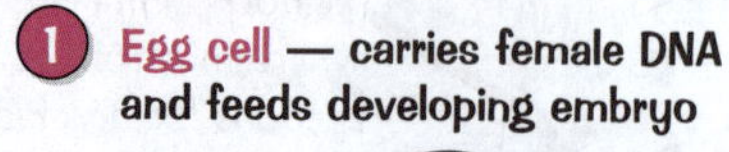

1 Egg cell — carries female DNA and feeds developing embryo

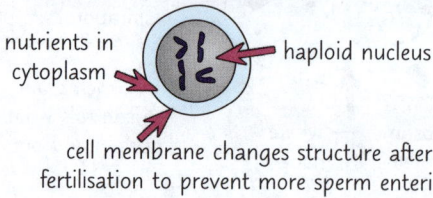

nutrients in cytoplasm

haploid nucleus

cell membrane changes structure after fertilisation to prevent more sperm entering

Haploid nuclei contain half the chromosomes of a normal body cell. When an egg and sperm cell join, they make a cell with the normal number of chromosomes.

2 Sperm cell — transports male DNA to egg

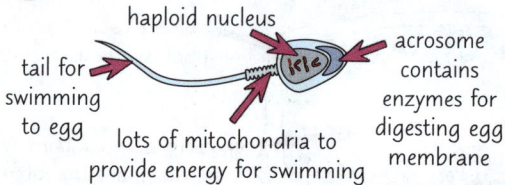

haploid nucleus

tail for swimming to egg

acrosome contains enzymes for digesting egg membrane

lots of mitochondria to provide energy for swimming

3 Ciliated epithelial cell — moves substances along internal surfaces (e.g. mucus in airways)

Enzymes

Enzymes catalyse (speed up) chemical reactions.

Each enzyme only catalyses one specific reaction because of the unique shape of its active site.

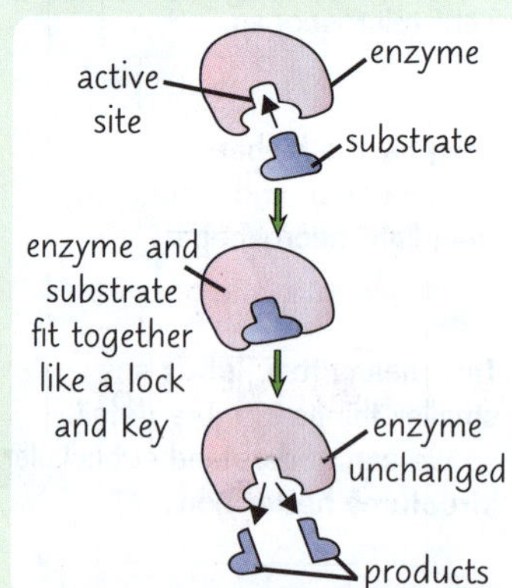

Factors Affecting Enzyme Activity

High temperatures and high and low pHs denature enzymes (change the shape of the active site so the enzyme no longer works).

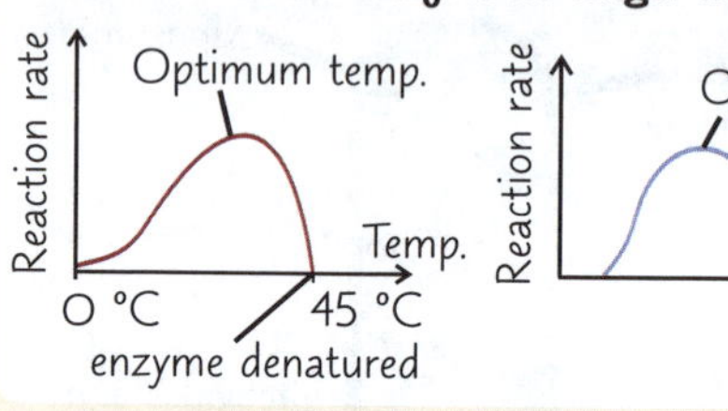

More substrate molecules means enzyme and substrate are more likely to meet.

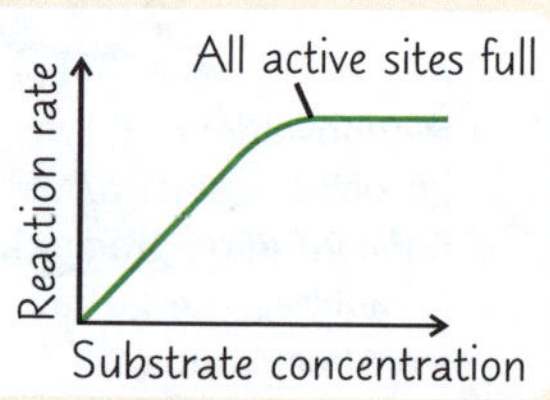

Enzymes and Transport in Cells

Enzymes in Organisms

Enzymes break big molecules into smaller ones, which are used for life processes.

Enzymes also catalyse synthesis reactions — building big molecules from smaller ones.

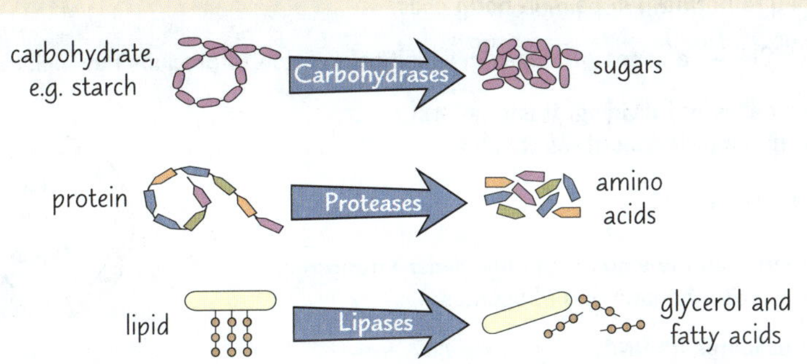

Diffusion

DIFFUSION — the net (overall) movement of particles from an area of higher concentration to an area of lower concentration.

Only very small molecules (e.g. glucose) can diffuse across cell membranes.

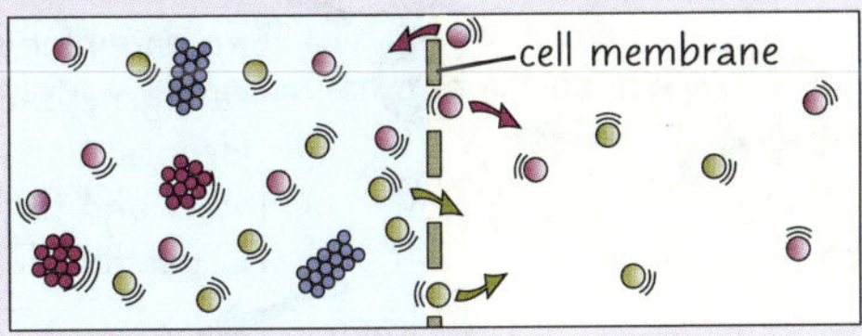

Osmosis

OSMOSIS — the net movement of water molecules across a partially permeable membrane from a region of higher water concentration to a region of lower water concentration.

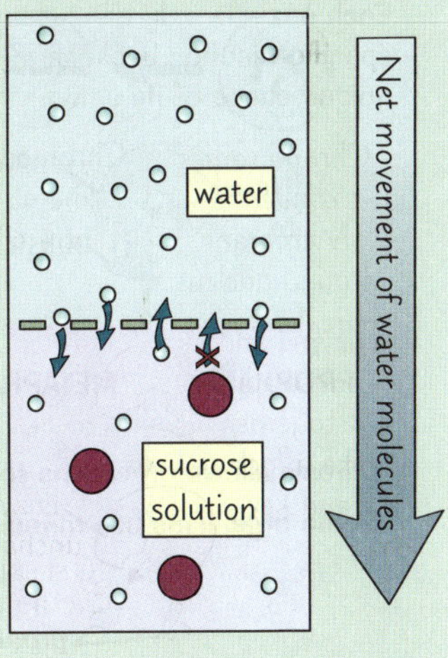

Active Transport

ACTIVE TRANSPORT — the movement of particles against a concentration gradient. It requires energy from respiration.

Transport this info into your head, even if it's going against your concentration gradient.

The Cell Cycle

Chromosomes and the Cell Cycle

CHROMOSOMES — coiled up lengths of DNA molecules, which carry **genes**. They're found in the nucleus and they're normally in pairs in body cells.

Cells with two copies of each chromosome are 'diploid'.

CELL CYCLE — a series of stages in which cells divide to produce new cells.

When a cell is not dividing, it is in **interphase**.
Before dividing, it does three things:

1. Grows in size.
2. Increases the amount of subcellular structures, e.g. mitochondria and ribosomes.
3. Duplicates its DNA.

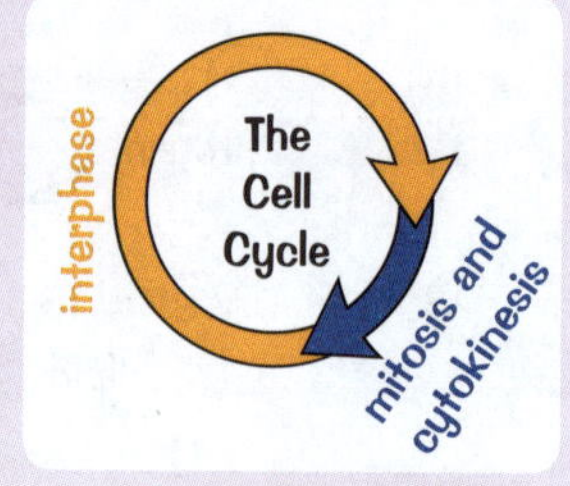
The Cell Cycle
interphase
mitosis and cytokinesis

Mitosis

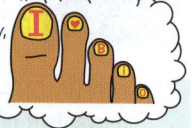

Mitosis is okay, but check out my toesies.

MITOSIS — the stage of the cell cycle when the cell **divides**.

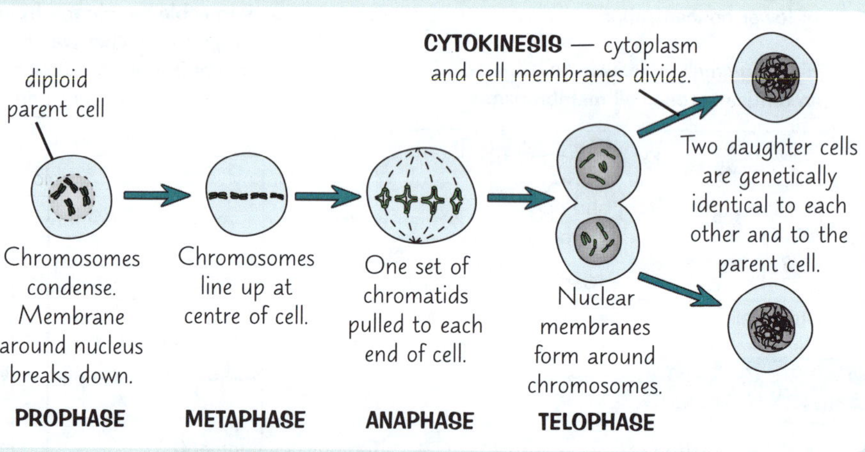
CYTOKINESIS — cytoplasm and cell membranes divide.
diploid parent cell
Two daughter cells are genetically identical to each other and to the parent cell.
Chromosomes condense. Membrane around nucleus breaks down.
Chromosomes line up at centre of cell.
One set of chromatids pulled to each end of cell.
Nuclear membranes form around chromosomes.
PROPHASE
METAPHASE
ANAPHASE
TELOPHASE

Mitosis allows organisms to **grow** or **replace cells** that have been damaged.
Some organisms use mitosis in **asexual reproduction**.

If there's a change in one of the genes that controls cell division, the cell may start dividing uncontrollably. This can result in cancer.

Growth and Stem Cells

Three Methods of Growth

Plants and animals grow due to:

1. **CELL DIFFERENTIATION** — the process by which a cell changes to become specialised for its job.

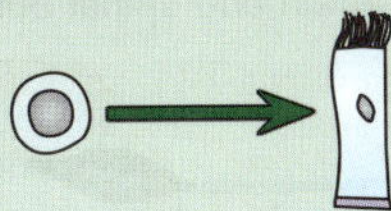

2. **CELL DIVISION** (mitosis)

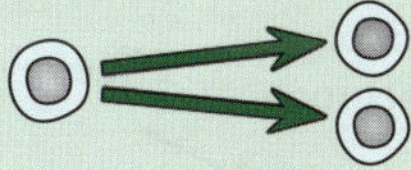

3. **CELL ELONGATION** (plants only)

Percentile Charts

Percentile charts are used to monitor a child's growth.

Mass, length and head circumference are monitored over time.

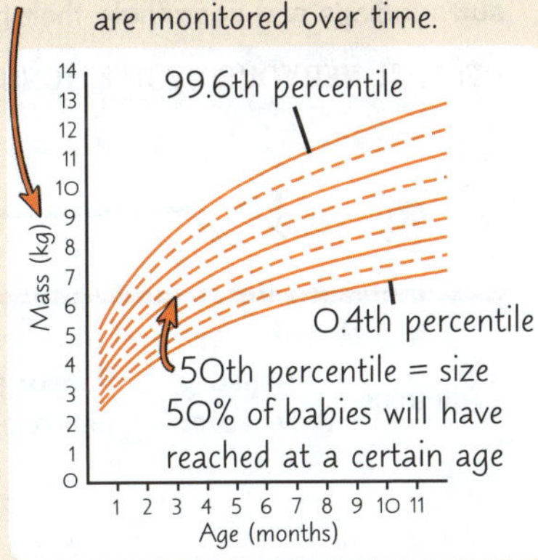

Doctors may be concerned if, e.g. a baby's size was below the 0.4th percentile or changed by more than two percentile lines over time.

Stem Cells

STEM CELLS — undifferentiated cells that can divide to produce lots more stem cells, and can differentiate into many other types of cell.

Stem cells from...	Can become...
adult animal	many kinds of cell, e.g. blood cells
human embryo	any kind of human cell
plant meristem	any kind of plant cell

Stem cells can be grown in a lab and made to differentiate.
The specialised cells can be transferred into people and so can be used in medicine:

Potential Benefits	Potential Risks
• Could replace cells that have been damaged by disease or injury, e.g. new cardiac muscle cells could treat heart disease.	• Tumour development. • Disease transmission (if donor stem cells are infected with a virus). • Rejection by patient's immune system.

The Nervous System and Neurones

The Nervous System

NEURONES — cells that carry information as electrical impulses in the nervous system.

The nervous system means that humans can react to their surroundings and coordinate their behaviour.

All this revision's really getting on my neurones...

CENTRAL NERVOUS SYSTEM (CNS) — consists of the brain and spinal cord.

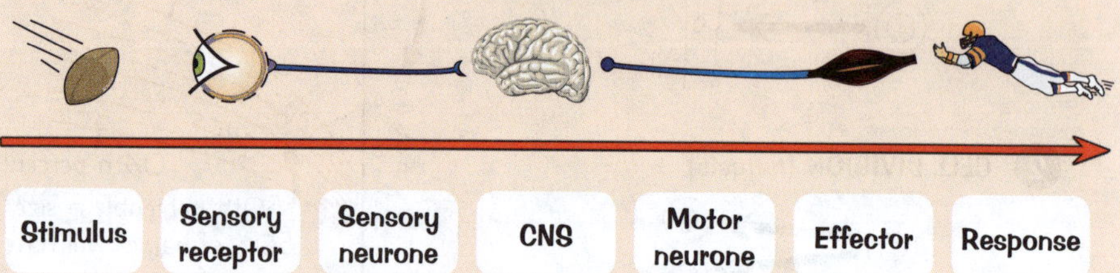

Stimulus → **Sensory receptor** → **Sensory neurone** → **CNS** → **Motor neurone** → **Effector** → **Response**

Effectors can be muscles (which respond to nervous impulses by contracting) or glands (which secrete hormones).

Three Types of Neurone

1. **SENSORY NEURONE — carries impulses from receptor cells to the CNS.**

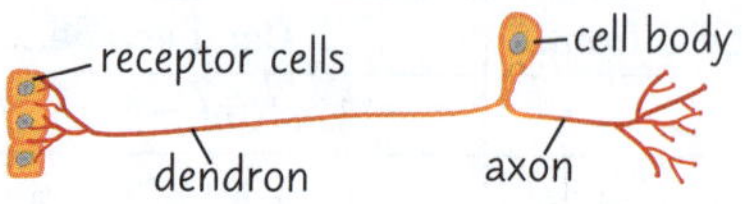

2. **MOTOR NEURONE — carries impulses from the CNS to effector cells.**

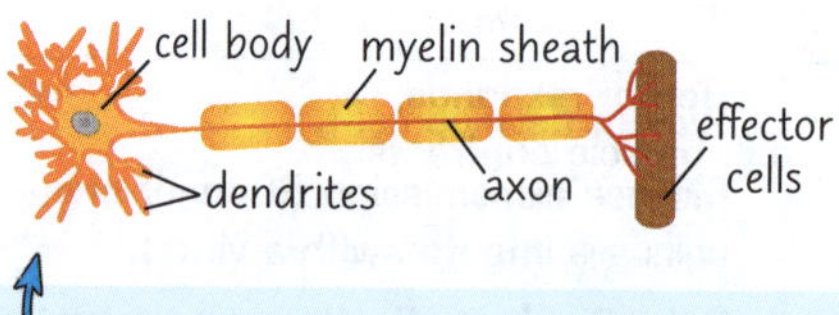

Not all motor neurones have myelin sheaths. Sensory and relay neurones can be myelinated too.

3. **RELAY NEURONE — carries impulses from sensory neurones to motor neurones.**

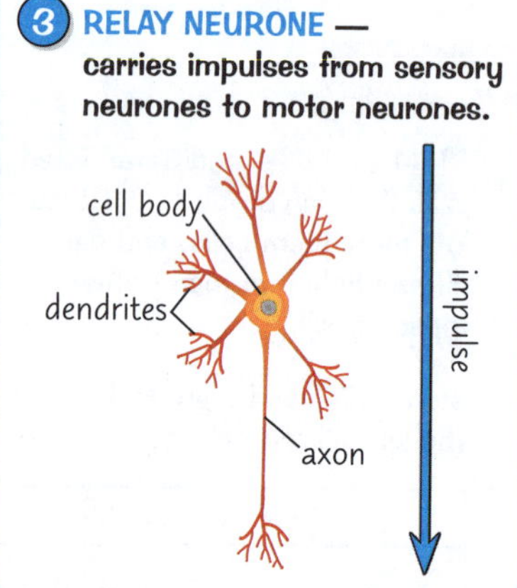

The myelin sheath acts as an insulator, speeding up the electrical impulse.

Synapses and Reflexes

Synapses

SYNAPSE — the connection between two neurones.

A nerve signal is transferred across a synapse by the diffusion of **neurotransmitters**.

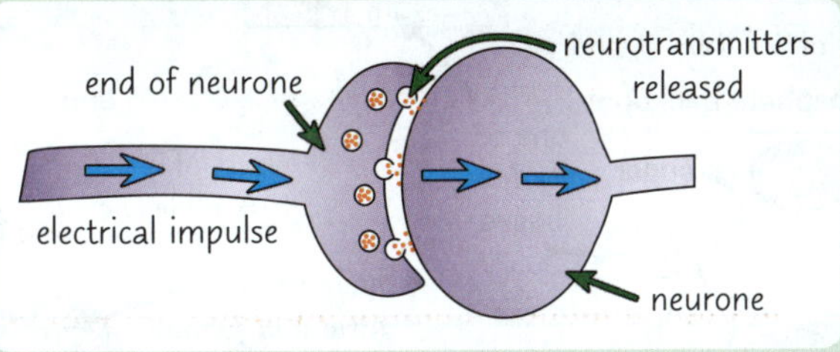

neurotransmitters released
end of neurone
electrical impulse
neurone

Reflex Arcs

REFLEXES — rapid, automatic responses to certain stimuli that don't involve the conscious part of the brain. They can reduce the chance of injury.

REFLEX ARC — the passage of information in a reflex, from receptor to effector.

Five steps in a reflex arc:

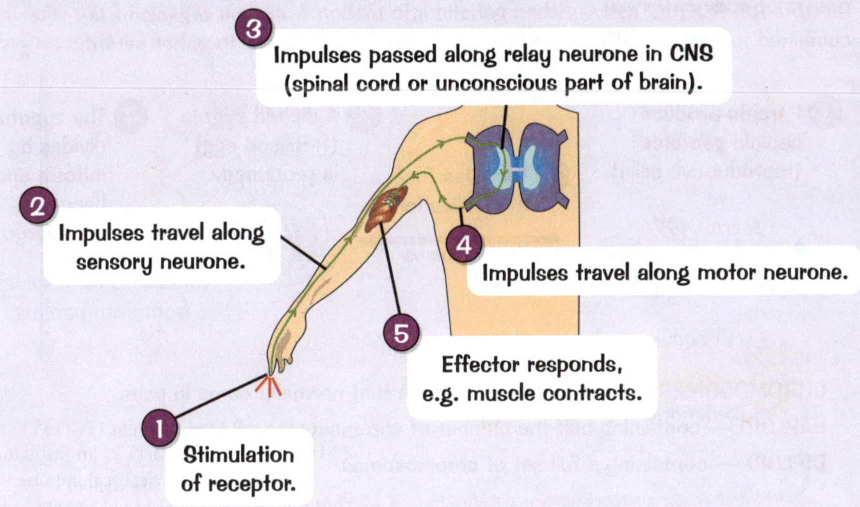

1 Stimulation of receptor.
2 Impulses travel along sensory neurone.
3 Impulses passed along relay neurone in CNS (spinal cord or unconscious part of brain).
4 Impulses travel along motor neurone.
5 Effector responds, e.g. muscle contracts.

DNA and Sexual Reproduction

The Structure of DNA

DNA — a polymer made up of two strands coiled into a double helix.

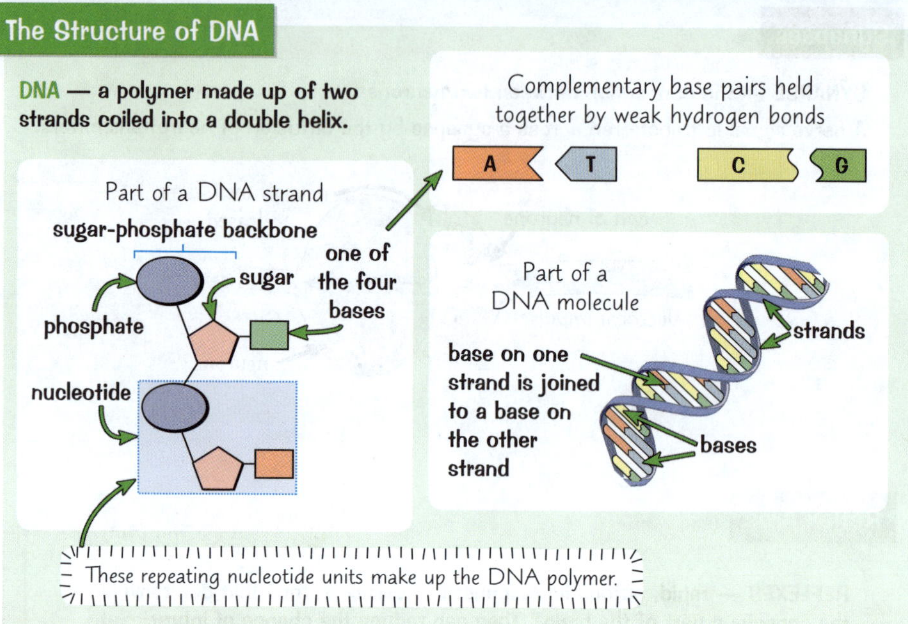
Part of a DNA strand
sugar-phosphate backbone
phosphate
sugar
one of the four bases
nucleotide
These repeating nucleotide units make up the DNA polymer.
Complementary base pairs held together by weak hydrogen bonds
A
T
C
G
Part of a DNA molecule
strands
base on one strand is joined to a base on the other strand
bases

Sexual Reproduction

SEXUAL REPRODUCTION — when genetic information from two organisms is combined to produce offspring which are genetically different to either parent.

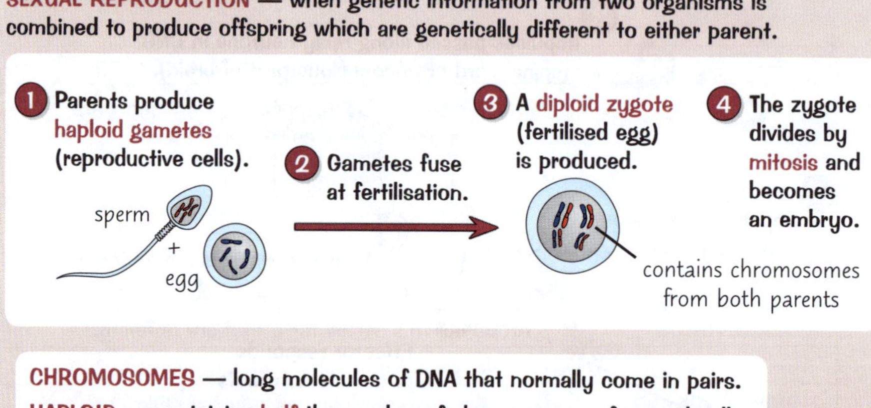
1 Parents produce haploid gametes (reproductive cells).
sperm
+
egg
2 Gametes fuse at fertilisation.
3 A diploid zygote (fertilised egg) is produced.
contains chromosomes from both parents
4 The zygote divides by mitosis and becomes an embryo.

CHROMOSOMES — long molecules of DNA that normally come in pairs.

HAPLOID — containing half the number of chromosomes of normal cells.

DIPLOID — containing a full set of chromosomes.

Normal cells are diploid.

Meiosis, DNA and Genetic Terms

Meiosis

Meiosis is a type of cell division that produces four haploid daughter cells.

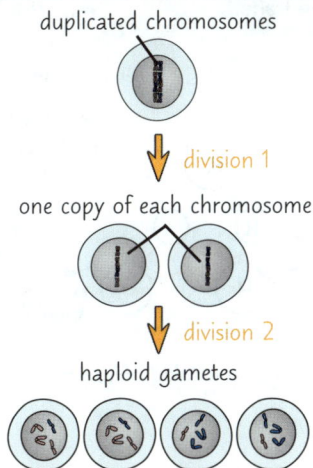

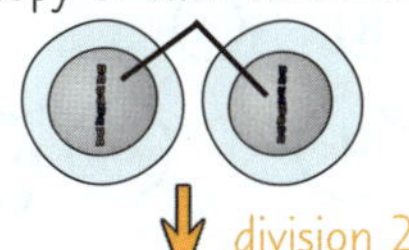

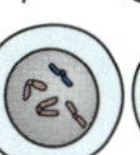
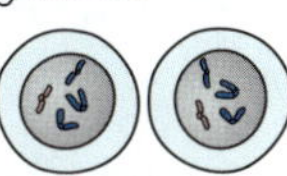

All the gametes produced by meiosis are genetically different.

Extracting DNA From Fruit

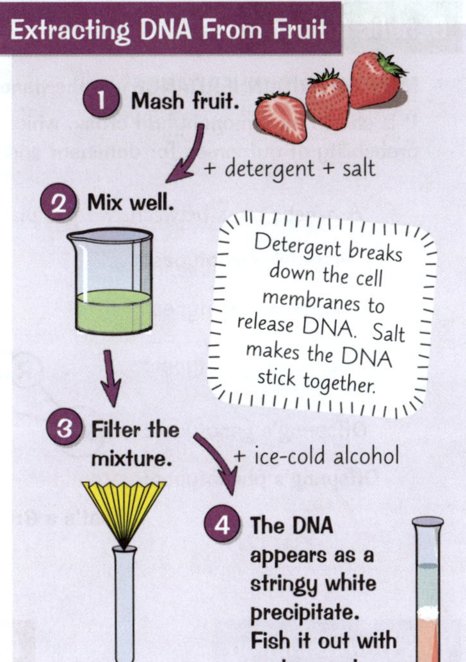

1 Mash fruit.
+ detergent + salt
2 Mix well.
Detergent breaks down the cell membranes to release DNA. Salt makes the DNA stick together.
3 Filter the mixture.
+ ice-cold alcohol
4 The DNA appears as a stringy white precipitate. Fish it out with a glass rod.

Genetic Terms

GENOME	All of an organism's DNA.
GENE	A small section of DNA found on a chromosome that codes for a particular protein.
ALLELE	A version of a gene.
DOMINANT	An allele that is always expressed.
RECESSIVE	An allele that is only expressed when two copies are present.
HOMOZYGOUS	Both of an organism's alleles for a trait are the same.
HETEROZYGOUS	An organism's alleles for a trait are different.
GENOTYPE	An organism's combination of alleles.
PHENOTYPE	The characteristics an organism has.

- Some characteristics are controlled by a single gene but most are controlled by multiple genes.
- Body cells have two alleles of every gene — one on each chromosome.

Genetic Diagrams

Genetic Crosses

MONOHYBRID INHERITANCE — inheritance of a single characteristic.

It is shown by a monohybrid cross, which is used to work out the probability of outcomes for dominant and recessive traits.

A genetic cross between two pea plants that are heterozygous for pea type.

Parents' phenotypes: Round Round

Parents' genotypes: Rr Rr

Gametes' genotypes: R r R r

Offspring's genotypes: RR Rr Rr rr

Offspring's phenotypes: Round Round Round Wrinkly

r = recessive allele for wrinkly peas

I'm not old, I was born like this!

That's a 3:1 ratio of round to wrinkly offspring.

Sex Determination

Human body cells have 23 pairs of chromosomes.

The 23rd pair determines sex.

A Punnett square for X and Y chromosome sex determination.

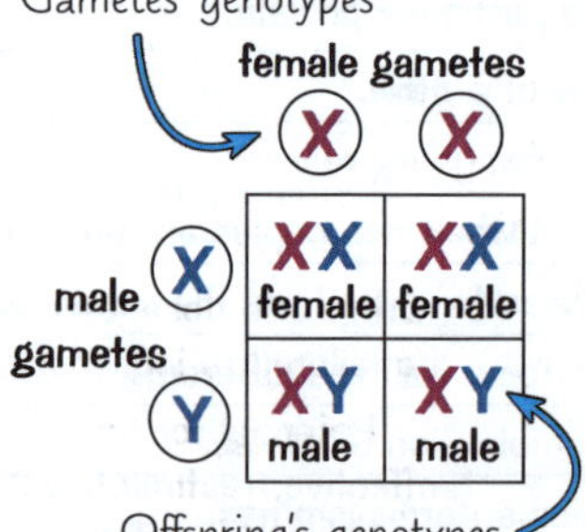

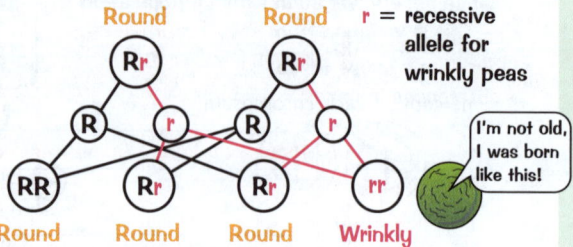

That's a 1:1 ratio of male to female offspring.

Family Pedigrees

Horizontal lines link parents.

Vertical lines connect parents to children.

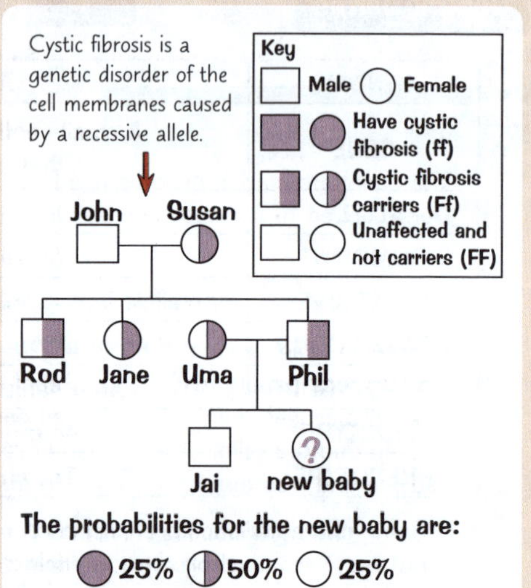

Variation & the Human Genome Project

Variation

VARIATION — differences in the characteristics of organisms.

MUTATION — a random change to the base sequence of DNA.

The base sequence of a gene determines what protein is made.

Genetic variation

Differences in the genes individuals inherit cause genetic variation within a population — this is variation from sexual reproduction.

Mutations cause these differences in genes.

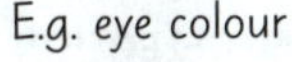
E.g. eye colour

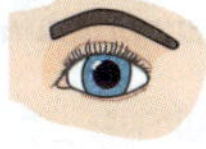

There's lots of variation within species due to mutations.

	Most mutations	Some mutations	Very few mutations
Effect on phenotype	None	Slight	Significant

Environmental variation

Differences in the conditions in which organisms develop cause variation — they get acquired characteristics.

E.g. leaf colour

Genetic and environmental variation

For most characteristics, variation is caused by both genetics and the environment.

E.g. plant height

The Human Genome Project

The complete human genome has been worked out.
Genes linked to diseases can be identified. This helps with...

Prediction and prevention

Knowing which genes predispose people to what diseases, can help doctors tailor advice and treatment.

Testing and treatment for inherited disorders

People can be tested early and we can develop better treatments.

Developing new and better medicines

Drugs and dosages can be tailored to individuals.

Potential for more effective treatments with fewer side-effects.

Linking genes to diseases could lead to increased stress, gene-ism or discrimination by employers and insurers.

Natural Selection and Evolution

Evolution by Natural Selection

Darwin came up with the theory of evolution by natural selection.

EVOLUTION — the slow and continuous change of organisms from one generation to the next.

NATURAL SELECTION — the process by which a characteristic gradually becomes more (or less) common in a population.

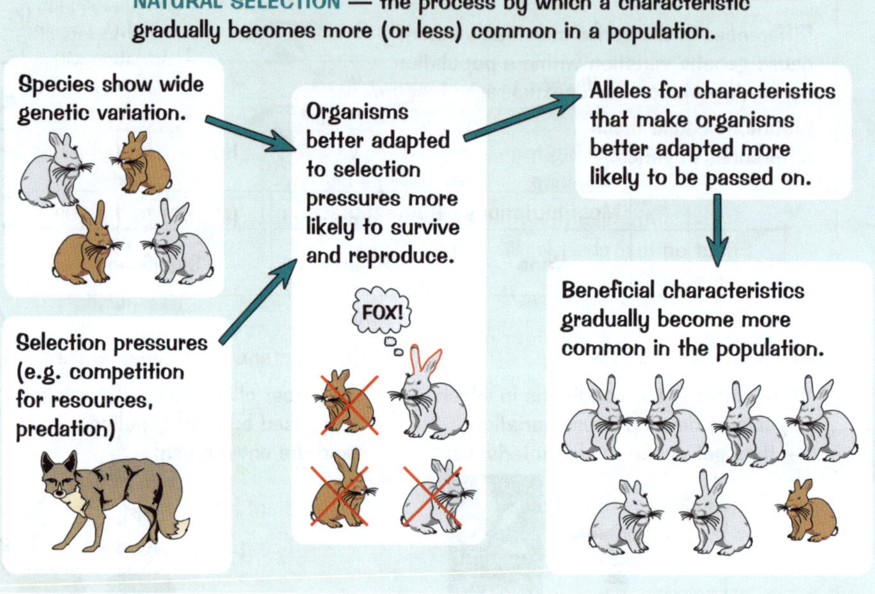

Species show wide genetic variation.
Selection pressures (e.g. competition for resources, predation)
Organisms better adapted to selection pressures more likely to survive and reproduce.
FOX!
Alleles for characteristics that make organisms better adapted more likely to be passed on.
Beneficial characteristics gradually become more common in the population.

Antibiotic-Resistant Bacteria

Antibiotic resistance in bacteria supports Darwin's theory of evolution.

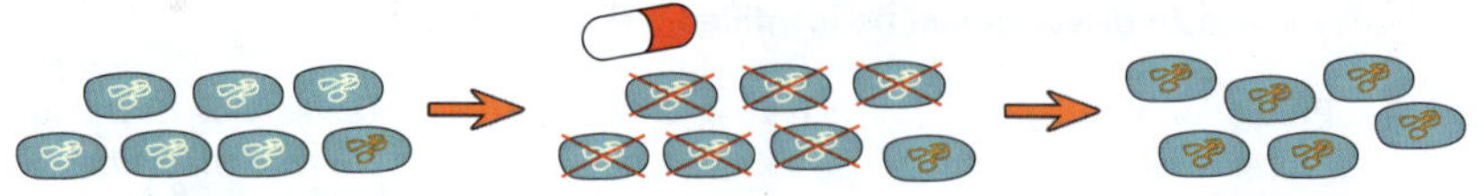

The emergence of other resistant organisms (e.g. rats resistant to poison) also supports Darwin's theory.

Evidence for Human Evolution

Hominid Fossils

Three fossils that provide evidence for human evolution:

'Ardi' and 'Lucy' were found in Ethiopia and Leakey's fossils were found in Kenya.

	1 Ardi	2 Lucy	3 Turkana Boy (one of Leakey's fossils)
Age (millions of years)	4.4	3.2	1.6
Species	*Ardipithecus ramidus*	*Australopithecus afarensis*	*Homo erectus*
Feet	Ape-like big toe for climbing	Arched for walking. No ape-like big toe.	Human-like (adapted for walking)
Limbs	Ape-like (long arms, short legs)	Between human and ape	Human-like (short arms, long legs)
Brain size	Like chimpanzee's	Bit bigger than chimpanzee's	Like human's

Leakey also found fossils of other *Australopithecus* and *Homo* species.

Stone Tools

Homo **species used more complex stone tools as they evolved:**

2.5 million years ago — Time (timeline not to scale) — present

smaller — Brain size — larger

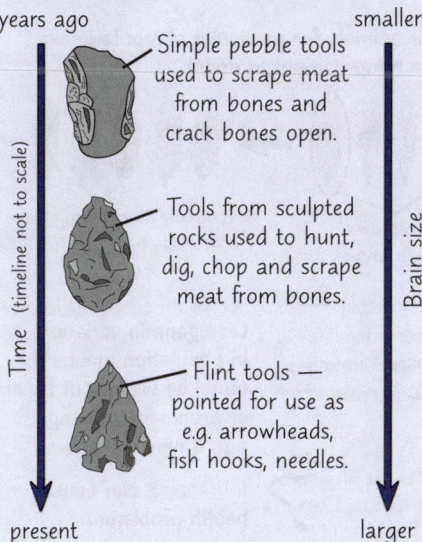

- Simple pebble tools used to scrape meat from bones and crack bones open.
- Tools from sculpted rocks used to hunt, dig, chop and scrape meat from bones.
- Flint tools — pointed for use as e.g. arrowheads, fish hooks, needles.

Three Ways to Date Tools

1. **Structural features, e.g. simpler tools are usually older.**

2. **Rock layers**

deeper layer = older tool

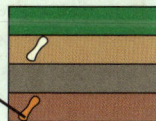

3. **Carbon-14 dating — used to date carbon-containing material found with tool.**

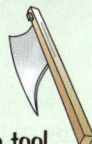

I once dated a tool... It broke my heart.

Classification and Selective Breeding

Traditional Classification System

CLASSIFICATION — organising living organisms into groups based on their features.

Traditionally, organisms were classified based on observable characteristics.

They were split into five kingdoms...

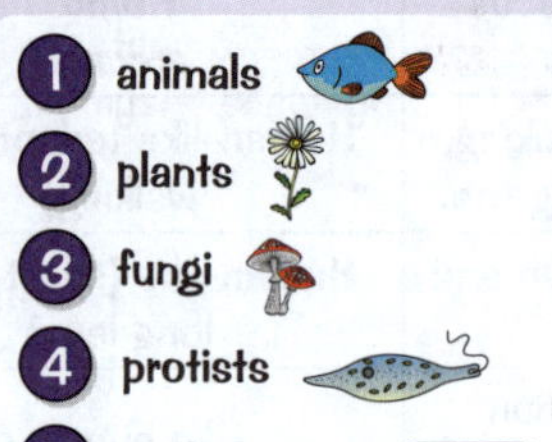

1 animals
2 plants
3 fungi
4 protists
5 prokaryotes

...then subdivided into smaller groups.

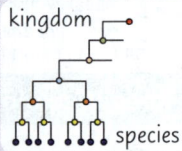

kingdom
species

Modern Classification System

Now, organisms' genes can be analysed — the more similar the base sequence of a gene, the more closely related the organisms.

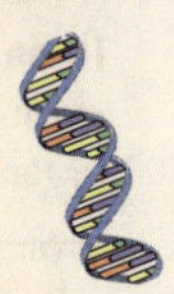

Organisms are now split into three domains before being subdivided into the smaller groups of the five kingdom system.

1	Bacteria	true bacteria
2	Archaea	a different type of prokaryotic cell first found in extreme places
3	Eukarya	including protists, fungi, plants and animals

Selective Breeding

SELECTIVE BREEDING — breeding plants or animals for particular characteristics (e.g. disease resistance in crops or a gentle temperament in dogs).

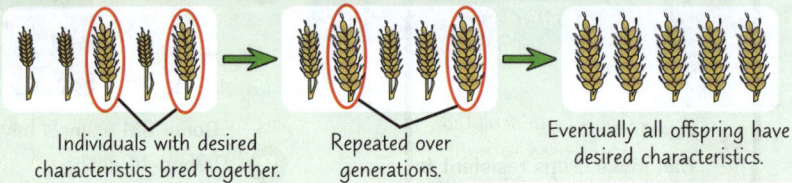

Individuals with desired characteristics bred together.

Repeated over generations.

Eventually all offspring have desired characteristics.

Benefits:

Agriculture: crops and animals can be bred to produce bigger yields, e.g. more meat.

Medical research: e.g. scientists can breed organisms with a characteristic they want to study.

Risks:

RIP

Less genetic variation in population means it could be wiped out by an environmental change, e.g. a new disease.

Inbreeding can cause health problems.

Genetic Engineering

Genetic Engineering Process

GENETIC ENGINEERING — transfer of a gene responsible for a desirable characteristic from one organism's genome into another organism.

It produces genetically modified organisms (GMOs).

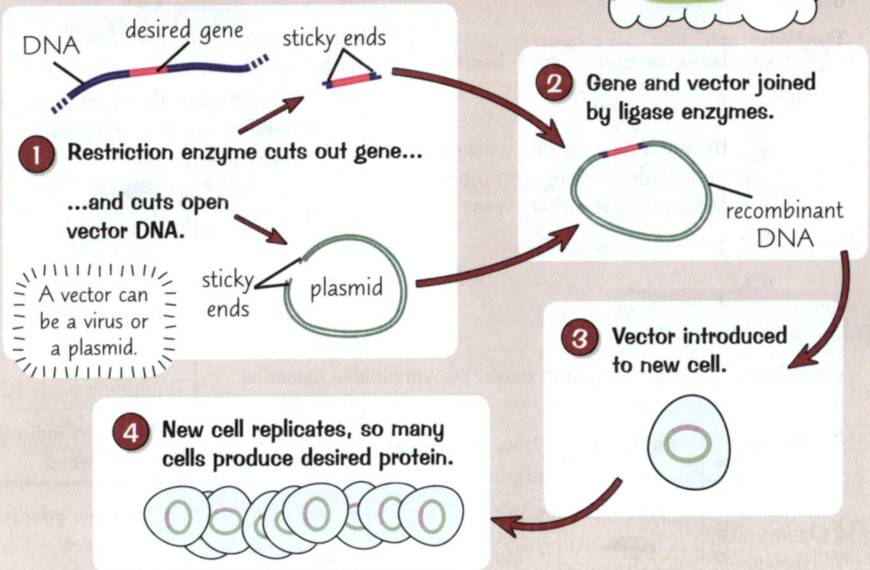

sticky ends

DNA

desired gene

sticky ends

1 Restriction enzyme cuts out gene...

...and cuts open vector DNA.

A vector can be a virus or a plasmid.

sticky ends

plasmid

2 Gene and vector joined by ligase enzymes.

recombinant DNA

3 Vector introduced to new cell.

4 New cell replicates, so many cells produce desired protein.

Benefits and Risks of Genetic Engineering

Benefits:

Agriculture:

Can make crops resistant to drought, pests or herbicides.

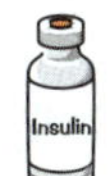

Medicine:

Bacteria produce human insulin, which is used to treat diabetes.

Sheep and cows could produce human antibodies to treat illnesses, e.g. arthritis.

The antibodies are extracted from the animal, e.g. from its milk.

Risks:

Some GM animals have health problems.

GM crops could negatively affect food chains, or transplanted genes could get out into environment.

Health and Disease

Health

HEALTH — a state of complete physical, mental and social well-being, and not merely the absence of disease or infirmity.

Diseases can cause ill health.

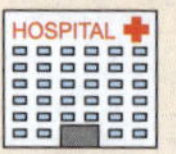

Having a disease can weaken your body, making you more susceptible to other diseases.

Two Types of Disease

1. **COMMUNICABLE DISEASE** — a disease that can spread from person to person or between animals and people.

2. **NON-COMMUNICABLE DISEASE** — a disease that cannot spread between people or between animals and people.

Infectious Diseases

PATHOGENS — organisms that cause communicable diseases.

Disease	Pathogen	How it's spread	Signs / symptoms	Ways to reduce spread
Chalara ash dieback	Fungus	• Wind • Transfer of diseased trees	• Leaf loss • Bark lesions (wounds)	• Remove infected ash trees • Restrict imports
Malaria	Protist	Mosquito vectors	• Damage to red blood cells • Damage to liver	• Mosquito nets • Insect repellent
Cholera	Bacterium	Contaminated water sources	Diarrhoea	Have clean water supplies
Tuberculosis	Bacterium	Airborne droplets (coughs and sneezes)	• Coughing • Lung damage	Infected people should: • Avoid crowds • Sleep alone • Ventilate homes

STIs and Defences Against Disease

Sexually Transmitted Infections (STIs)

SEXUALLY TRANSMITTED INFECTION — infection spread through sexual contact.

STI	Pathogen	How it's spread	Symptoms / effects	Ways to reduce spread
Chlamydia	Bacterium	Sexual contact, including genital contact	• Often none • Can cause infertility	• Wear a condom • Screen individuals • Avoid sexual contact
HIV	Virus	Exchanging bodily fluids (e.g. blood, semen)	• Kills white blood cells • Reduces immune response • Leads to AIDS • Vulnerability to other infections	• Wear a condom • Avoid sharing needles • Take medication • Screen individuals

Human Defences Against Disease

PHYSICAL BARRIERS

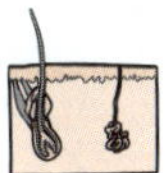

Skin acts as a barrier to pathogens.

Hairs and mucus in the nose trap particles containing pathogens.

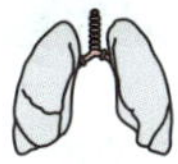

Mucus in trachea and bronchi traps pathogens, and cilia waft mucus up to throat so it can be swallowed.

CHEMICAL BARRIERS

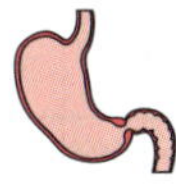

Hydrochloric acid in the stomach kills pathogens.

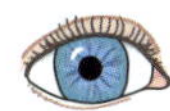

Lysozymes in tears kill bacteria.

The Immune System

Specific Immune Response

SPECIFIC IMMUNE RESPONSE — the immune response to a specific pathogen.

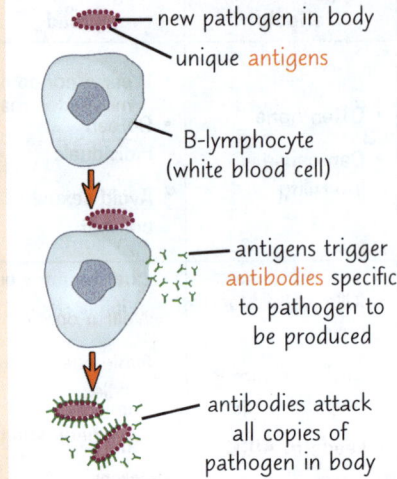

new pathogen in body

unique antigens

B-lymphocyte (white blood cell)

antigens trigger antibodies specific to pathogen to be produced

antibodies attack all copies of pathogen in body

Memory lymphocytes also produced — these stay in body for long time and 'remember' antigen.

Secondary Immune Response

Key
exposure to antigen

Secondary immune response — faster and stronger. Memory lymphocytes trigger fast production of antibodies.

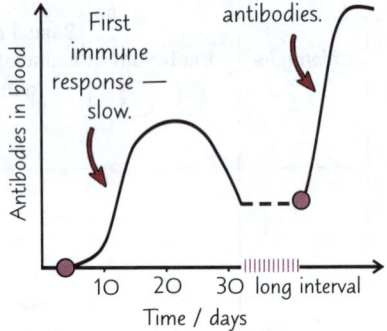

First immune response — slow.

Antibodies in blood

10
20
30
long interval

Time / days

The secondary response often gets rid of a pathogen before a person has any symptoms.

Immunisation

IMMUNISATION — a process that makes an individual resistant to becoming ill from a specific communicable disease.

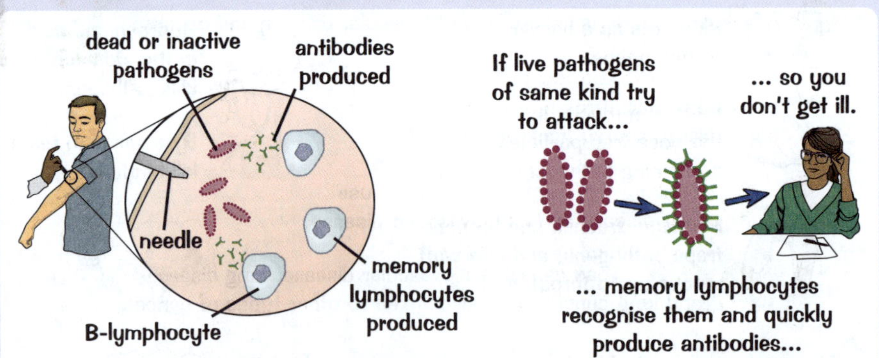
dead or inactive pathogens
antibodies produced
needle
B-lymphocyte
memory lymphocytes produced
If live pathogens of same kind try to attack...
... memory lymphocytes recognise them and quickly produce antibodies...
... so you don't get ill.

Medicines and Lifestyle Factors

Antibiotics

- Antibiotics only kill bacteria.
- They inhibit processes in bacterial cells, but not in the host organism.

Developing New Medicines

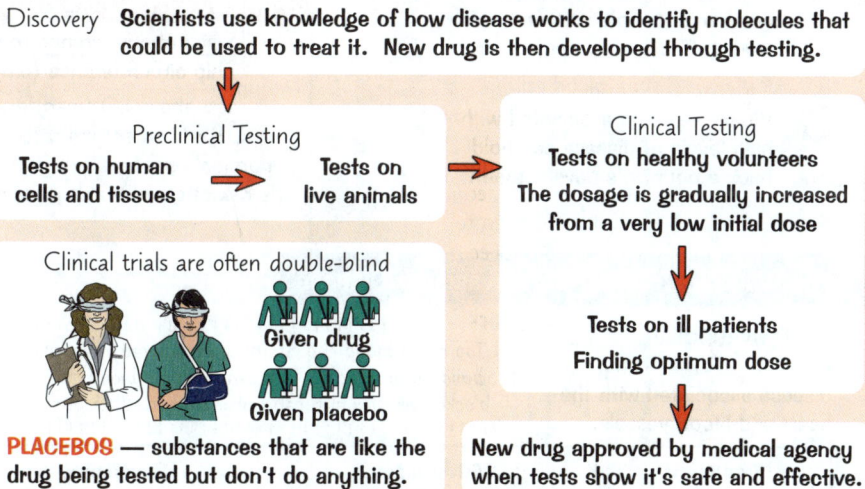

Discovery — Scientists use knowledge of how disease works to identify molecules that could be used to treat it. New drug is then developed through testing.

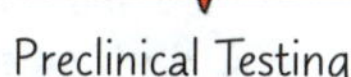

Preclinical Testing

Tests on human cells and tissues

Tests on live animals

Clinical Testing

Tests on healthy volunteers

The dosage is gradually increased from a very low initial dose

Tests on ill patients

Finding optimum dose

New drug approved by medical agency when tests show it's safe and effective.

Clinical trials are often double-blind

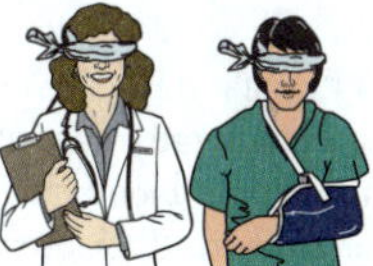

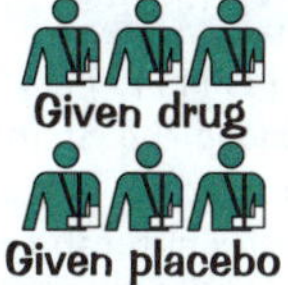

Given drug

Given placebo

PLACEBOS — substances that are like the drug being tested but don't do anything.

Four Risk Factors for Non-Communicable Diseases

RISK FACTORS — things that are linked to an increase in the likelihood that a person will develop a certain disease during their lifetime.

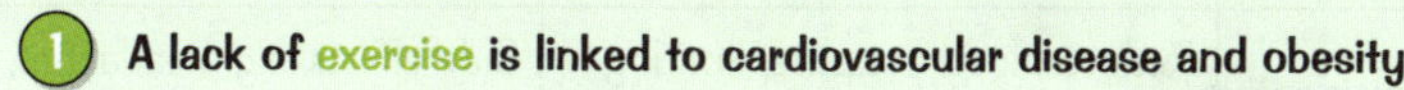

1. A lack of exercise is linked to cardiovascular disease and obesity.

2. A poor diet with too few or too many nutrients can lead to malnutrition or related disorders, e.g. obesity, scurvy (lack of vitamin C).

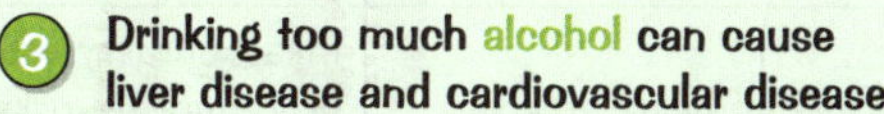

3. Drinking too much alcohol can cause liver disease and cardiovascular disease.

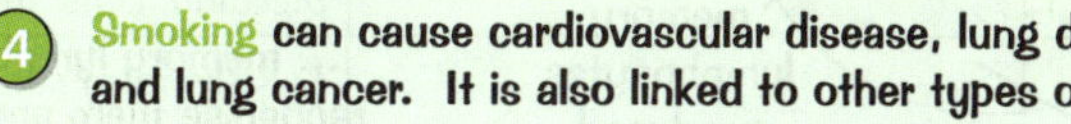

4. Smoking can cause cardiovascular disease, lung disease and lung cancer. It is also linked to other types of cancer.

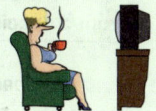

Many non-communicable diseases are caused by several risk factors interacting.

Non-Communicable Diseases

Effects of Non-Communicable Diseases

1. **Local** — high levels of disease puts pressure on local hospitals.
2. **National** — expensive for NHS to treat everyone and reduces number of people who can work (affects economy).
3. **Global** — costs associated with high levels of disease can hold back a country's development.

Two Measures of Obesity

1. **BMI** = $\frac{\text{mass (kg)}}{(\text{height (m)})^2}$

   Result is used to classify body, e.g. < 18.5 = underweight, > 30 = obese.

2. **Waist-to-hip ratio** = $\frac{\text{waist circumference (cm)}}{\text{hip circumference (cm)}}$

   A ratio above 1.0 (men) and 0.85 (women) indicates abdominal obesity, which increases the risk of other health problems.

Three Ways of Treating Cardiovascular Disease

CARDIOVASCULAR DISEASE (CVD) — any disease associated with the heart and blood vessels.

Too much blood cholesterol can cause fatty deposits to build up in arteries. This can lead to a blood clot and blocked vessel, which can cause a heart attack or stroke.

Treatment	Advantages	Disadvantages
1 **Lifestyle changes** (e.g. exercise)	Reduces risk of heart attack and stroke.	None.
2 **Life-long medication** Statins	Reduce cholesterol, slowing down formation of fatty deposits.	Side effects, including possible liver damage.
Anticoagulants	Make blood clots less likely.	Can cause excessive bleeding.
Antihypertensives	Reduce blood pressure, limiting damage to blood vessels.	Side effects, e.g. headaches, fainting.
3 **Surgical procedures** Stent (tube put in artery)	Keeps arteries open so blood flow isn't blocked.	• Scar tissue may form. • Have to take drugs to stop blood clotting.
Coronary bypass surgery (healthy blood vessel put in heart)	Reduces risk of heart attack.	Heart surgery is a major procedure — risk of bleeding, clots, infection.
Donor heart	Can treat heart failure.	• Risks from surgery. • Drugs have to be taken to stop body rejecting it.

Photosynthesis

The Photosynthesis Reaction

PHOTOSYNTHESIS — an endothermic reaction that happens in plants and algae, in which energy is transferred to chloroplasts from the environment by light.

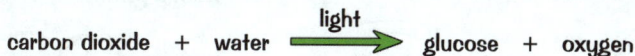

carbon dioxide + water $\xrightarrow{\text{light}}$ glucose + oxygen

Photosynthetic organisms make biomass from glucose. The energy in the biomass is passed on through food chains, so photosynthetic organisms are the main producers of food for nearly all life on Earth.

Three Limiting Factors of Photosynthesis

LIMITING FACTOR (of photosynthesis) — thing that stops photosynthesis happening any faster.

1 Temperature

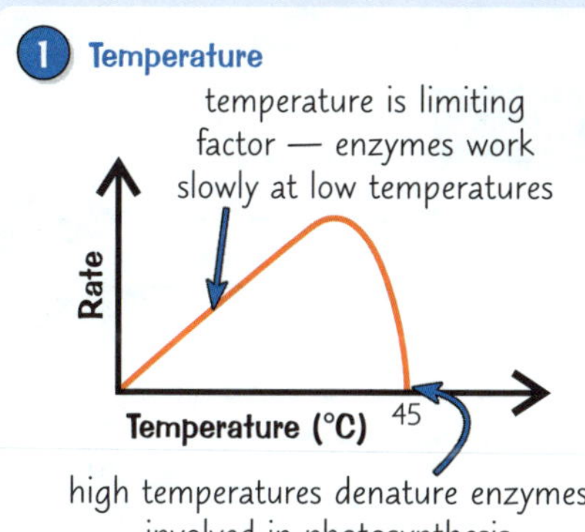
temperature is limiting factor — enzymes work slowly at low temperatures
Rate
Temperature (°C)
45
high temperatures denature enzymes involved in photosynthesis

2 CO_2 concentration

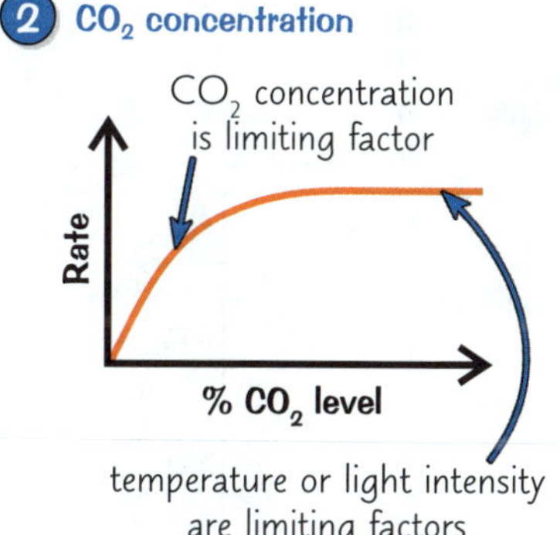
CO_2 concentration is limiting factor
Rate
% CO_2 level
temperature or light intensity are limiting factors

3 Light intensity

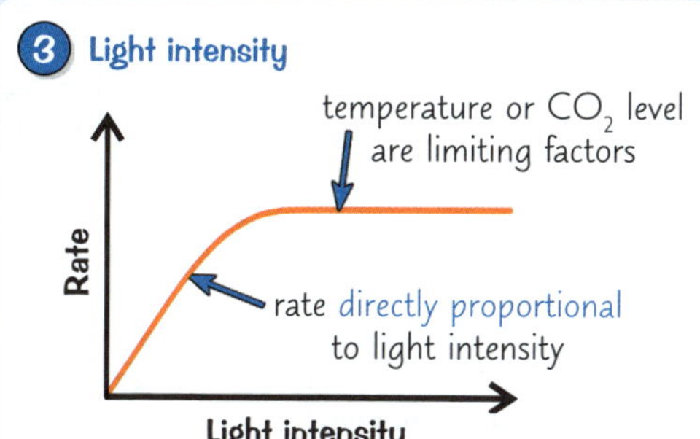
temperature or CO_2 level are limiting factors
Rate
rate directly proportional to light intensity
Light intensity

Light intensity and the distance from a light source are inversely proportional to each other.

The inverse square law links light intensity with distance from a light source:

$$\text{Light intensity} \propto \frac{1}{\text{distance (d)}^2}$$

E.g. doubling the distance means light intensity is four times smaller.

Plant Cells

Root Hair Cells

Plant roots are covered in millions of root hair cells.

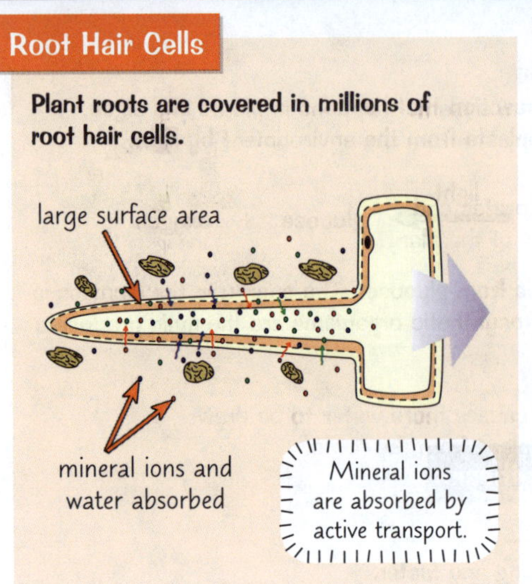
large surface area
mineral ions and water absorbed
Mineral ions are absorbed by active transport.

Stomata

STOMATA — pores that let gases and water vapour escape from a plant.

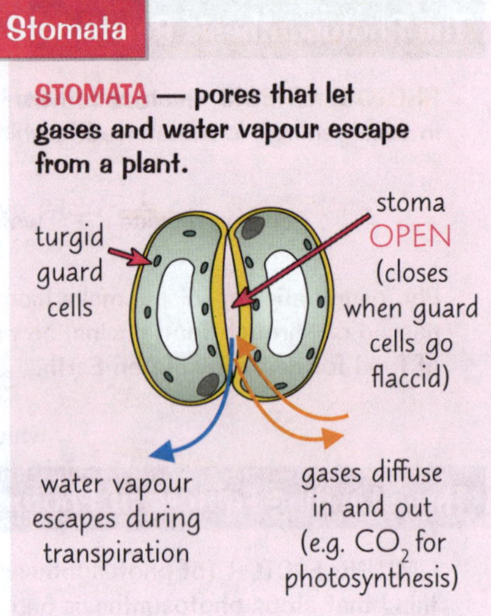
turgid guard cells
stoma OPEN (closes when guard cells go flaccid)
water vapour escapes during transpiration
gases diffuse in and out (e.g. CO_2 for photosynthesis)

Xylem

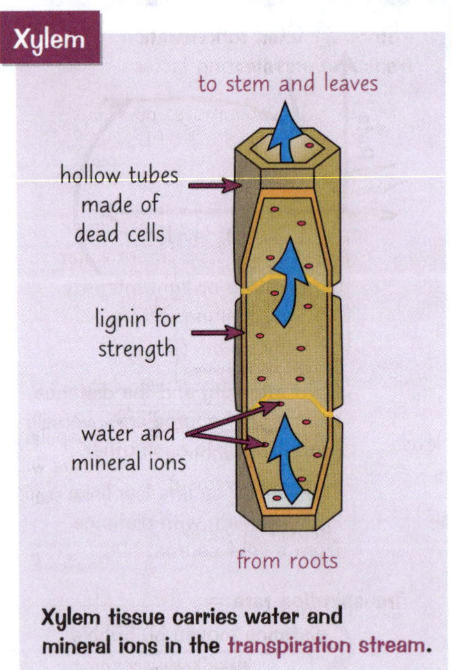
to stem and leaves
hollow tubes made of dead cells
lignin for strength
water and mineral ions
from roots

Xylem tissue carries water and mineral ions in the transpiration stream.

Phloem

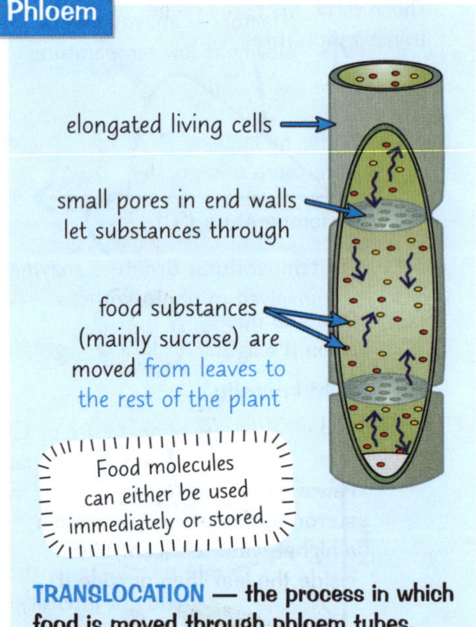
elongated living cells
small pores in end walls let substances through
food substances (mainly sucrose) are moved from leaves to the rest of the plant
Food molecules can either be used immediately or stored.

TRANSLOCATION — the process in which food is moved through phloem tubes. It requires energy.

Transpiration

Transpiration Basics

TRANSPIRATION — the loss of water from a plant.

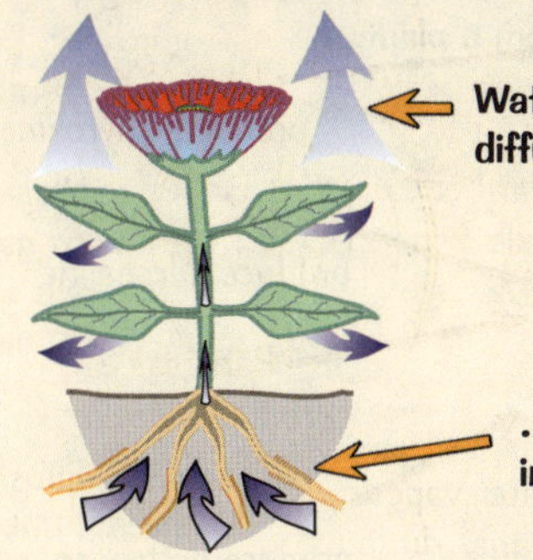

Water evaporates and diffuses out of the plant...

...which causes more water to be drawn into the plant from the roots.

It transpired that Jay did indeed have a favourite plant.

Transpiration Rate

These three things increase transpiration rate:

1. Warm temperatures

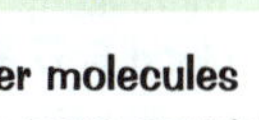

Water molecules have more energy.

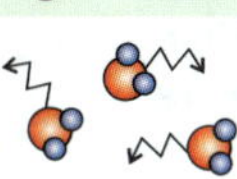

2. High light intensity

Stomata open when it's light.

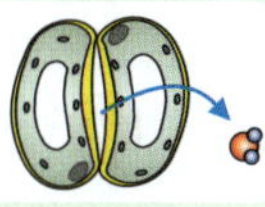

3. Good air flow

Fewer water molecules surround the leaves (so there's a higher water concentration inside the leaf than outside it).

Transpiration Rate Calculations

Potometer used to estimate transpiration rate:

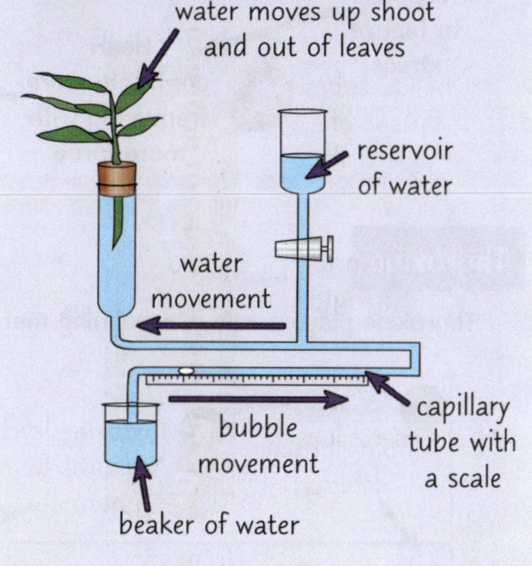

Transpiration rate = $\dfrac{\text{distance moved by bubble}}{\text{time taken}}$

Hormones

The Endocrine System

ENDOCRINE GLANDS — glands that secrete chemicals (known as hormones) directly into the bloodstream, which carries them to the target organs.

The effects of hormones are slower than nerves but last longer.

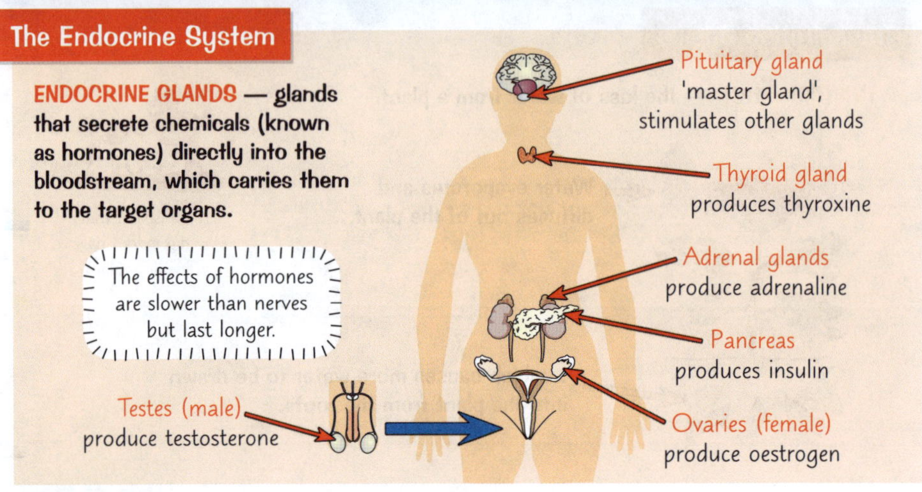

Pituitary gland
'master gland', stimulates other glands
Thyroid gland
produces thyroxine
Adrenal glands
produce adrenaline
Pancreas
produces insulin
Testes (male)
produce testosterone
Ovaries (female)
produce oestrogen

Adrenaline

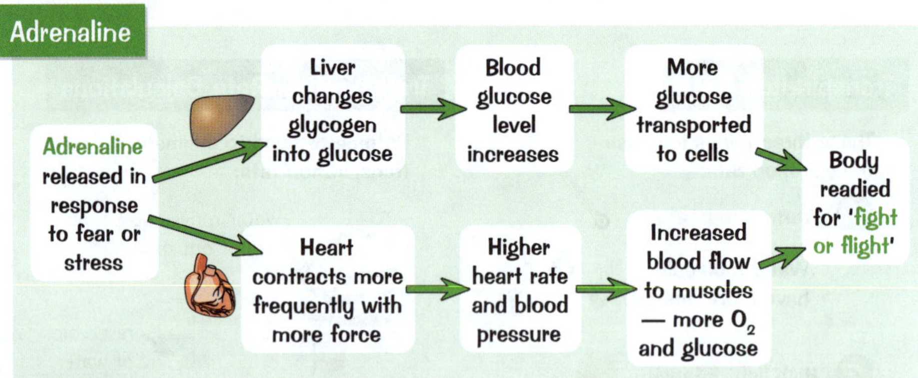

Adrenaline released in response to fear or stress
Liver changes glycogen into glucose
Blood glucose level increases
More glucose transported to cells
Heart contracts more frequently with more force
Higher heart rate and blood pressure
Increased blood flow to muscles — more O_2 and glucose
Body readied for 'fight or flight'

Thyroxine

Thyroxine plays a role in regulating metabolic rate.

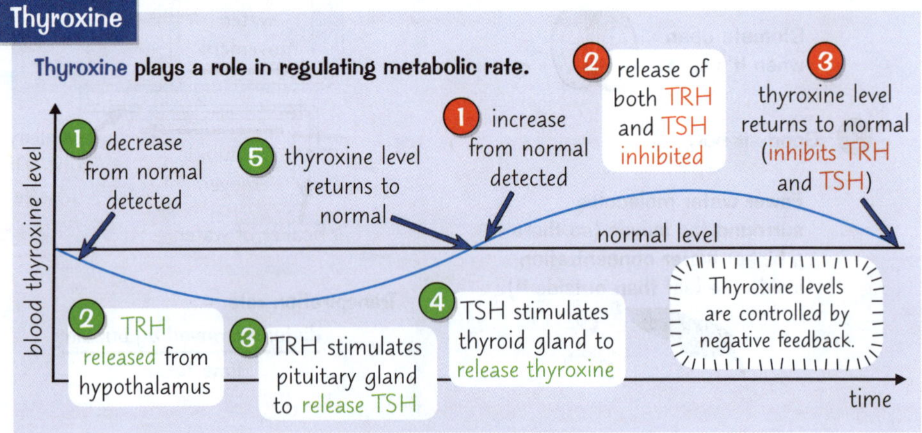

blood thyroxine level
time
normal level
1 decrease from normal detected
2 TRH released from hypothalamus
3 TRH stimulates pituitary gland to release TSH
4 TSH stimulates thyroid gland to release thyroxine
5 thyroxine level returns to normal
1 increase from normal detected
2 release of both TRH and TSH inhibited
3 thyroxine level returns to normal (inhibits TRH and TSH)

Thyroxine levels are controlled by negative feedback.

The Menstrual Cycle

Stages of the Menstrual Cycle

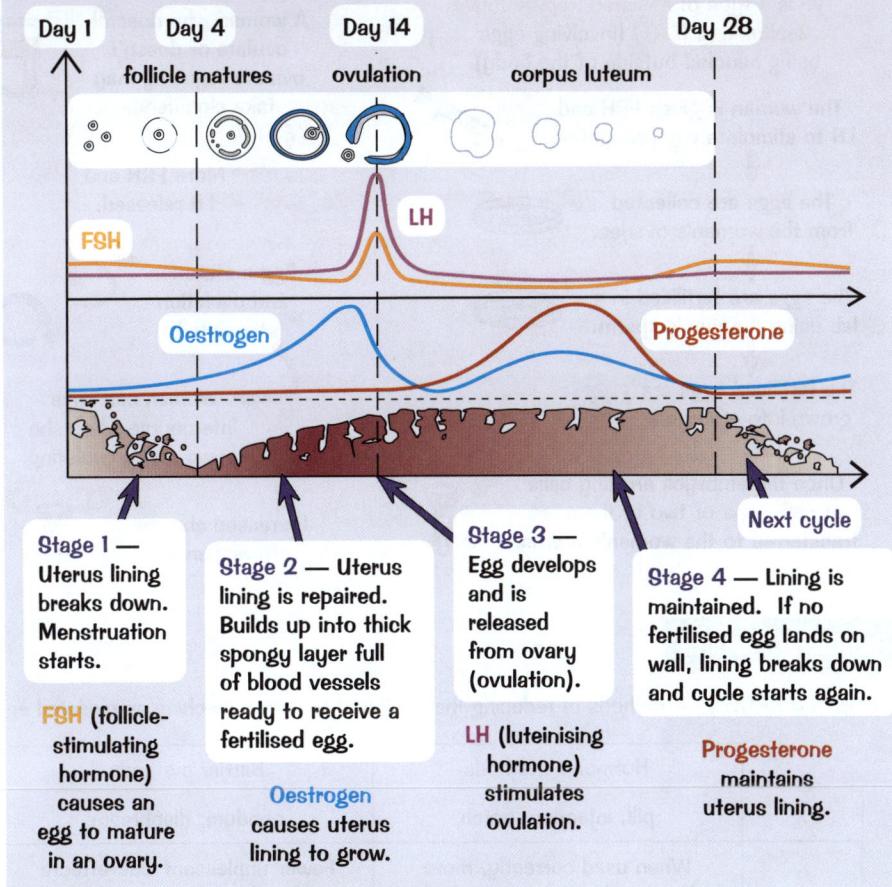

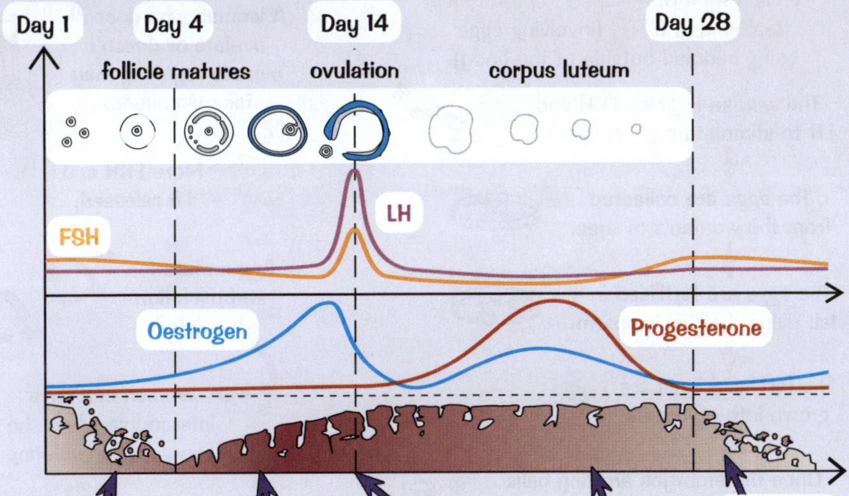

Day 1 Day 4 Day 14 Day 28

follicle matures ovulation corpus luteum

LH

FSH

Oestrogen

Progesterone

Next cycle

Stage 1 — Uterus lining breaks down. Menstruation starts.

Stage 2 — Uterus lining is repaired. Builds up into thick spongy layer full of blood vessels ready to receive a fertilised egg.

Stage 3 — Egg develops and is released from ovary (ovulation).

Stage 4 — Lining is maintained. If no fertilised egg lands on wall, lining breaks down and cycle starts again.

FSH (follicle-stimulating hormone) causes an egg to mature in an ovary.

Oestrogen causes uterus lining to grow.

LH (luteinising hormone) stimulates ovulation.

Progesterone maintains uterus lining.

Hormone Feedback in the Menstrual Cycle

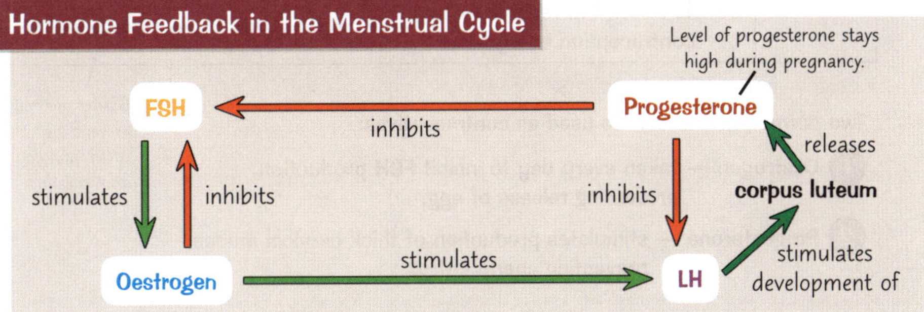

Controlling Fertility

In Vitro Fertilisation (IVF)

IVF is a type of Assisted Reproductive Technology (ART) (involving eggs being handled outside of the body).

The woman is given FSH and LH to stimulate egg production.

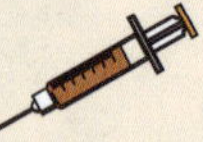

↓

The eggs are collected from the woman's ovaries.

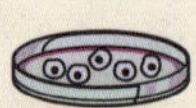

↓

The eggs are fertilised in a lab using the man's sperm.

↓

The fertilised eggs are grown into embryos.

↓

Once the embryos are tiny balls of cells, one or two of them are transferred to the woman's uterus.

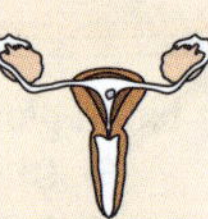

Clomifene Therapy

A woman who doesn't ovulate or doesn't ovulate regularly may take clomifene.

→ More FSH and LH released.

→ Egg maturation and ovulation stimulated.

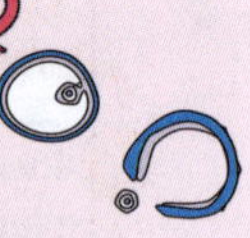

→ Woman can have intercourse when she knows she is ovulating.

→ Increased chance of pregnancy.

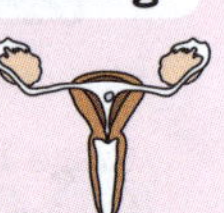

Reducing Fertility

CONTRACEPTION — methods of reducing the likelihood of sperm reaching an ovulated egg.

	Hormonal methods	Barrier methods
E.g.	pill, injection, patch	condom, diaphragm
Benefits	When used correctly, more effective than barrier methods.	Fewer unpleasant side-effects than hormonal methods.
	Couple doesn't have to think about contraception every time.	Condoms can protect against STIs.

Barrier methods prevent the sperm and egg from meeting.

Two hormones that can be used as contraceptives:

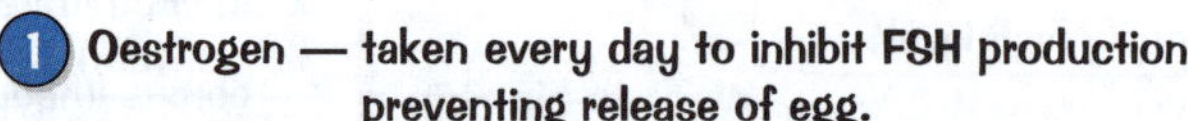

1. Oestrogen — taken every day to inhibit FSH production, preventing release of egg.
2. Progesterone — stimulates production of thick cervical mucus, preventing sperm entry.

Homeostasis — Blood Glucose

Homeostasis

HOMEOSTASIS — the regulation of the conditions inside your body and cells. It maintains a stable internal environment in response to changes in internal and external conditions.

Stable internal environment in here.

It's important to maintain constant conditions for cells to function properly.

Controlling Blood Glucose

Five steps the body takes to reduce blood glucose:

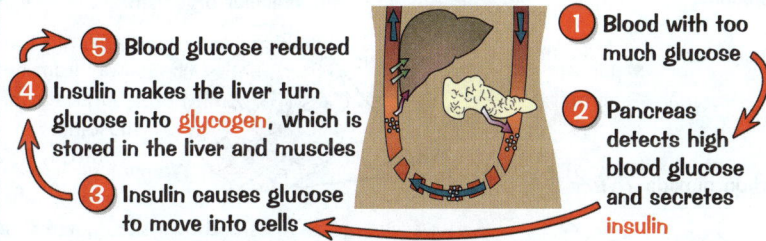

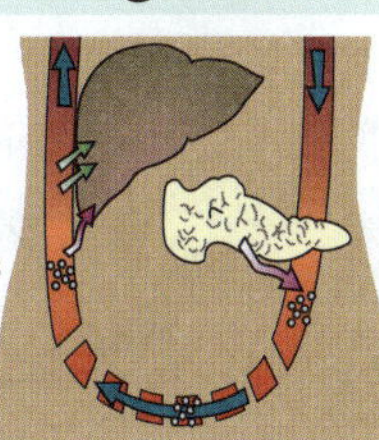

1. Blood with too much glucose
2. Pancreas detects high blood glucose and secretes **insulin**
3. Insulin causes glucose to move into cells
4. Insulin makes the liver turn glucose into **glycogen**, which is stored in the liver and muscles
5. Blood glucose reduced

Five steps the body takes to increase blood glucose:

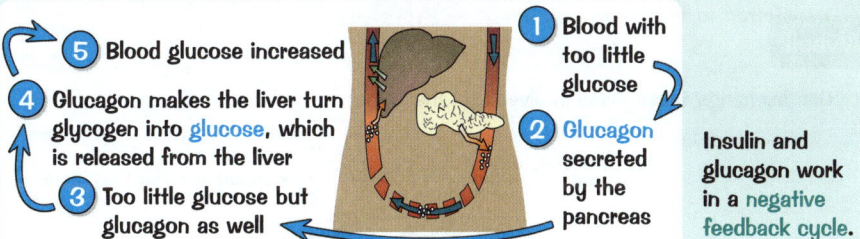

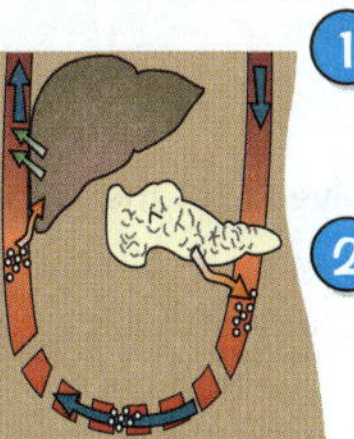

1. Blood with too little glucose
2. **Glucagon** secreted by the pancreas
3. Too little glucose but glucagon as well
4. Glucagon makes the liver turn glycogen into **glucose**, which is released from the liver
5. Blood glucose increased

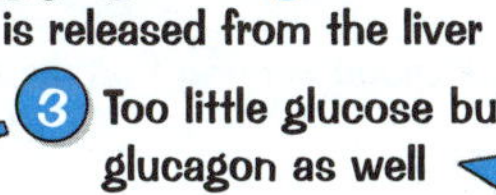

Insulin and glucagon work in a **negative feedback cycle**.

Diabetes

	Type 1	Type 2
Cause	Pancreas produces little or no insulin	Cells no longer respond to insulin properly
Effect	Blood glucose can rise to dangerously high levels	
Treatment	Insulin therapy, e.g. injections	Healthy diet and regular exercise

There is a correlation between obesity and type 2 diabetes. Two ways of measuring obesity:

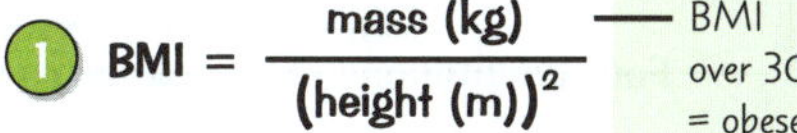

1. $$\text{BMI} = \frac{\text{mass (kg)}}{(\text{height (m)})^2}$$

BMI over 30 = obese

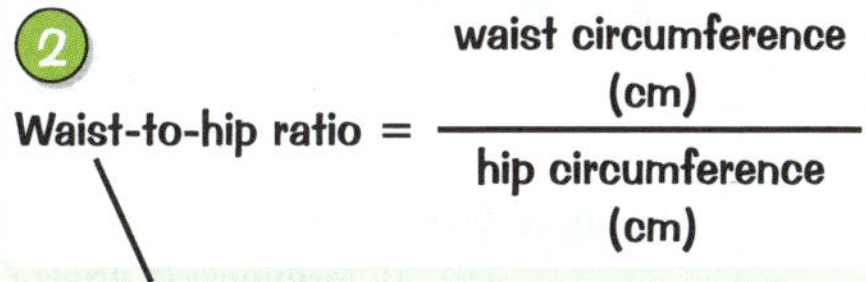

2. $$\text{Waist-to-hip ratio} = \frac{\text{waist circumference (cm)}}{\text{hip circumference (cm)}}$$

A ratio above 1.0 (men) and 0.85 (women) = increased risk of type 2 diabetes

Exchange of Materials

Six Materials Exchanged

Organisms need to exchange materials with their environment:

1. **oxygen**

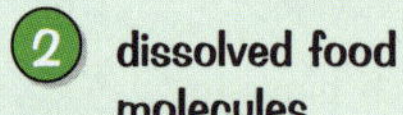
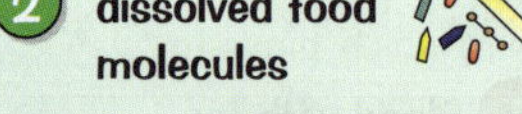

2. **dissolved food molecules**

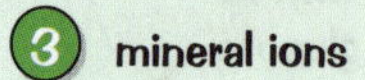

3. **mineral ions**

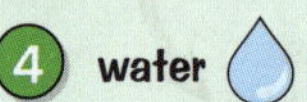

4. **water**

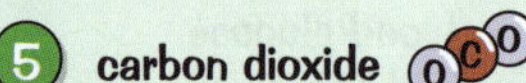

5. **carbon dioxide**

6. **urea** (animals only)

Surface Area to Volume Ratio

Single-celled organism

large SA : vol ratio → enough substances can pass across outer surface to meet needs of organism

Multicellular organism

small SA : vol ratio → many cells too far away from outer surface to get substances in and out this way

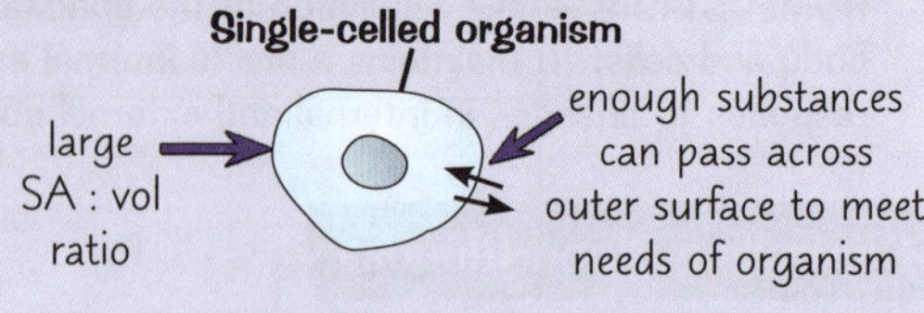

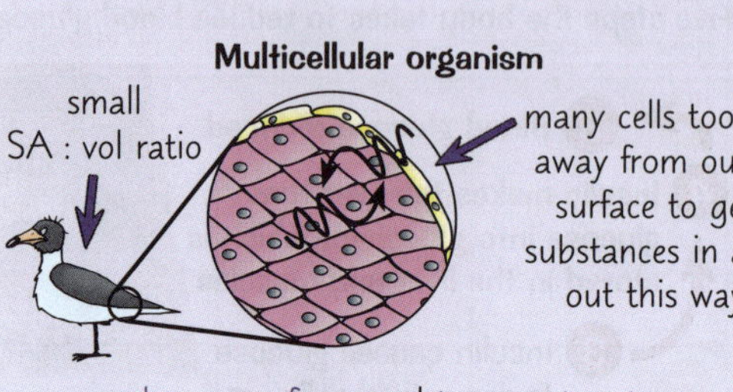

exchange surfaces and transport systems are needed so needs of every cell can be met

Alveoli

Gas exchange takes place in alveoli (in the lungs).

air goes in and out

alveolus

blood coming from rest of body (lots of CO_2)

gases diffuse between alveolus and blood

CO_2

O_2

blood going to rest of body (lots of O_2)

capillary

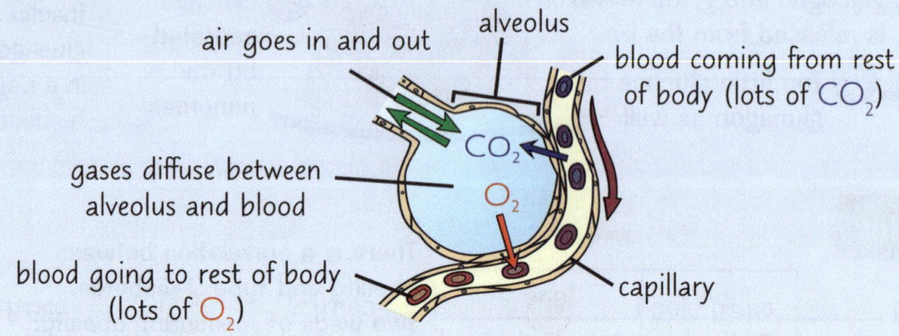

Four adaptations of alveoli for gas exchange:

1. **Big surface area** (so lots can diffuse at once)

2. **Thin walls** (so short diffusion distance)

3. **Good blood supply** (maintains CO_2 and O_2 concentration gradients)

4. **Moist lining** (so gases can dissolve)

Blood and Blood Vessels

Four Blood Components

Component	Function	Description
1 Red blood cells (erythrocytes)	**Carry oxygen around the body.**	no nucleus so more room for O_2; biconcave shape = big surface area = lots of O_2 absorbed; contains haemoglobin, which binds to O_2
2 White blood cells	**Defend against infection.**	lymphocyte → antitoxins, antibodies; phagocyte — phagocytosis
3 Platelets	**Help blood to clot at a wound.**	fragments of cells; a plate, a platelet
4 Plasma	**Carries everything in the blood.**	liquid; amino acids, hormones, red blood cells, urea, glucose, antibodies, antitoxins, white blood cells, proteins, platelets, CO_2

Three Types of Blood Vessel

1 **Arteries carry blood away from the heart.**

thick muscle and elastic layers because blood pressure is high

2 **Capillaries carry blood close to body cells to exchange substances.**

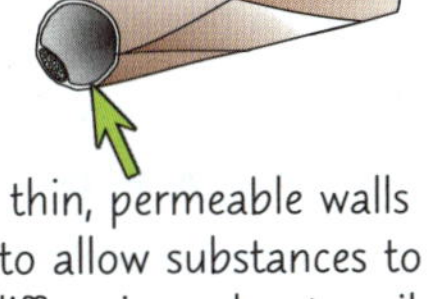

thin, permeable walls to allow substances to diffuse in and out easily

3 **Veins carry blood back to the heart.**

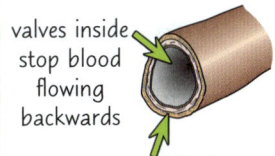

valves inside stop blood flowing backwards

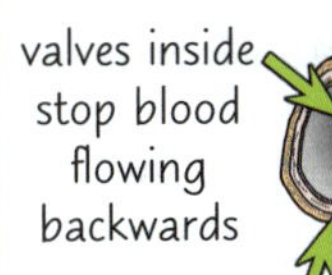

thinner walls than arteries because blood pressure is lower

The Heart and Respiration

The Heart

The circulatory system is made up of the heart, blood vessels and blood.
Humans have a double circulatory system (two circuits):

Circuit 1 — heart (right ventricle) → lungs → heart

Circuit 2 — heart (left ventricle) → rest of body → heart

KEY:
= oxygenated blood
= deoxygenated blood

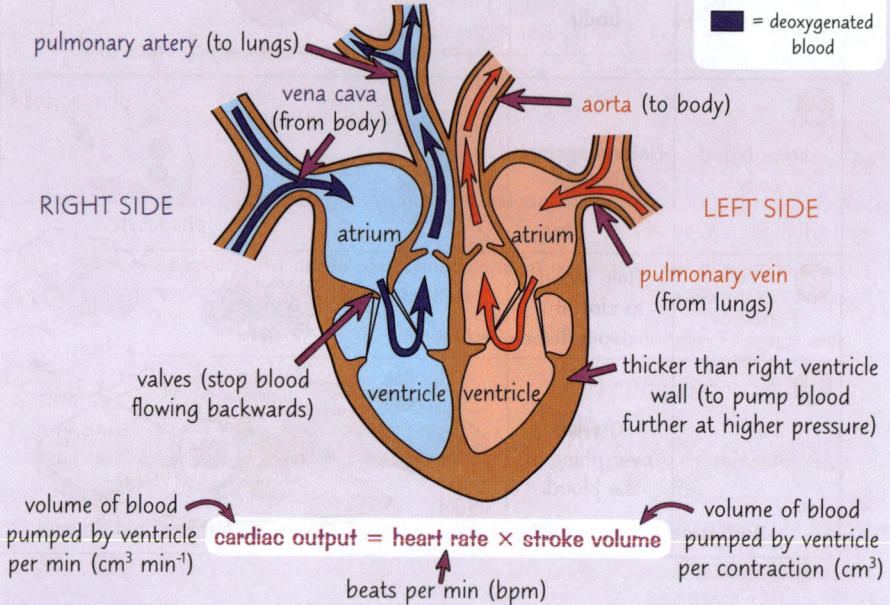

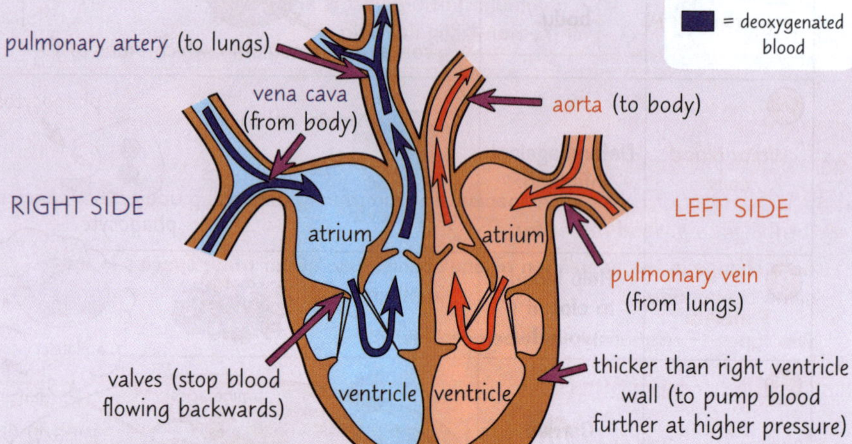

pulmonary artery (to lungs)

vena cava (from body)

aorta (to body)

RIGHT SIDE

LEFT SIDE

atrium

atrium

pulmonary vein (from lungs)

valves (stop blood flowing backwards)

ventricle

ventricle

thicker than right ventricle wall (to pump blood further at higher pressure)

cardiac output = heart rate × stroke volume

cardiac output: volume of blood pumped by ventricle per min ($cm^3\ min^{-1}$)

heart rate: beats per min (bpm)

stroke volume: volume of blood pumped by ventricle per contraction (cm^3)

Respiration

RESPIRATION — the process of transferring energy from glucose.
It's an exothermic reaction that goes on continuously in living cells.
The energy transferred is used for metabolic processes.

AEROBIC RESPIRATION — respiration with oxygen.

glucose + oxygen → carbon dioxide + water

The most efficient type of respiration (transfers the most energy).

ANAEROBIC RESPIRATION — respiration without oxygen.

In muscle cells:

glucose → lactic acid

In plant and fungal cells:

glucose → ethanol + carbon dioxide

Ecosystems and Organism Interactions

Levels of Organisation

Habitat — the place where an organism lives.

INDIVIDUAL	A single organism.
POPULATION	All the organisms of one species in a habitat.
COMMUNITY	The populations of different species living in a habitat.
ECOSYSTEM	A community of organisms along with all the non-living conditions.

Interdependence

INTERDEPENDENCE — each species in a community depending upon other species for things, e.g. food or shelter.

So a change in the population of one species can affect other species in the same community.

Two types of relationship between organisms:

1. MUTALISM

Both organisms benefit.

2. PARASITISM

Parasite benefits but the host doesn't.

Factors Affecting Communities

Both biotic (living) and abiotic (non-living) factors can affect organisms in a community:

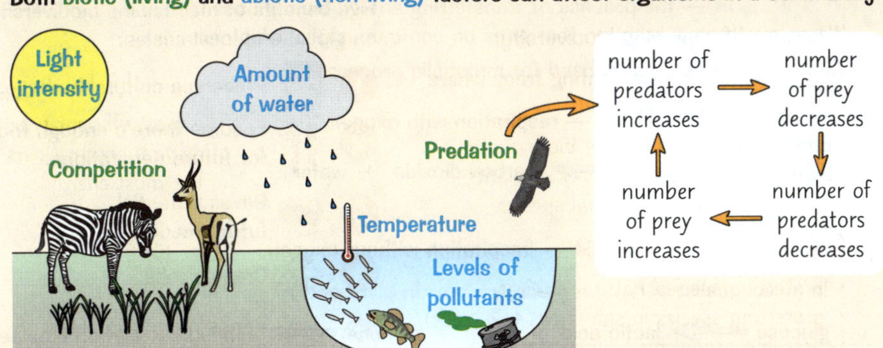

Human Impacts on Biodiversity

Eutrophication

BIODIVERSITY — the variety of living organisms in an ecosystem.

EUTROPHICATION — a process in which an excess of nutrients builds up in water, which can lead to a reduction in biodiversity:

1. Fertilisers add excess nitrates.
2. Excess nitrates cause algae to grow fast and block out light.
3. Plants can't photosynthesise — they die and decompose.
4. Microorganisms that eat decomposing plants multiply and use up oxygen.
5. Organisms that need oxygen die.

Fish Farms

Four ways fish farming can reduce biodiversity:

1. **Waste and food from the nets can enter open water and cause eutrophication.**
2. **Parasites can escape from the farm and infect wild animals (which can kill them).**
3. **Predators can be trapped in the nets and die.**
4. **Farmed fish can escape and compete with wild populations (e.g. for food).**

Non-Indigenous Species

Non-indigenous species don't naturally occur in an area.

They can cause native species to die out because:

they can out-compete native species.

they can bring new diseases to a habitat.

Maintaining Biodiversity

Two ways of improving biodiversity:

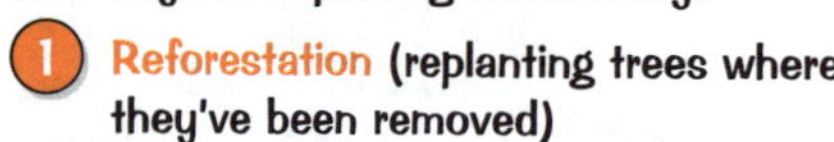

1. **Reforestation (replanting trees where they've been removed)**

Forests generally have high biodiversity as they contain a wide variety of plants, which support lots of animal species.

2. **Conservation schemes** — for example:

- protecting species' natural habitat,
- protecting species in safe areas (e.g. zoos),
- breeding organisms to increase population.

Five benefits of maintaining biodiversity on global and local scales:

1. **Preserves cultural heritage.**

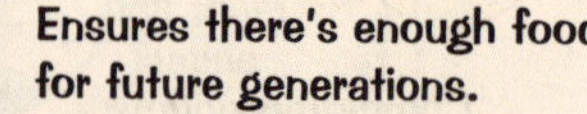

2. **Ensures there's enough food for future generations.**

3. **Saves potential future medicines.**

4. **Creates jobs.**

5. **Brings money to areas through ecotourism.**

Cycling of Materials

Recycling Materials

Materials are cycled through the abiotic and biotic parts of an ecosystem.

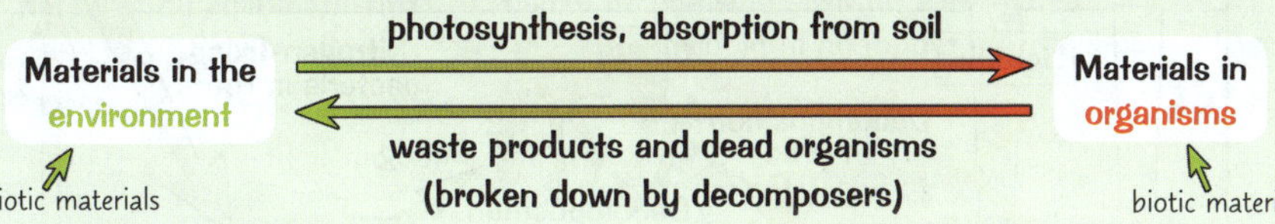

The Water Cycle

POTABLE WATER — water that's drinkable.

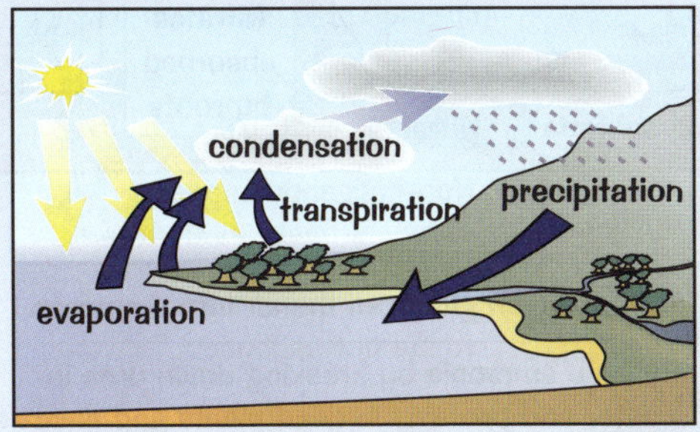

In times of drought, potable water can be produced from salt water by desalination:

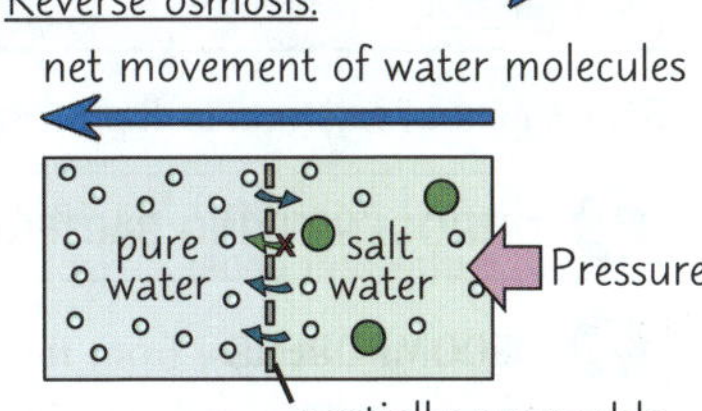

Thermal desalination can also be used to get pure water — salt water is boiled then the steam is condensed and collected.

The Carbon Cycle

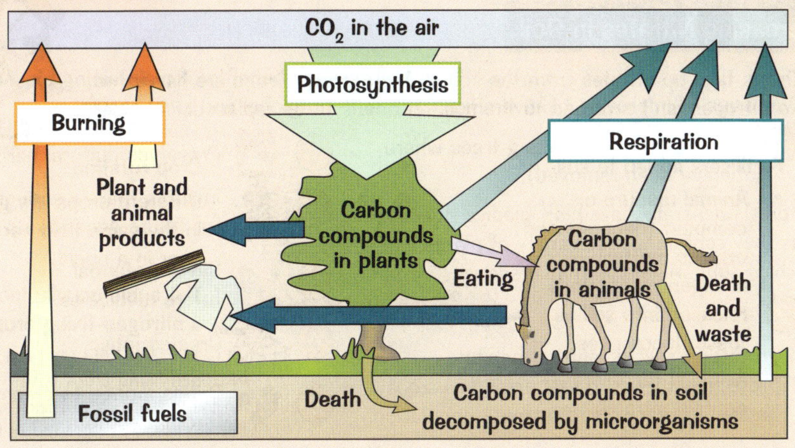

Nitrogen

The Nitrogen Cycle

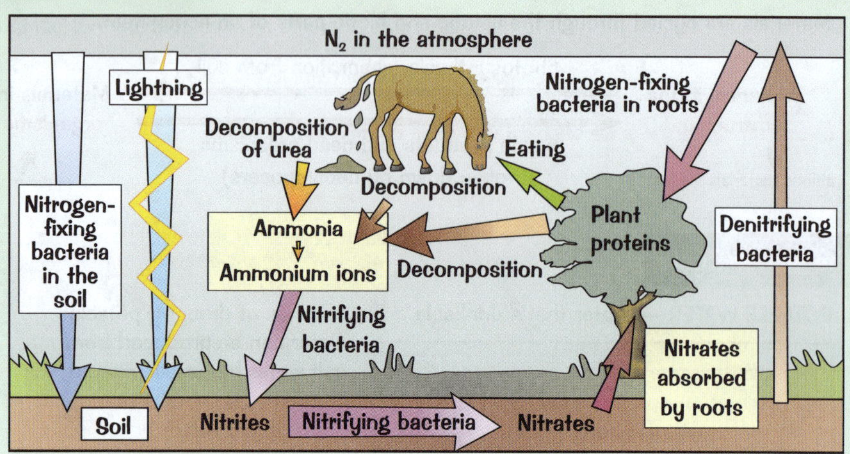

Four types of bacteria in the nitrogen cycle:

1 NITROGEN-FIXING BACTERIA	Turn nitrogen gas from the air into ammonia.
2 DECOMPOSERS	Release ammonia by breaking down urea in waste, and proteins in dead plants and animals.
3 NITRIFYING BACTERIA	Turn ammonia into nitrites, then into nitrates.
4 DENITRIFYING BACTERIA	Turn nitrates into nitrogen gas.

Increasing Nitrates in Soil

Crops take up nitrates from the soil as they grow. Crops are harvested, so nitrogen isn't returned to the soil. It needs to be replaced:

Fertilisers added to soil

- Animal manure or compost (decomposed organic matter) — nitrogen compounds released into soil as these decompose.
- Artificial fertilisers — contain nitrates.

Crop rotation

Different crops are grown in the same field each year in a cycle.

The cycle usually includes a nitrogen-fixing crop.

Nitrogen-fixing crops have nitrogen-fixing bacteria in their roots.

Chemical Equations

Chemical Formulas and Equations

CHEMICAL FORMULA — shows the proportion of atoms of each element in a compound.

E.g. CO_2 ← 2 oxygen atoms for every carbon atom

CHEMICAL EQUATION — shows the overall change in a reaction.

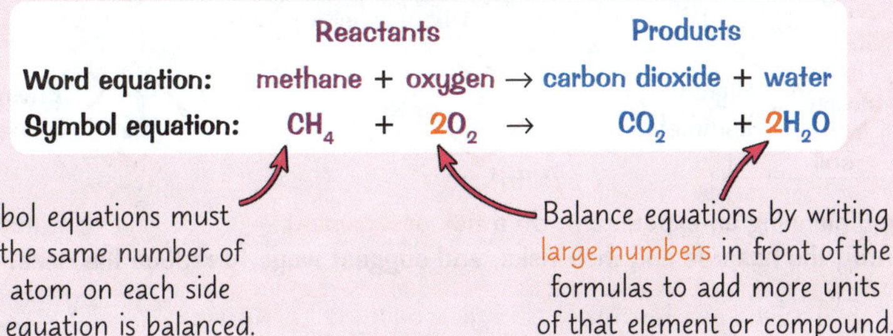

Reactants
Products
Word equation: methane + oxygen → carbon dioxide + water
Symbol equation: CH_4 + $2O_2$ → CO_2 + $2H_2O$
Symbol equations must have the same number of each atom on each side so the equation is balanced.
Balance equations by writing large numbers in front of the formulas to add more units of that element or compound.

State Symbols

(s)	solid
(l)	liquid
(g)	gas
(aq)	aqueous

'Aqueous' means dissolved in water.

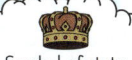

Symbol of state.

Common Chemical Formulas

Name	Formula
Water	H_2O
Ammonia	NH_3
Carbon dioxide	CO_2
Hydrogen	H_2
Chlorine	Cl_2
Oxygen	O_2

Name	Formula
Ammonium	NH_4^+
Hydroxide	OH^-
Nitrate	NO_3^-
Carbonate	CO_3^{2-}
Sulfate	SO_4^{2-}

Ionic Equations

IONIC EQUATIONS — show only the particles that react and the products they form.

aqueous calcium chloride	+	aqueous sodium hydroxide	→	calcium hydroxide	+	aqueous sodium chloride
$Ca^{2+}_{(aq)}$	+	$2OH^-_{(aq)}$	→	$Ca(OH)_{2(s)}$

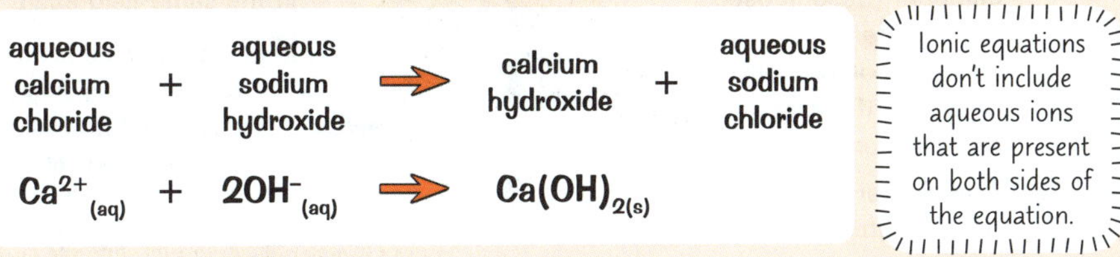

Ionic equations don't include aqueous ions that are present on both sides of the equation.

Hazards and History of the Atom

Hazard Symbols

HAZARD SYMBOLS — warn you about the dangers of a substance.

Understanding hazard symbols means you can use suitable safe-working procedures when working with the substances.

Oxidising

Corrosive

Toxic

Highly flammable

Harmful

Environmental hazard

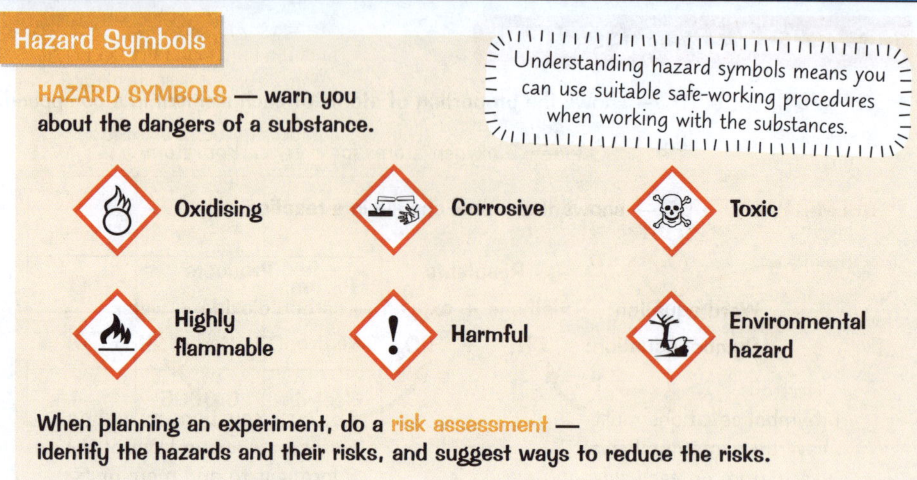

When planning an experiment, do a risk assessment — identify the hazards and their risks, and suggest ways to reduce the risks.

The History of the Atom

Start of 1800s — John Dalton described atoms as solid spheres.

1897 — 'Plum pudding' model — ball of positive charge containing small negative electrons.

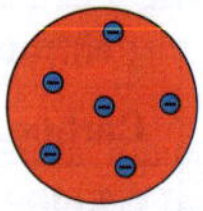

1909 — Nuclear model — a positive nucleus surrounded by a cloud of electrons (and mostly empty space).

α-particles are fired at thin sheet...

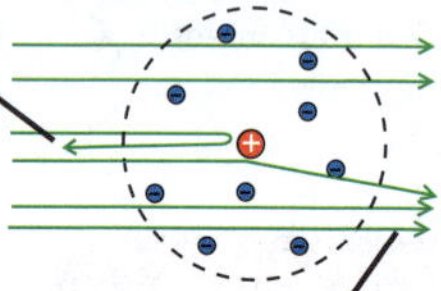

...some are deflected backwards...
...most particles pass straight through.

1913 — Bohr model — electrons orbit nucleus in fixed shells.

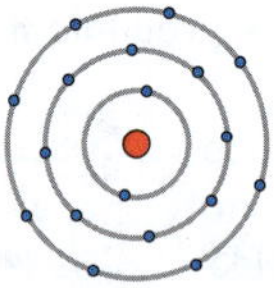

Later experiments — Nucleus contains protons that are positively charged and neutrons that are neutral.

You don't need to worry about remembering specific dates.

Atoms, Elements and Isotopes

Atomic Structure

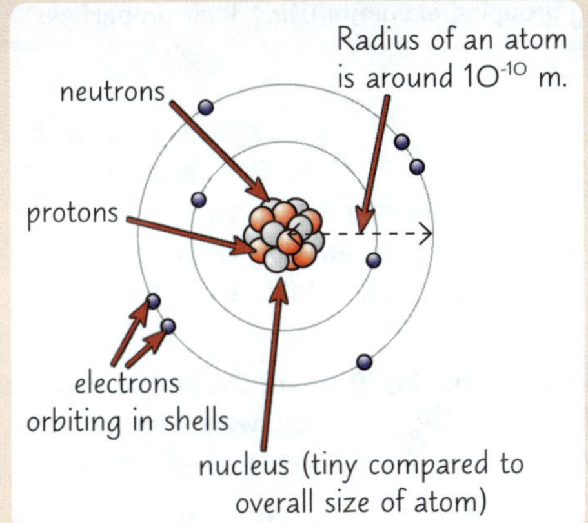

Atoms have no overall charge because they have the same number of protons as electrons.

Particle	Relative mass	Relative charge
Proton	1	+1
Neutron	1	0
Electron	0.0005	–1

Most of the mass of an atom is in the nucleus.

Nuclear Symbols

NUCLEAR SYMBOL — used to describe atoms:

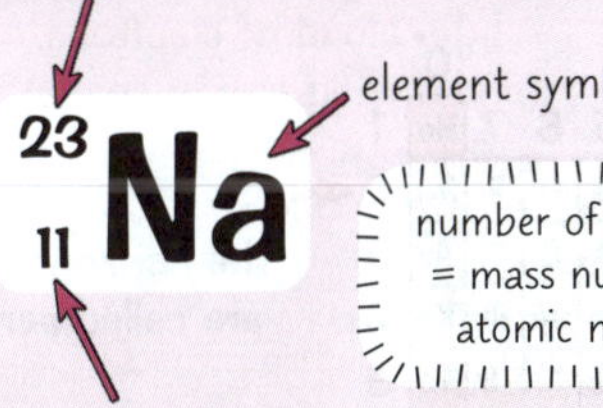

number of neutrons = mass number – atomic number

Elements

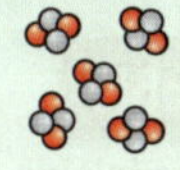

ELEMENTS — substances made up of atoms with the same number of protons.

Different elements have different numbers of protons, so each element has a unique atomic number.

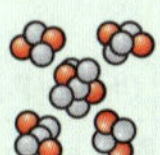

ISOTOPES of an element — atoms with the same number of protons but different numbers of neutrons.

Relative Atomic Mass

RELATIVE ATOMIC MASS (A_r) — the average mass of one atom of an element, compared to $^1/_{12}$ of the mass of one atom of carbon-12:

$$A_r = \frac{\text{sum of (isotope abundance} \times \text{isotope mass number)}}{\text{total abundance of all isotopes}}$$

A_r might not be a whole number because it's an average taking into account all the different isotopes.

The Periodic Table

Mendeleev's Table

Mendeleev made his **Table of Elements** by grouping elements using their properties.

If he ordered the elements by atomic mass, he could arrange them so his groups of elements with similar chemical properties formed columns.

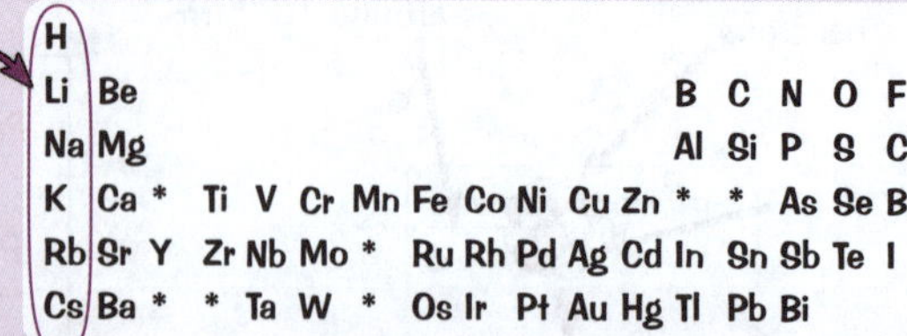

H																
Li	Be											B	C	N	O	F
Na	Mg											Al	Si	P	S	Cl
K	Ca	*	Ti	V	Cr	Mn	Fe	Co	Ni	Cu	Zn	*	*	As	Se	Br
Rb	Sr	Y	Zr	Nb	Mo	*	Ru	Rh	Pd	Ag	Cd	In	Sn	Sb	Te	I
Cs	Ba	*	*	Ta	W	*	Os	Ir	Pt	Au	Hg	Tl	Pb	Bi		

Mendeleev swapped some elements round in places where ordering by atomic mass didn't fit the pattern.

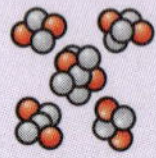

Some of the atomic masses he used were wrong due to the presence of isotopes.

Mendeleev left gaps in the table to keep elements with similar properties together.

He predicted the properties of missing elements using the other elements in the columns.

The Modern Periodic Table

Hydrogen is sometimes put in Group 1.

The elements are ordered by increasing atomic number.

1	2											3	4	5	6	7	0	
			H														He	1
Li	Be											B	C	N	O	F	Ne	2
Na	Mg											Al	Si	P	S	Cl	Ar	3
K	Ca	Sc	Ti	V	Cr	Mn	Fe	Co	Ni	Cu	Zn	Ga	Ge	As	Se	Br	Kr	4
Rb	Sr	Y	Zr	Nb	Mo	Tc	Ru	Rh	Pd	Ag	Cd	In	Sn	Sb	Te	I	Xe	5
Cs	Ba	Lanthanides and Actinides	Hf	Ta	W	Re	Os	Ir	Pt	Au	Hg	Tl	Pb	Bi	Po	At	Rn	6
Fr	Ra																	7

The horizontal rows are called periods.

Elements with similar properties form vertical groups.

If you know how one element in a group reacts, you can predict how the others will react.

Position in the periodic table tells you the electronic configuration:

Group number = the number of electrons in the outer shell.

Period number = the number of shells with electrons in.

Electronic Configurations and Ions

Electronic Configurations

Electrons occupy shells — sometimes called energy levels.
Electrons fill each shell up before occupying a new one, starting with the lowest energy.

Shell	Electrons allowed in shell
1	2
2	8
3	8

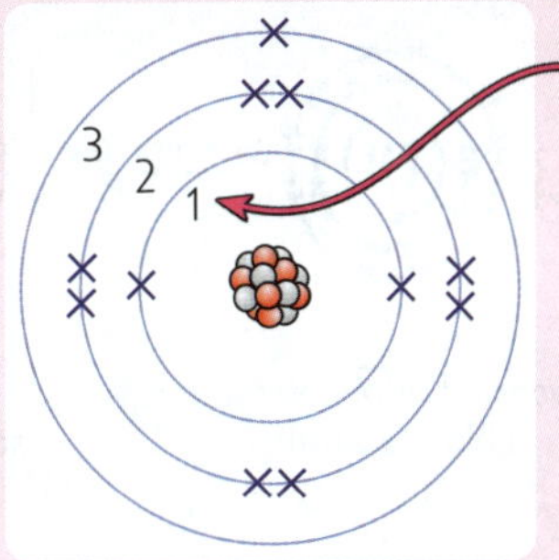

Lowest energy shells are closest to the nucleus.

Electronic configurations can also be represented using numbers — this one is 2.8.1.

Forming Ions

IONS — charged particles made when electrons are transferred.

	Electron transfer	Group	Charge of ion
Metals	lose electrons to form positive ions (cations)	1	1+
		2	2+
Non-metals	gain electrons to form negative ions (anions)	6	2–
		7	1–

Charge on ion = number of electrons gained or lost.

E.g. 2+ means 2 electrons lost (so there are 2 more protons than electrons).

The ions formed by elements in these groups have full outer shells.

Ionic Formulas

The overall charge of any ionic compound is zero.

Calcium nitrate = $Ca(NO_3)_2$ (2+ on Ca, 1– on NO_3)

Overall charge is 0 as there are 2 nitrate ions for each calcium ion.

Name ends in...	Anion contains...
-ate	...oxygen and at least one other element.
-ide	...only one element.

Except for hydroxide ions, OH^-.

Ionic Substances and Bonding Models

Ionic Bonding

IONIC BONDING — the electrostatic attraction between oppositely charged ions.
Ionic bonds form when electrons are transferred from metal atoms to non-metal atoms.

Sodium Chloride

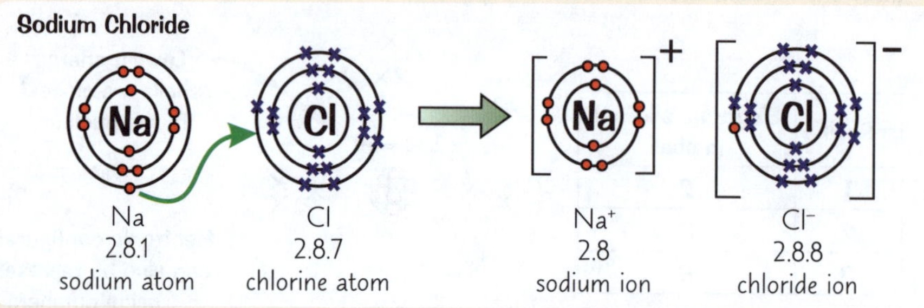

Giant Ionic Lattice

Strong electrostatic forces of attraction between oppositely charged ions act in all directions.

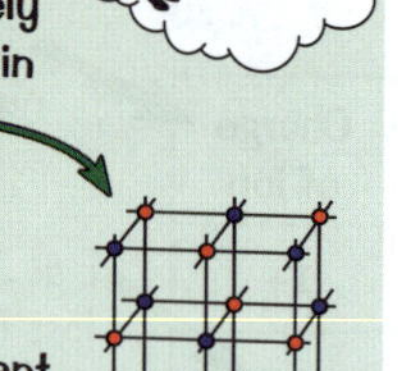

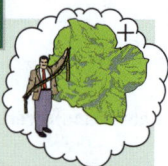

Closely-packed regular arrangement of ions.

Three Properties of Ionic Compounds

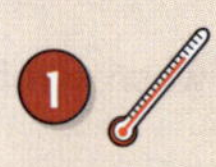

1. **High melting and boiling points — lots of energy needed to overcome the strong attraction between the ions.**

2. **Soluble in water.**

3. **Conduct electricity only when molten or dissolved — ions free to move and carry electric charge.**

Models

Ball and stick diagrams:

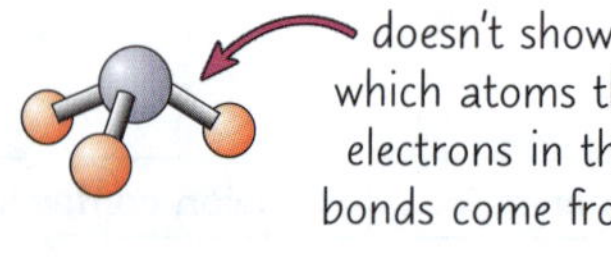

doesn't show which atoms the electrons in the bonds come from.

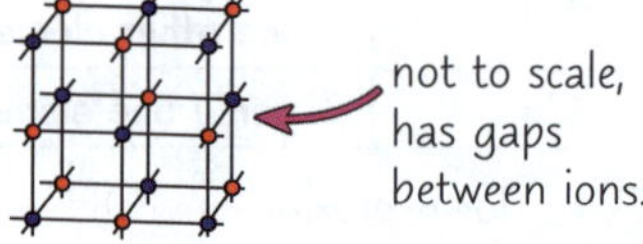

not to scale, has gaps between ions.

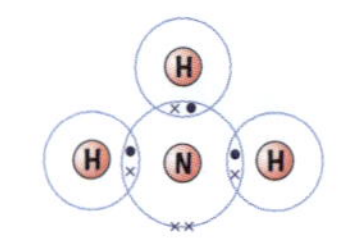

Dot and cross diagrams — don't show relative sizes of atoms or their arrangement in space.

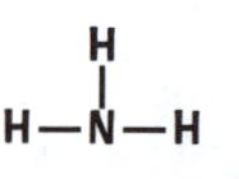

Displayed formula (2D) — doesn't show 3D structure or sizes of atoms.

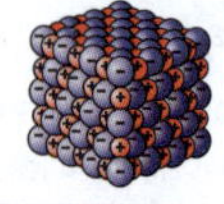

3D model — only shows outer layer.

Molecular Substances

Simple Molecular Substances

COVALENT BOND — a shared pair of electrons between two non-metal atoms.

Simple molecular substances are made up of molecules containing a few covalently-bonded atoms.

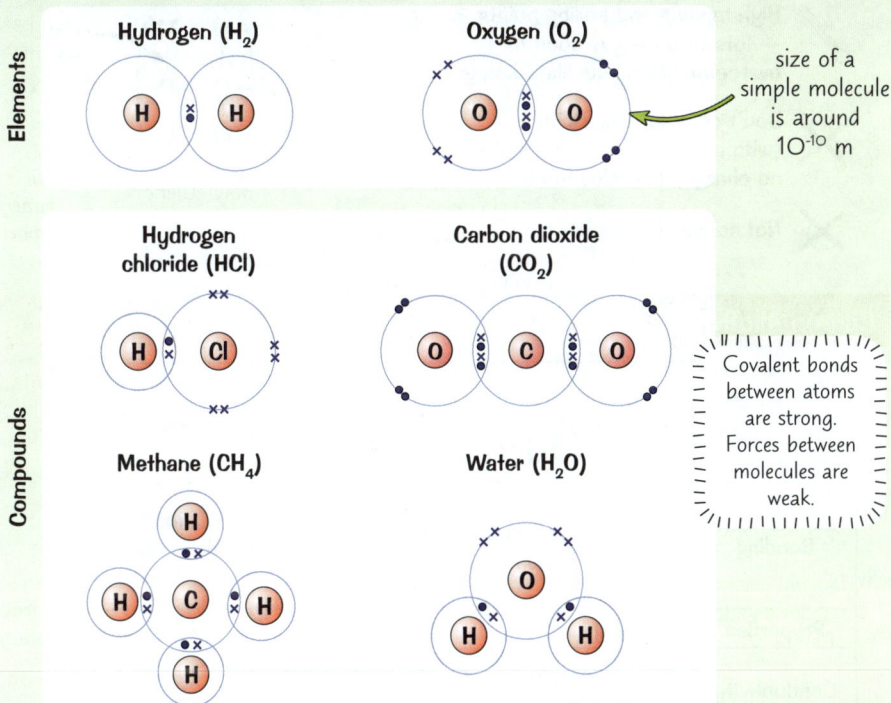

Elements

Hydrogen (H_2)

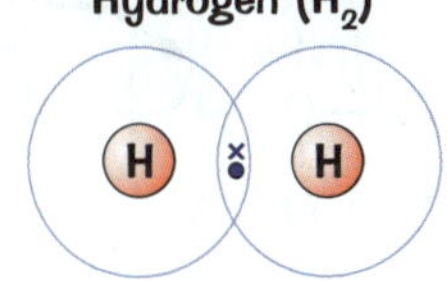

Oxygen (O_2)

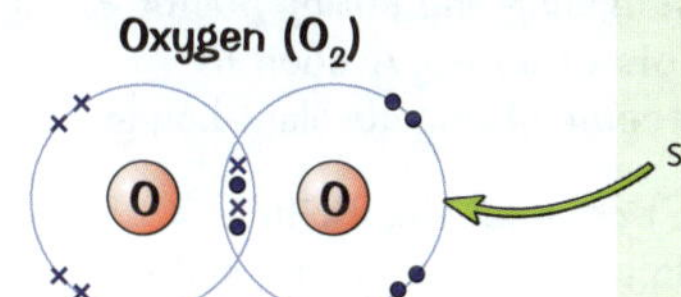

size of a simple molecule is around 10^{-10} m

Compounds

Hydrogen chloride (HCl)

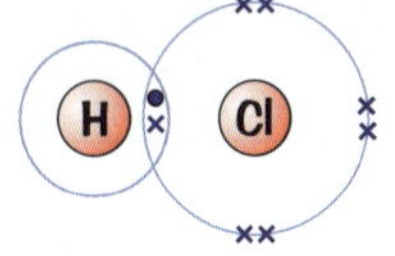

Carbon dioxide (CO_2)

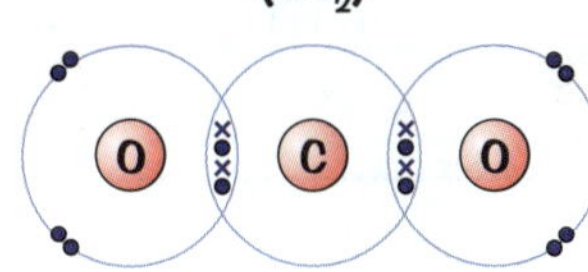

Covalent bonds between atoms are strong. Forces between molecules are weak.

Methane (CH_4)

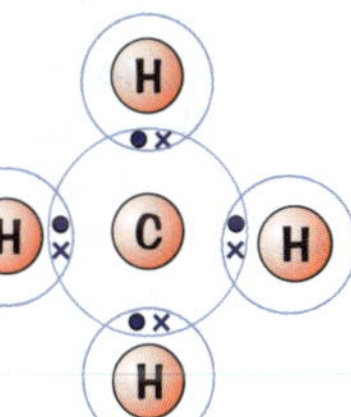

Water (H_2O)

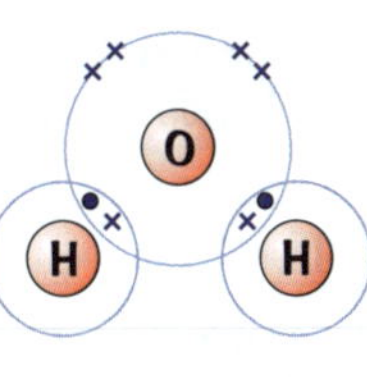

Three Properties of Simple Molecular Substances

1. 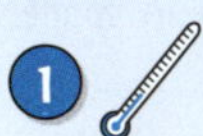 **Low melting and boiling points — mostly gases or liquids at room temperature.**
2. 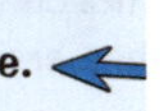 **Don't conduct electricity — there are no charged particles to carry charge.**
3.  **Some are soluble in water, and some aren't.**

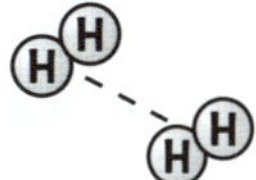

As molecules get smaller, less energy is needed to break the weaker forces between them.

These properties are also typical of non-metal elements.

More Covalent Substances

Giant Covalent Structures

GIANT COVALENT STRUCTURES — solids containing atoms which are all bonded to each other by strong covalent bonds.

High melting and boiling points — lots of energy needed to overcome strong covalent bonds.

Don't conduct electricity (with a couple of exceptions) — no charged particles to carry charge.

Not soluble in water.

Examples include diamond and graphite.

Polymers

POLYMERS — very long chains of covalently bonded carbon atoms.

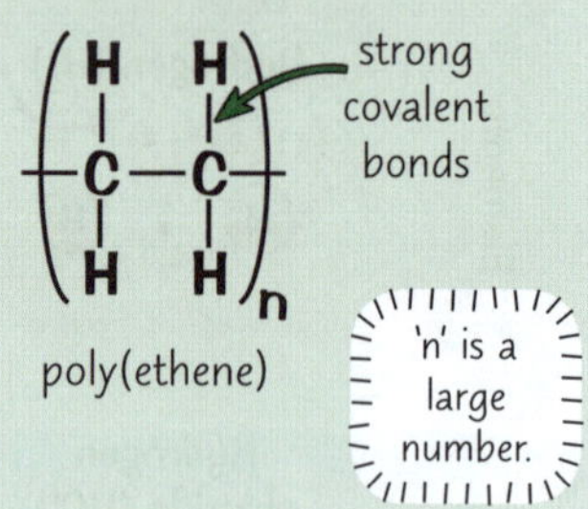

poly(ethene)

Carbon Allotropes

	Diamond	Graphite	Graphene
Bonding	C atoms form four covalent bonds	C atoms form three covalent bonds. No covalent bonds between layers	C atoms form three covalent bonds
Properties	Very hard	Soft, slippery	Strong, light
Conductivity	Doesn't conduct electricity	Conducts electricity and thermal energy	Conducts electricity
Uses	Cutting tools	Electrodes, lubricant	

Each carbon atom in graphite and graphene has one delocalised electron.

FULLERENES — have hollow shapes, giving them large surface areas.

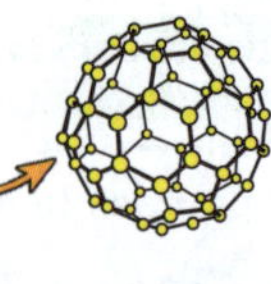

Buckminsterfullerene (C_{60}) is spherical.

Nanotubes are cylindrical fullerenes. They have delocalised electrons so they can conduct electricity.

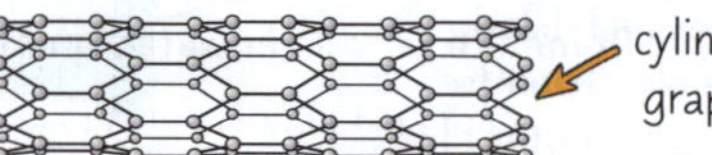

Metallic Bonding, Metals & Non-Metals

Metallic Bonding

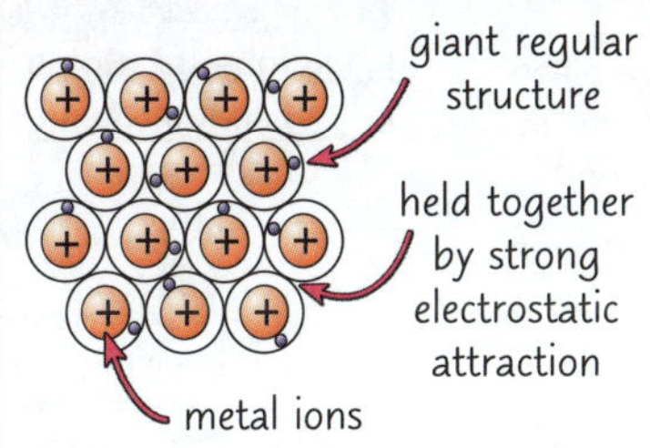

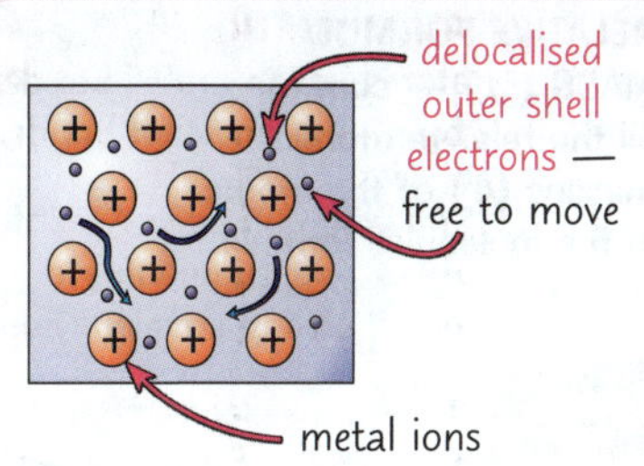

Six Properties of Metals

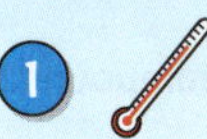
1. High melting and boiling points as lots of energy needed to overcome strong metallic bonds. Generally solids at room temperature.

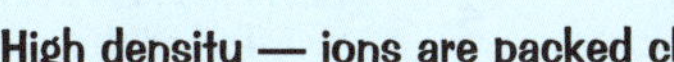
2. High density — ions are packed close together.

3. Not soluble in water.

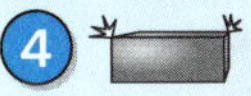
4. Shiny appearance.

5. Good electrical conductors — delocalised electrons carry charge.

6. Soft and malleable — layers in metals slide over each other.

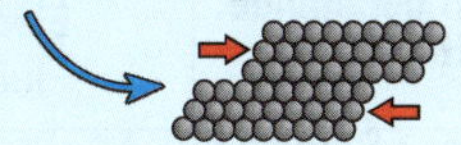

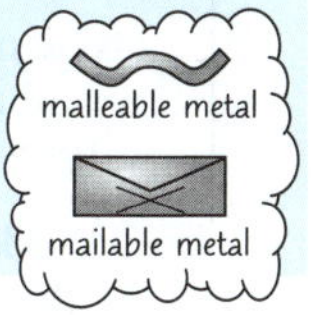

Chemical Properties of Metals and Non-Metals

METALS — outer shell under half-filled, lose electrons to get a full outer shell.

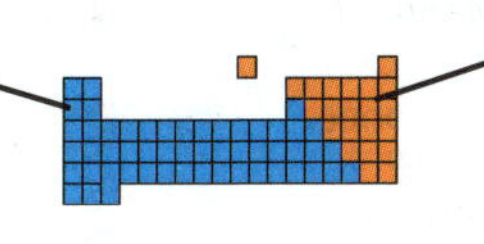

NON-METALS — outer shell over half-filled, gain electrons to get a full outer shell.

Mass, Moles and Limiting Reactants

Relative Formula Mass

RELATIVE FORMULA MASS (M_r) — sum of all the relative atomic masses (A_r) of the atoms in the molecular formula.

Percentage Mass

$$\text{Percentage mass of an element in a compound} = \frac{A_r \times \text{number of atoms of that element}}{M_r \text{ of compound}} \times 100$$

The Mole

Guacamole recipe: take 6.02×10^{23} avocados...

One mole = 6.02×10^{23} particles of a substance.

This is the Avogadro constant.

The particles could be e.g. atoms, molecules or ions.

Mass in grams of one mole of atoms of an element = the A_r of the element.

Mass in grams of one mole of molecules of a compound = the M_r of the compound.

$$\text{Number of moles (mol)} = \frac{\text{mass in g}}{M_r \text{ or } A_r}$$

Number of particles = moles × 6.02×10^{23}

To find the number of particles in a given mass, first find the number of moles.

Balancing Equations Using Masses

If you know the masses of reactants and products:

Divide mass by M_r to find the number of moles of each substance.

↓

Divide each number of moles by the smallest number of moles.

↓

If results aren't all whole numbers, multiply them by the same number so that they are whole.

↓

Put these numbers in front of the chemical formulas.

Limiting Reactants

LIMITING REACTANT — a reactant that gets completely used up in a reaction, so limits the amount of product formed.

All the other reactants are in excess.

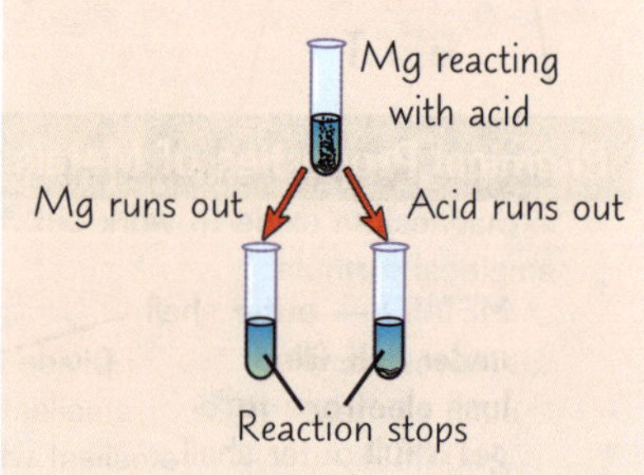

Concentration and Empirical Formulas

Concentration

CONCENTRATION — amount of substance dissolved in a certain volume of solution.

Increase the...	Concentration...
...amount of solute	...increases
...volume of solution	...decreases

$$\text{Concentration} = \frac{\text{mass of solute}}{\text{volume of solution}}$$

Units = $g\ dm^{-3}$

Empirical Formula

EMPIRICAL FORMULA — the smallest whole number ratio of atoms in a compound.

molecular formula $C_6H_{12}O_6$ ⟷ empirical formula CH_2O

To find molecular formula from empirical formula:

1. Find M_r of empirical formula.
2. Divide M_r of compound by M_r of empirical formula.
3. Multiply atoms in empirical formula by result.

Empirical Formula Experiment

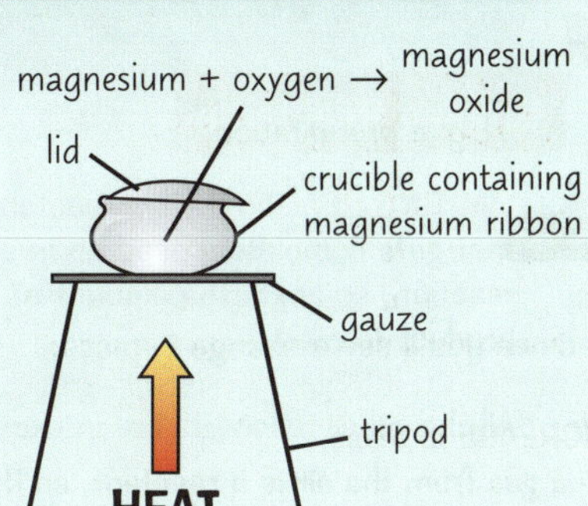

You need to weigh:

1. **Empty crucible and its lid.**
2. **Crucible, lid and contents before heating.**
3. **Crucible, lid and contents after heating.**

Mass of magnesium = 2 – 1

Mass of oxygen = 3 – 2

Use the mass of each element in magnesium oxide to work out empirical formula:

This method works for any compound if you know how much of each element is present.

Divide mass of each element by its A_r. → **Divide each result by smallest number to get smallest whole number ratio.** → **This gives the number of atoms of each element in empirical formula.**

Equations and Conservation of Mass

Calculating Masses Using Balanced Equations

To work out the mass of product formed from a given mass of a reactant:

Cong writes his balanced equations unconventionally.

Write a balanced equation for the reaction.

↓

Divide the mass of the reactant by its M_r to find the number of moles.

↓

Use the balanced equation to find the number of moles of the product.

This is assuming that all the reactant gets used up in the reaction.

↓

Multiply this number of moles by the M_r of the product to work out its mass.

You can also find the mass of a reactant from the mass of a product using this method.

Conservation of Mass

No atoms are created or destroyed in a chemical reaction, so the total masses of reactants and products are also the same — MASS IS CONSERVED.

If you weigh a sealed reaction vessel, you shouldn't see a change in mass:

If you weigh an unsealed reaction vessel, sometimes you'll see a change in mass:

DECREASE in mass
— a gas is made during the reaction and escapes the vessel, so its mass is no longer accounted for.

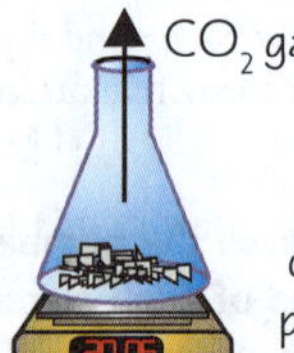

E.g. the thermal decomposition of calcium carbonate produces CO_2 gas.

INCREASE in mass
— a gas from the air is a reactant, so its mass is added to the mass in the vessel (none of the products are gaseous).

E.g. the reaction of magnesium with O_2 gas only produces a solid.

States of Matter

Particle Model

	Solid	Liquid	Gas
Particle Diagram			
Particle Arrangement	Regular	Random	Random
Particle Movement	Fixed position, can vibrate	Move around each other	Move quickly in all directions
Relative Energy of Particles	Low	Medium	High

Changes of State

Changes between states of matter are physical changes.

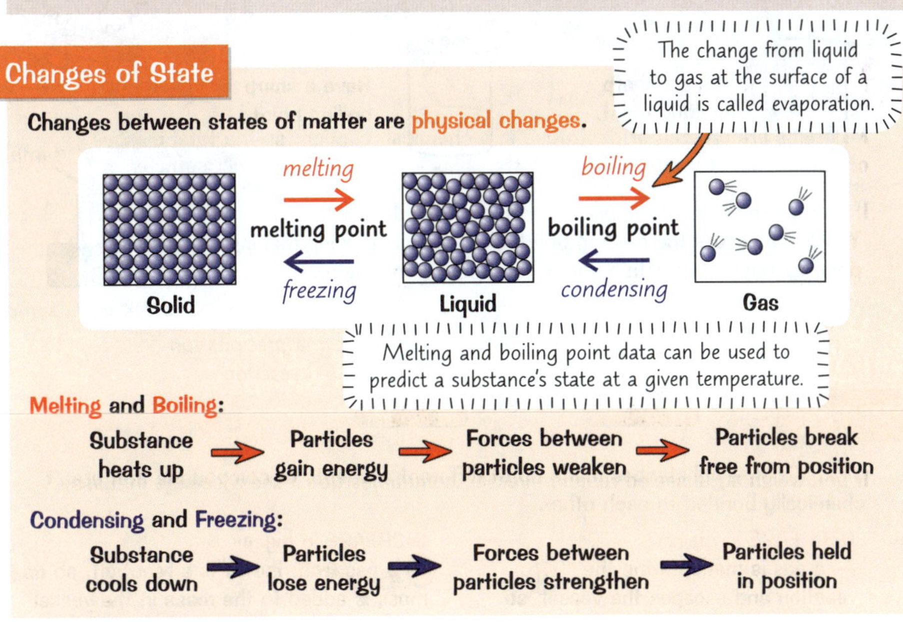

The change from liquid to gas at the surface of a liquid is called evaporation.
melting
melting point
freezing
boiling
boiling point
condensing
Solid
Liquid
Gas
Melting and boiling point data can be used to predict a substance's state at a given temperature.

Melting and Boiling:

Substance heats up → Particles gain energy → Forces between particles weaken → Particles break free from position

Condensing and Freezing:

Substance cools down → Particles lose energy → Forces between particles strengthen → Particles held in position

Chemical Changes

Chemical changes happen in chemical reactions.

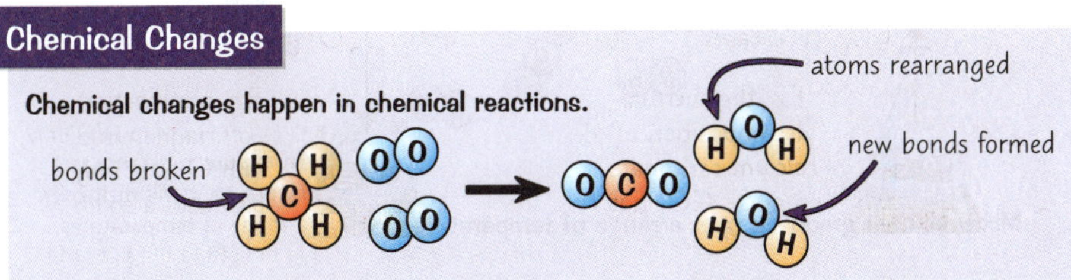

Purity

Definitions of Purity

	Everyday Definition	Chemical Definition
PURE SUBSTANCE	Clean or natural.	A substance containing only one element or compound.

Pure Substances

A chemically pure substance will:

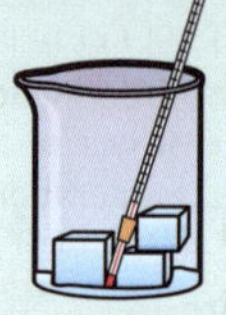

Have a sharp melting point.

Have a sharp boiling point.

You can measure the melting point of a substance using melting point apparatus, or with a water bath and thermometer.

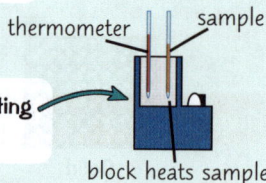

thermometer

sample

block heats sample

Mixtures

MIXTURES — substances made up of different elements or compounds that aren't chemically bonded to each other.

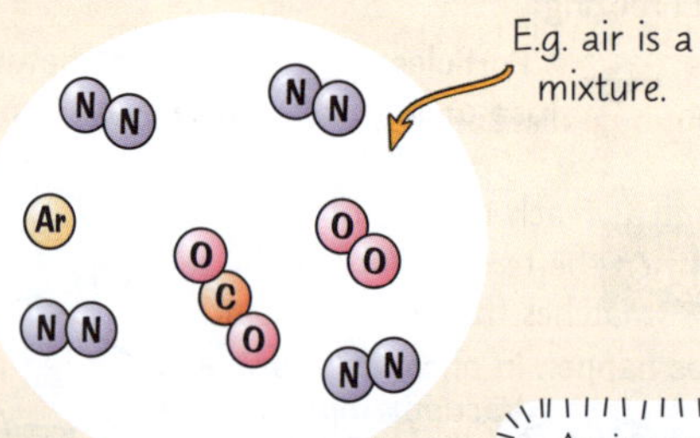

E.g. air is a mixture.

Mixtures melt gradually over a range of temperatures.

An impure substance is a mixture, so it will melt over a range of temperatures.

Separation Techniques

Filtration

FILTRATION — separates insoluble solids from liquids and solutions.

It can be used to separate out a solid product, or purify a liquid by removing insoluble impurities.

filter paper
Solid left in the filter paper.

Evaporation

EVAPORATION — separates soluble salts from solution.

evaporating dish

Crystals form and dry out as solvent evaporates.

Slowly heat solution.

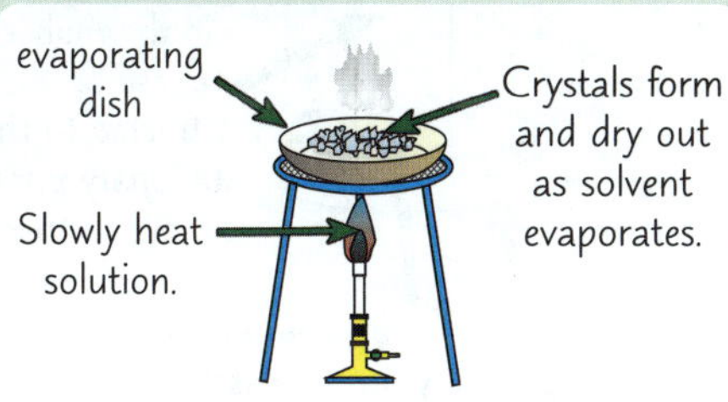

Crystallisation

CRYSTALLISATION — also separates soluble salts from solution.

Heat solution, but cool it when crystals start to form.

↓

Large crystals form as solution cools.

↓

Filter out crystals and leave to dry.

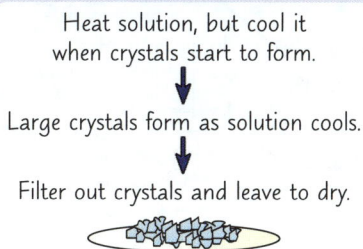

Two Types of Distillation

1. **Simple distillation**

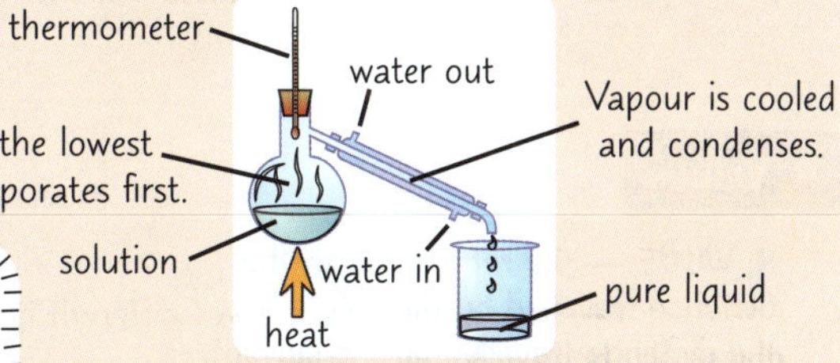

thermometer

water out

The part with the lowest boiling point evaporates first.

Vapour is cooled and condenses.

solution

water in

heat

pure liquid

Simple distillation can't separate liquids with similar boiling points, but fractional distillation can.

2. **Fractional distillation**

thermometer

condenser

Liquids reach the top of the column when the temperature at the top matches their boiling point.

fractions collected separately

fractionating column filled with glass rods

mixture of liquids

heat

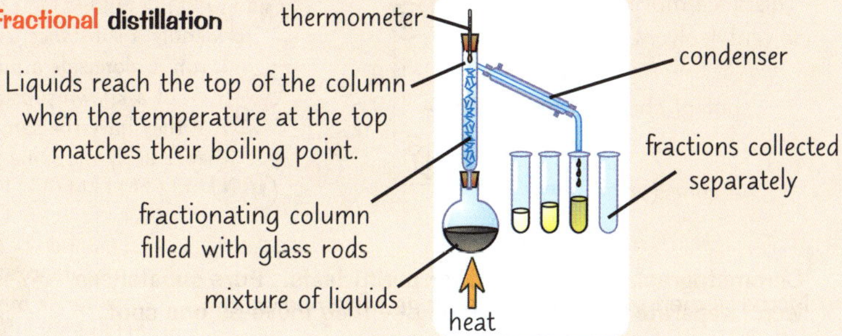

Chromatography

Paper Chromatography

CHROMATOGRAPHY — a method used to separate a mixture of soluble substances.

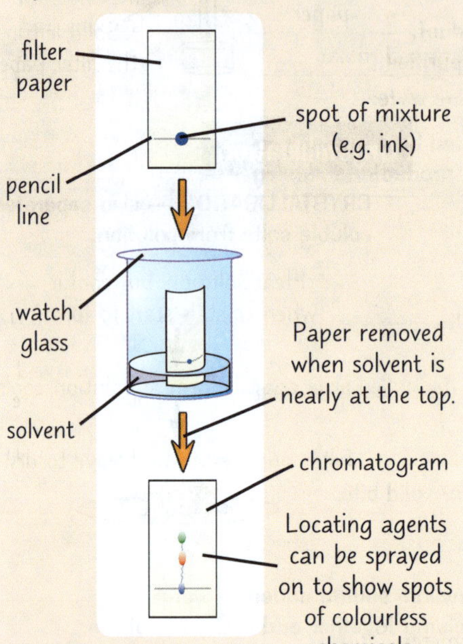

Two Phases of Chromatography

1. **STATIONARY PHASE — where the molecules can't move.** e.g. chromatography paper

Different components of the sample separate out.

Substances that are more soluble in the mobile phase or less attracted to the stationary phase move further.

Insoluble components stay on the baseline.

2. **MOBILE PHASE — where the molecules can move (the solvent).** e.g. water or ethanol

R_f Values

R_f VALUE — the ratio between the distance travelled by the solute and the distance travelled by the solvent.

$$R_f = \frac{\text{distance travelled by solute (B)}}{\text{distance travelled by solvent (A)}}$$

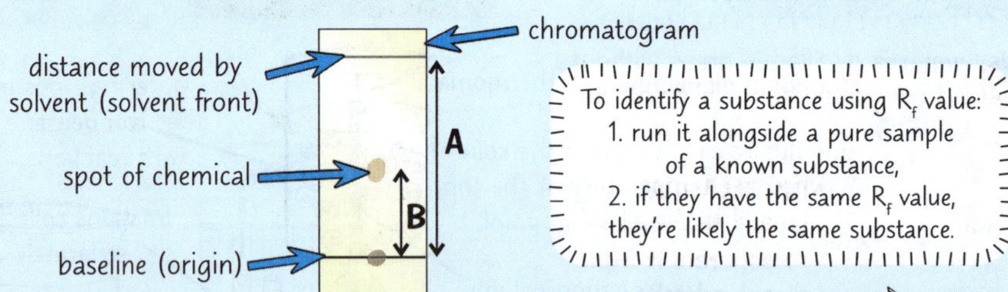

To identify a substance using R_f value:
1. run it alongside a pure sample of a known substance,
2. if they have the same R_f value, they're likely the same substance.

Chromatography can be used for purity tests. Pure substances won't separate in chromatography — they move as one spot.

Lou was excited to calculate his Ref value.

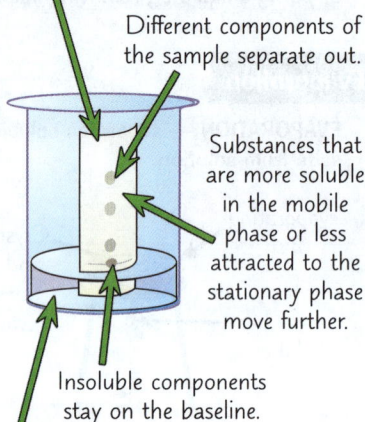

Water Treatment

Sources of Water

POTABLE WATER — water that is safe to drink.

Potable water is not chemically pure. It can contain low levels of dissolved salts and microbes.

Type of Water	Source
Ground water	Underground rocks
Salt water	Sea water
Waste water	Water contaminated by a human process, e.g. as a by-product in industry

Treating Water

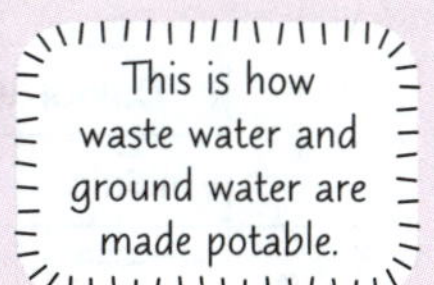

This is how waste water and ground water are made potable.

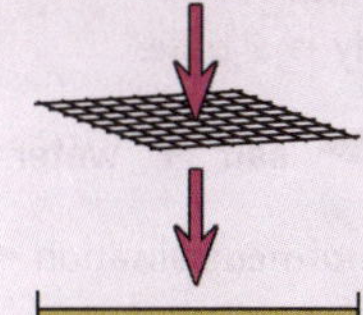

Mesh
— removes any large debris such as twigs.

Sand and gravel filtration
— removes any smaller solid bits.

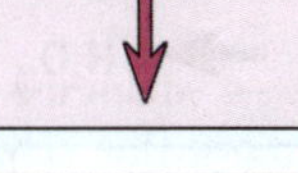

Sedimentation
— iron sulfate or aluminium sulfate added to water, making fine particles clump together and settle at bottom.

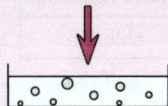

Chlorination
— chlorine gas bubbled through to kill harmful bacteria and other microbes.

Distilling Sea Water

Sea water is distilled in areas without much fresh water to make it potable.

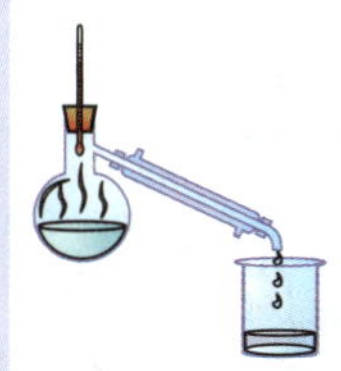

DISTILLATION — boiling the water to separate it from dissolved salts.

This uses lots of energy.

Water for Analysis

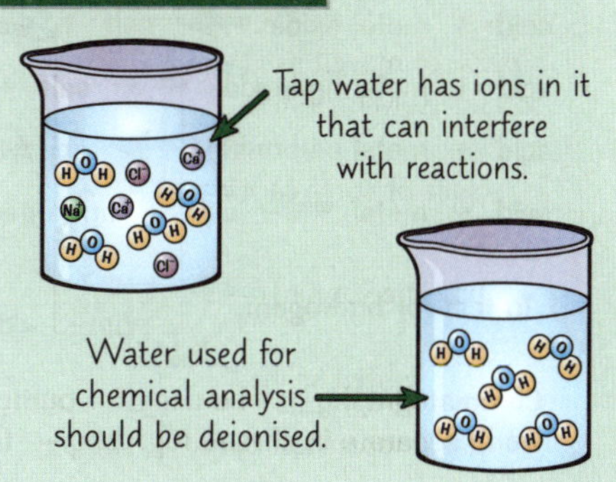

Tap water has ions in it that can interfere with reactions.
Water used for chemical analysis should be deionised.

Acids and Bases

The pH Scale

Alkalis are soluble bases.

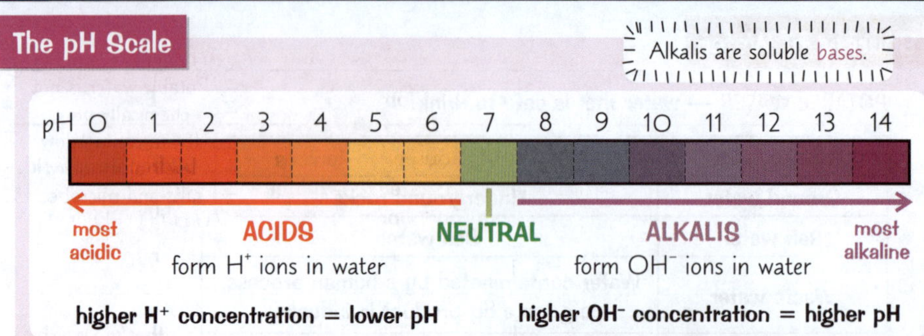
pH 0 1 2 3 4 5 6 7 8 9 10 11 12 13 14
most acidic
ACIDS
form H⁺ ions in water
NEUTRAL
ALKALIS
form OH⁻ ions in water
most alkaline
higher H⁺ concentration = lower pH
higher OH⁻ concentration = higher pH

Indicators

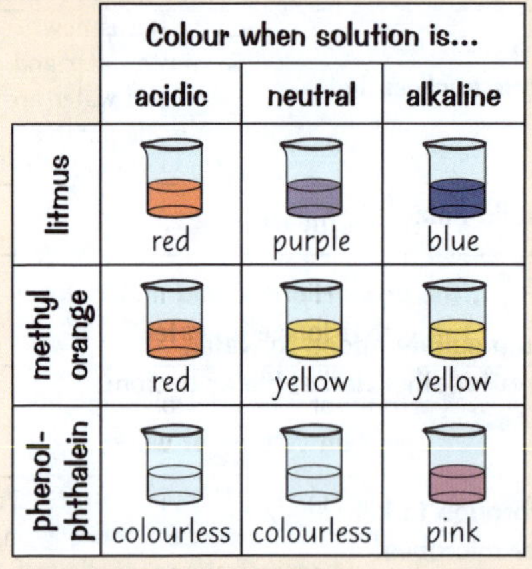

	Colour when solution is...		
	acidic	neutral	alkaline
litmus	red	purple	blue
methyl orange	red	yellow	yellow
phenol-phthalein	colourless	colourless	pink

Neutralisation Reactions

Any substance that reacts with acid this way is a base.

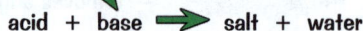

acid + base → salt + water

The products of neutralisation reactions are neutral.

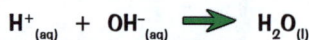

$$H^+_{(aq)} + OH^-_{(aq)} \rightarrow H_2O_{(l)}$$

Acid Used	Salt Produced
HCl	chloride
H_2SO_4	sulfate
HNO_3	nitrate

Reactions of Acids

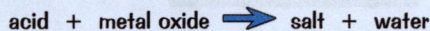

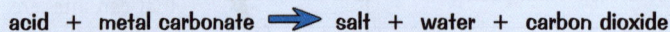

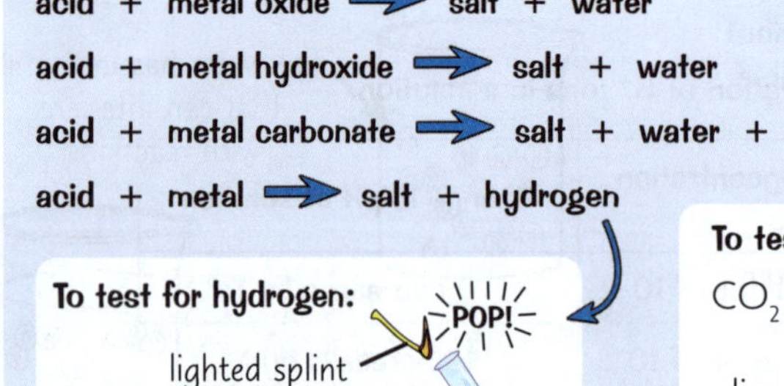
acid + metal oxide → salt + water
acid + metal hydroxide → salt + water
acid + metal carbonate → salt + water + carbon dioxide
acid + metal → salt + hydrogen
To test for hydrogen:
POP!
lighted splint
H₂ gas in open test tube

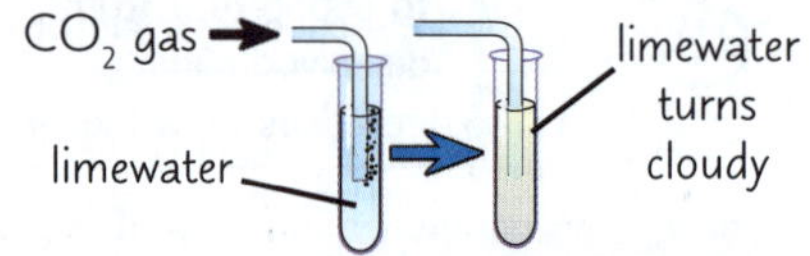
To test for carbon dioxide:
CO₂ gas
limewater
limewater turns cloudy

Strong and Weak Acids

Acid Strength

	Definition	Examples
STRONG ACID	An acid that completely ionises (dissociates) in water to produce hydrogen ions. E.g. $HCl \rightarrow H^+ + Cl^-$	hydrochloric acid sulfuric acid nitric acid
WEAK ACID	An acid that partially ionises (dissociates) in water to produce hydrogen ions. E.g. $CH_3COOH \rightleftharpoons H^+ + CH_3COO^-$	ethanoic acid citric acid carbonic acid

Strength vs Concentration

	A measure of...
ACID STRENGTH	...the proportion of acid molecules that ionise in water.
ACID CONCENTRATION	...the number of acid molecules in a certain volume of water.

Dilute acids have a low concentration.
Concentrated acids have a high concentration.

The pH will decrease with increasing acid concentration regardless of whether it's a strong or weak acid.

pH and H^+ Ion Concentration

pH — a measure of the concentration of H^+ ions in a solution.

Change in H^+ ion concentration of solution	Change in pH of solution
↑ increases by a factor of 10	↓ decreases by 1
↓ decreases by a factor of 10	↑ increases by 1

For a given concentration of acid, as the acid strength increases, pH decreases.

Insoluble and Soluble Salts

Solubility

You can use these rules to predict whether a product will be aqueous or a precipitate.

Substance	Soluble?
common salts of sodium, potassium and ammonium	yes
nitrates	yes
common chlorides	yes (except silver chloride and lead chloride)
common sulfates	yes (except lead, barium and calcium sulfate)
common carbonates and hydroxides	no (except for sodium, potassium and ammonium ones)

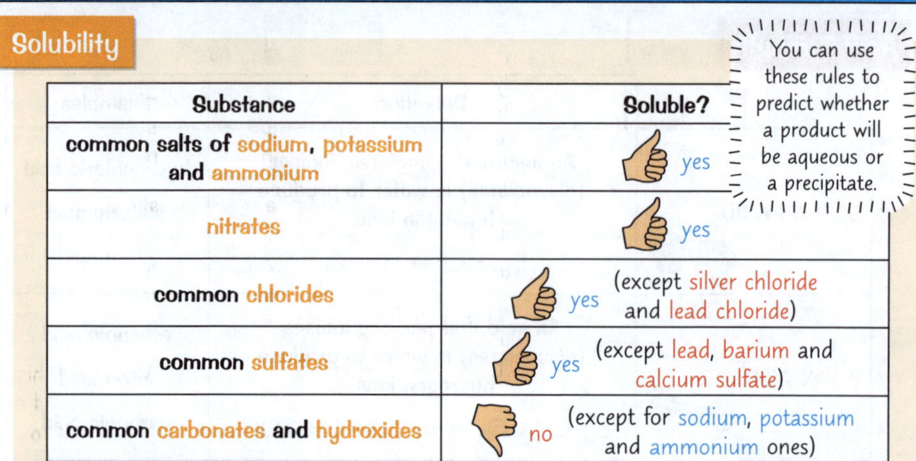

Making Insoluble Salts

soluble salts in solution

filter paper

filter funnel

precipitate

%#$@!

insolent salt

dry precipitate

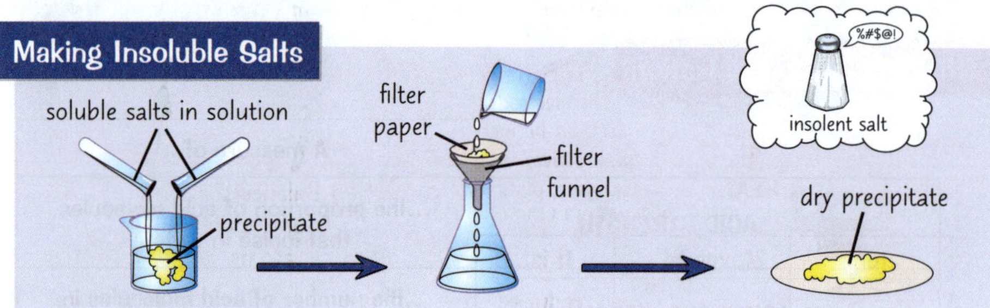

Making Soluble Salts

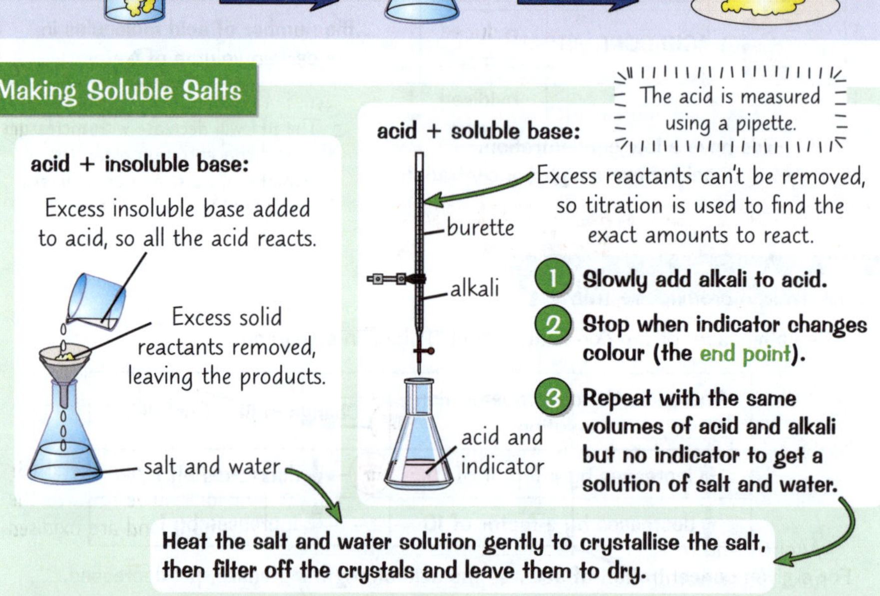

acid + insoluble base:
Excess insoluble base added to acid, so all the acid reacts.
Excess solid reactants removed, leaving the products.
salt and water
acid + soluble base:
The acid is measured using a pipette.
Excess reactants can't be removed, so titration is used to find the exact amounts to react.
burette
alkali
acid and indicator
1 Slowly add alkali to acid.
2 Stop when indicator changes colour (the end point).
3 Repeat with the same volumes of acid and alkali but no indicator to get a solution of salt and water.
Heat the salt and water solution gently to crystallise the salt, then filter off the crystals and leave them to dry.

Electrolysis

Electrochemical Cells

ELECTROLYSIS — passing an electric current through an electrolyte, causing it to decompose.

Electrolyte — a molten or dissolved ionic compound.

Electrolyte = dissolved ionic compound:

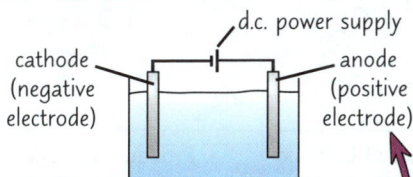

d.c. power supply
cathode (negative electrode)
anode (positive electrode)

Electrolyte = molten ionic compound:

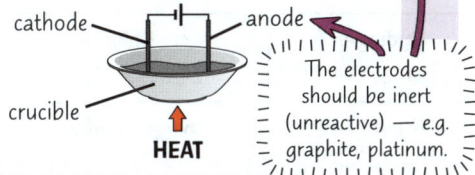

cathode
anode
crucible
HEAT

The electrodes should be inert (unreactive) — e.g. graphite, platinum.

Ion	Moves to...	It is...
cation (+ve)	cathode (–ve)	reduced (gains e^-)
anion (–ve)	anode (+ve)	oxidised (loses e^-)

Half Equations

HALF EQUATIONS — show how electrons are transferred during reactions.

To write a half equation:

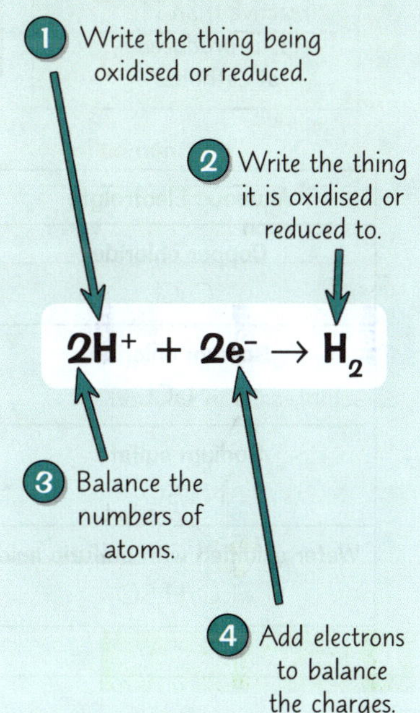

1 Write the thing being oxidised or reduced.
2 Write the thing it is oxidised or reduced to.
$2H^+ + 2e^- \rightarrow H_2$
3 Balance the numbers of atoms.
4 Add electrons to balance the charges.

Electrolysis of Molten Ionic Compounds

Positive metal (Pb^{2+}) ions move towards the cathode and are reduced.
$$Pb^{2+} + 2e^- \rightarrow Pb$$

Molten lead metal sinks to the bottom.

Bromine gas is given off.

Negative non-metal (Br^-) ions move towards the anode and are oxidised.
$$2Br^- \rightarrow Br_2 + 2e^-$$

Section 12 — Chemical Changes

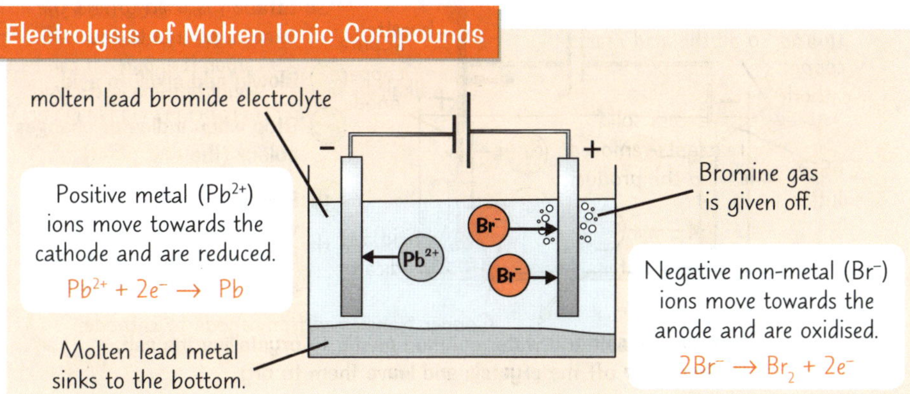

More on Electrolysis

Electrolysis of Aqueous Ionic Compounds

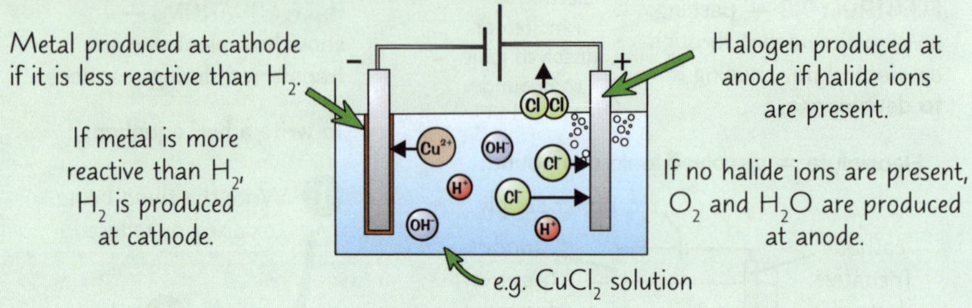
Metal produced at cathode if it is less reactive than H_2.
If metal is more reactive than H_2, H_2 is produced at cathode.
Halogen produced at anode if halide ions are present.
If no halide ions are present, O_2 and H_2O are produced at anode.
e.g. $CuCl_2$ solution

Aqueous Electrolyte	Product at Cathode	Product at Anode
Copper chloride $CuCl_2$	**Copper** $Cu^{2+} + 2e^- \rightarrow Cu$	**Chlorine** $2Cl^- \rightarrow Cl_2 + 2e^-$
Sodium chloride NaCl	**Hydrogen** $2H^+ + 2e^- \rightarrow H_2$	**Chlorine** $2Cl^- \rightarrow Cl_2 + 2e^-$
Sodium sulfate Na_2SO_4	**Hydrogen** $2H^+ + 2e^- \rightarrow H_2$	**Oxygen and water** $4OH^- \rightarrow O_2 + 2H_2O + 4e^-$
Water acidified with sulfuric acid H_2O/H_2SO_4	**Hydrogen** $2H^+ + 2e^- \rightarrow H_2$	**Oxygen and water** $4OH^- \rightarrow O_2 + 2H_2O + 4e^-$

Purifying Copper

Copper extracted from its ore by reduction with carbon is impure. It can be purified using electrolysis.

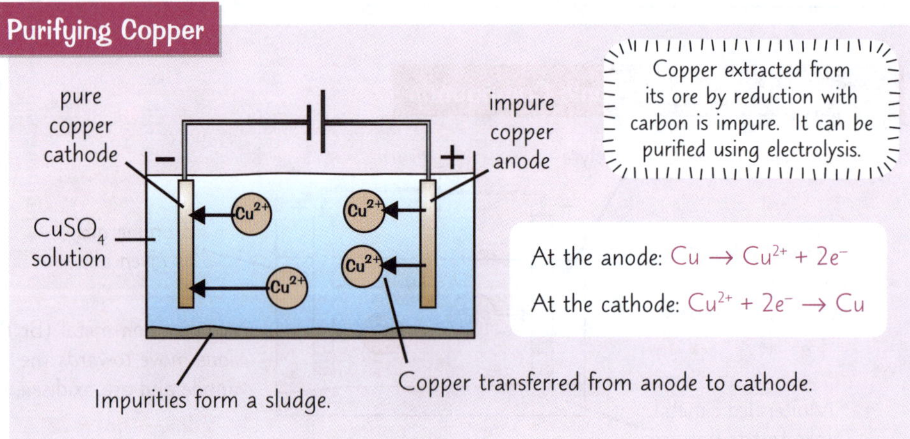
pure copper cathode
impure copper anode
$CuSO_4$ solution
Impurities form a sludge.
Copper transferred from anode to cathode.

At the anode: $Cu \rightarrow Cu^{2+} + 2e^-$

At the cathode: $Cu^{2+} + 2e^- \rightarrow Cu$

Reactivity of Metals

The Reactivity Series

- Easily form cations.
- Less resistant to oxidation.

↑ increasing reactivity

	Reaction with water	Reaction with dilute acid
Potassium	Vigorous — forms metal hydroxide and hydrogen	Explosive — forms salt and hydrogen
Sodium		
Calcium		
Magnesium	Reacts with steam but not water — forms metal oxide and hydrogen	Vigorous — forms salt and hydrogen
Aluminium		
CARBON		
Zinc	Reacts with steam but not water — forms metal oxide and hydrogen	Some bubbling — forms salt and hydrogen
Iron		
HYDROGEN		
Copper	No reaction	No reaction
Silver		
Gold		

- Do not easily form cations.
- More resistant to oxidation.

DISPLACEMENT REACTION — when a more reactive element takes the place of a less reactive metal in a compound.

You can use the reactions with acid and water, plus displacement reactions, to find a metal's position in the reactivity series.

Redox Reactions

REDOX REACTION — where one substance in a reaction is reduced and another is oxidised.

	Gain of...	or Loss of...
Oxidation =	oxygen	electrons
Reduction =	electrons	oxygen

Displacement reactions are redox reactions.

$$Ca_{(s)} + ZnSO_{4(aq)} \rightarrow CaSO_{4(aq)} + Zn_{(s)}$$

Ca is oxidised — it loses electrons.

Zn is reduced — it gains electrons.

Extracting Metals

Extraction Methods

Most metals are extracted from ores taken from the Earth's crust.

increasing reactivity

K
Na
Ca
Mg
Al
C
Zn
Fe
Cu
Ag
Au

Electrolysis — used for metals more reactive than carbon.

Electrolysis requires lots of energy so is expensive — only used for reactive metals.

Reduction using carbon — can only be used to extract metals less reactive than carbon.

Found as uncombined elements.

Heating the ore with carbon reduces it — oxygen is removed.

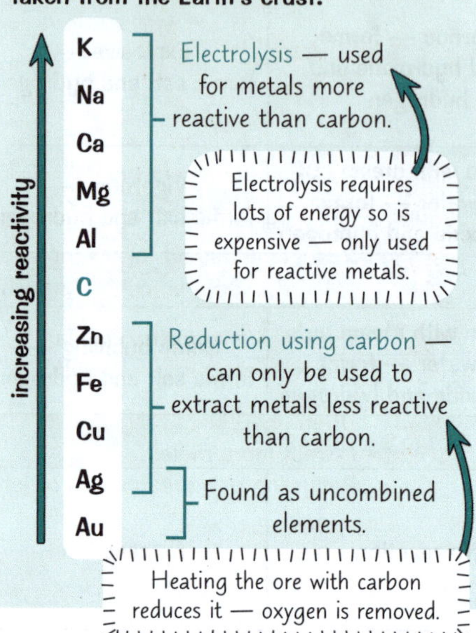

Extraction by Electrolysis

E.g. extraction of aluminium:

cathode

anode

O_2

Al^{3+}

O^{2-}

O^{2-}

Al

molten aluminium metal is formed

oxygen gas is formed

molten aluminium oxide mixed with cryolite (to lower the melting point)

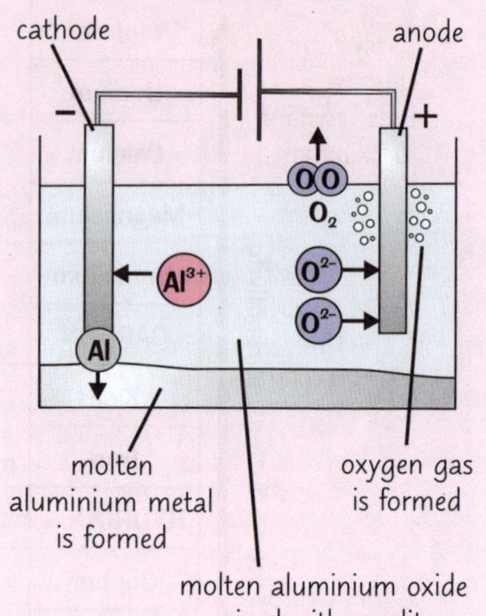

Biological Methods of Extraction

Phytoextraction

soil containing metal compounds

metal builds up in leaves

harvested plants are burned — ash contains metal compounds

Bacterial (Bioleaching)

low-grade ore

bacteria

leachate solution containing metal ions

Pure metal extracted

electrolysis

displacement reaction with more reactive metal

Bacteria get energy from bonds between atoms in the ore, separating out the metal in the process.

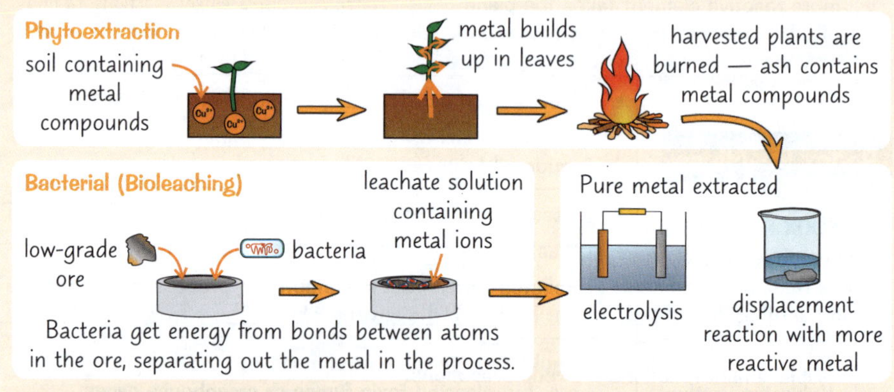

Compared to traditional methods:

- ✓ **Can be used to extract metals from low-grade ores or from waste.**
- ✓ **Less damaging to environment.**
- ✗ **Slow.**

Recycling and Life Cycle Assessments

Issues With Extracting Metals

Metals are non-renewable resources — they will eventually run out.

Mining metals damages the environment.

Fossil fuels need burning to provide lots of energy for extraction, causing pollution.

Fossil fuels are also non-renewable, so need to be conserved.

Benefits of Recycling Metals

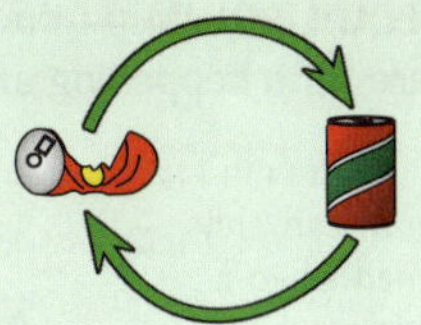

Reduces the amount of waste sent to landfill.

Reduces the need for mining — preserves finite amount of metal.

Uses less energy than mining and extracting raw materials.

Often cheaper to recycle than extract more metal.
Recycling also creates lots of jobs.

Life Cycle Assessments

LIFE CYCLE ASSESSMENT (LCA) — an assessment of the environmental impact of a product over each stage of its life.

Life Cycle Assessment Stage	Considerations
Raw Materials	• Metals need mining and extraction from ores. • Raw materials for chemical manufacture often come from crude oil (non-renewable resource).
Manufacturing	• Uses a lot of energy and can cause pollution. • Waste products need recycling or disposing of. • Polluted water from manufacturing processes shouldn't be put back into the environment.
Using the Product	• Could damage the environment, e.g. by releasing toxic fumes or greenhouse gases, or by contaminating streams and rivers.
Product Disposal	• Disposal in landfill takes up space and can cause pollution. • Incineration causes air pollution.

Reversible Reactions

Equilibrium

DYNAMIC EQUILIBRIUM — the forward and backward reactions are both happening at the same rate.

Reversible reaction — where the products can react to form the reactants again.

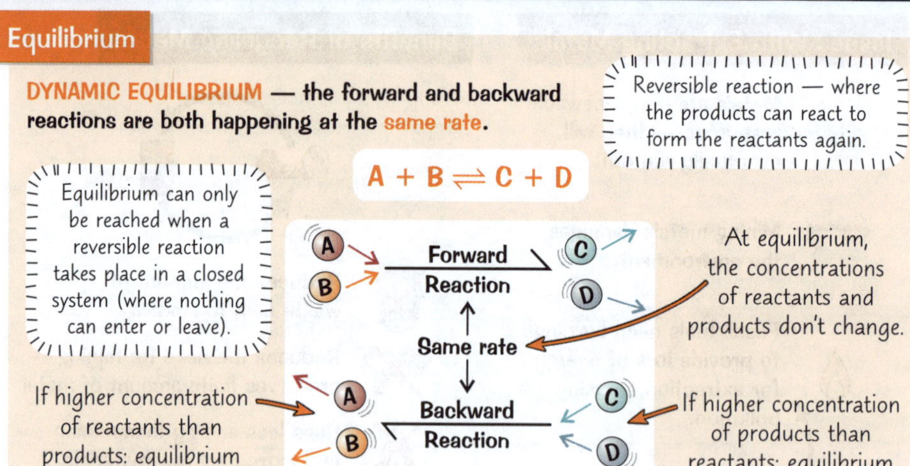

A + B ⇌ C + D
Equilibrium can only be reached when a reversible reaction takes place in a closed system (where nothing can enter or leave).
A
B
Forward Reaction
C
D
At equilibrium, the concentrations of reactants and products don't change.
Same rate
If higher concentration of reactants than products: equilibrium lies to the left.
A
B
Backward Reaction
C
D
If higher concentration of products than reactants: equilibrium lies to the right.

Haber Process

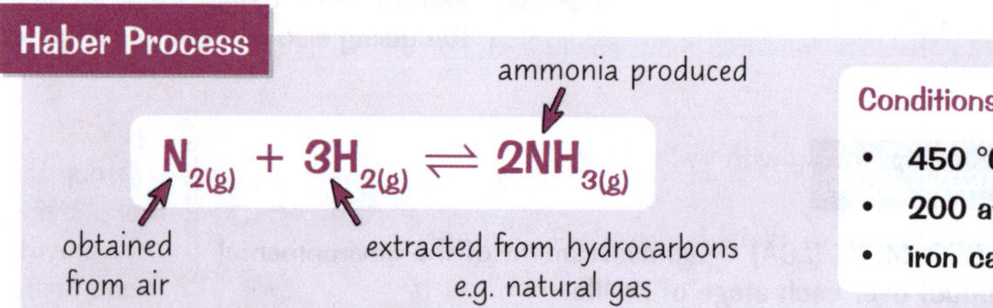

ammonia produced
$N_{2(g)} + 3H_{2(g)} \rightleftharpoons 2NH_{3(g)}$
obtained from air
extracted from hydrocarbons e.g. natural gas

Conditions:

- **450 °C**
- **200 atmospheres**
- **iron catalyst**

Le Chatelier's Principle

If the conditions of a reversible reaction at equilibrium are changed, the system tries to counteract that change.

If the reaction is endothermic in one direction, it will be exothermic in the other.

		The equilibrium shifts to favour the...
Temperature	increases	...endothermic direction to take in heat energy.
	decreases	...exothermic direction to release heat energy.
Pressure	increases	...side with fewer moles of gas to reduce the pressure.
	decreases	...side with more moles of gas to increase the pressure.

If concentration of a reagent is changed, the system will respond to reverse the change.

If the concentration of...	The system responds to...
...reactants increases	...make more products.
...reactants decreases	...make more reactants.

Group 1 and Group 0 Elements

Alkali Metals

ALKALI METALS — common name for Group 1 metals.

Group 1 elements all have one electron in their outer shell.

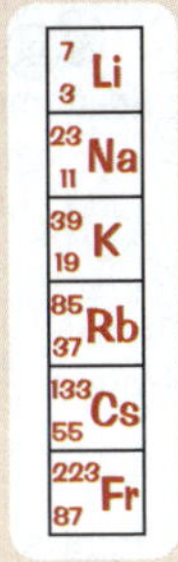

7 3 Li
23 11 Na
39 19 K
85 37 Rb
133 55 Cs
223 87 Fr

Properties of Group 1 Metals

Group 1 metals have different properties from most other metals:

They're much more reactive.

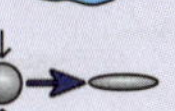
They're softer.

They have lower melting and boiling points.

Reactivity of Group 1 Elements

Readily lose single outer electron to form stable 1+ ion.

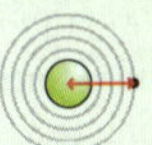
Reactivity increases down Group 1 as outer electron is further from nucleus and more easily lost.

Use the trend down Group 1 to predict how other alkali metals react with water.

Alkali metals react vigorously with water to make alkalis:

alkali metal + water → metal hydroxide + hydrogen

e.g. sodium + water → sodium hydroxide + hydrogen

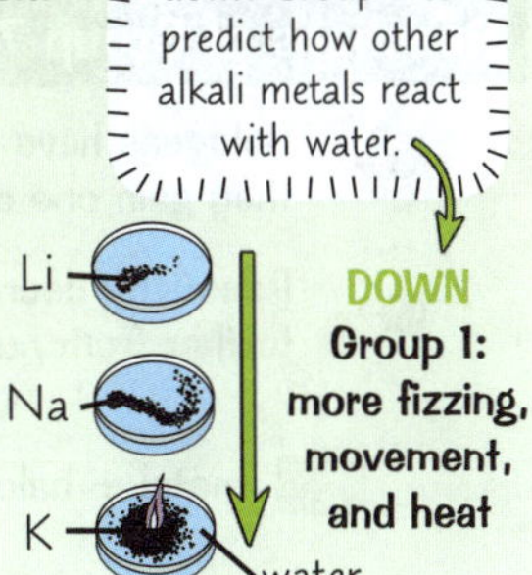

Group 0 Elements

GROUP 0 ELEMENTS — non-metals with full outer shells of electrons.

These elements are also known as the noble gases.

Full outer shells are very stable, so these elements are inert (unreactive).

All Group 0 elements are colourless monatomic gases at room temperature.

As you go DOWN Group 0:	
Density	increases
Melting and boiling points	increase

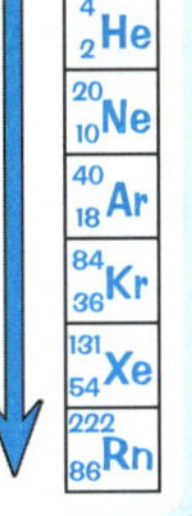

Property	Uses
Inert	Protect metals during welding
Non-flammable	Filament lamps, flash photography
Low density (just helium)	Fill balloons, airships

Group 7 Elements

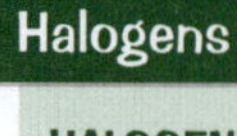

Halogens

HALOGENS — the non-metal elements in Group 7.

The halogens exist as diatomic molecules — two atoms joined by a covalent bond.

Halogen	Appearance at room temperature
Chlorine	green gas
Bromine	red-brown liquid which gives off orange vapour
Iodine	dark grey solid which gives off purple vapour

Chlorine gas turns damp blue litmus paper white.

Different states at room temperature show melting and boiling points increase down group.

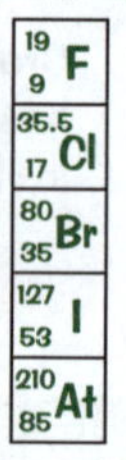

Reactions of Group 7 Elements

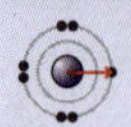

Halogens have seven outer shell electrons — they gain one electron to form a stable 1– ion.

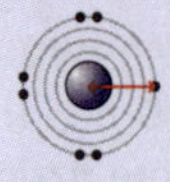

Reactivity decreases down Group 7 as outer shell is further from nucleus so it's harder to gain an electron.

Hydrogen halides form acidic solutions (e.g. hydrochloric acid) when dissolved in water.

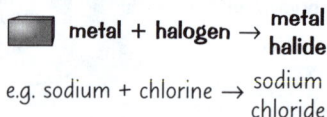

metal + halogen → metal halide

e.g. sodium + chlorine → sodium chloride

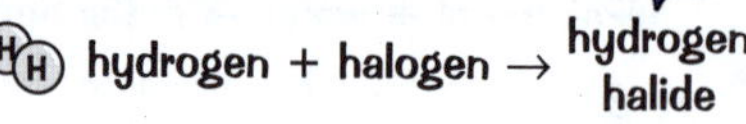

hydrogen + halogen → hydrogen halide

e.g. hydrogen + chlorine → hydrogen chloride

Halogen Displacement Reactions

Displacement reactions are redox reactions.

Start with →	$KCl_{(aq)}$ (colourless)	$KBr_{(aq)}$ (colourless)	$KI_{(aq)}$ (colourless)
add $Cl_{2(aq)}$ (colourless) →	no reaction	orange solution (Br_2)	brown solution (I_2)
add $Br_{2(aq)}$ (orange) →	no reaction	no reaction	brown solution (I_2)
add $I_{2(aq)}$ (brown) →	no reaction	no reaction	no reaction

Chlorine displaces bromine from an aqueous salt.

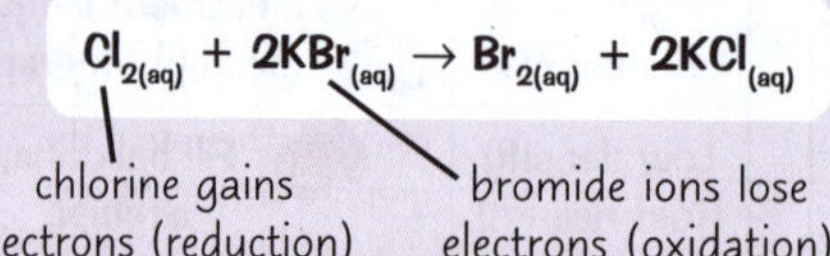

$$Cl_{2(aq)} + 2KBr_{(aq)} \rightarrow Br_{2(aq)} + 2KCl_{(aq)}$$

chlorine gains electrons (reduction)

bromide ions lose electrons (oxidation)

Results of displacement reactions show reactivity decreases down Group 7. You'd predict astatine wouldn't displace other halogens as it's at the bottom of Group 7.

Rates of Reaction

Measuring Rates of Reaction

RATE OF REACTION — how quickly a reaction happens.

$$\text{Rate of reaction} = \frac{\text{Amount of product formed}}{\text{Time}} \text{ or } \frac{\text{Amount of reactant used}}{\text{Time}}$$

Units of rate depend on what has been measured — they're in the form 'amount per time'.

Three common units of rate: $g\ s^{-1}$, $cm^3\ s^{-1}$, $mol\ dm^{-3}\ s^{-1}$

Three ways to measure rate of reaction:

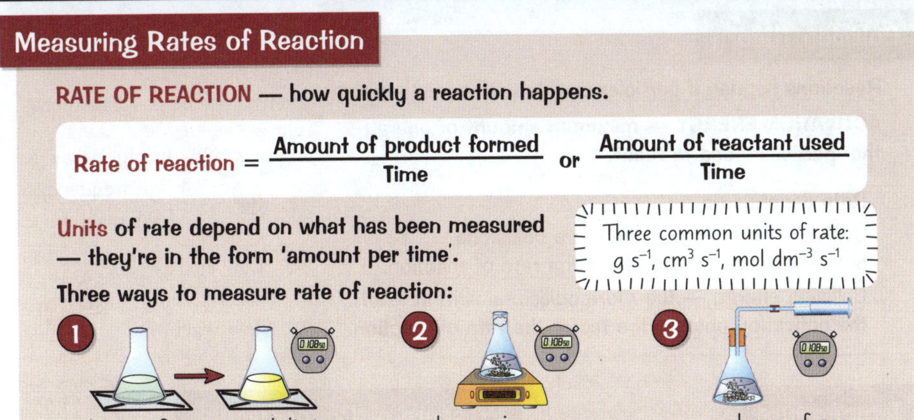

Comparing Rates of Reaction

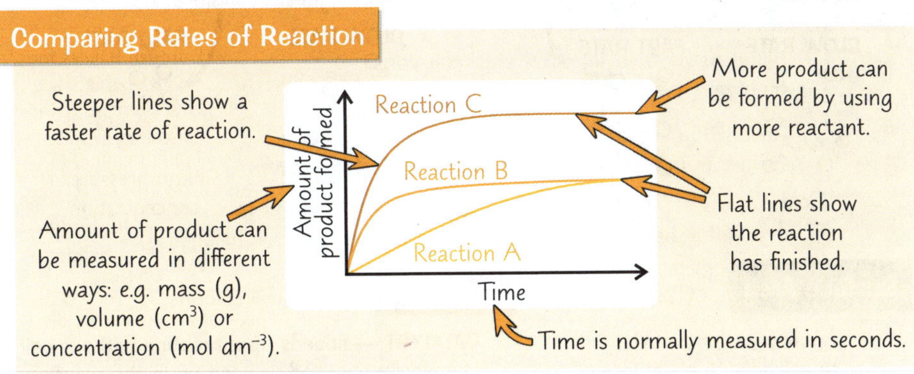

Steeper lines show a faster rate of reaction.
Amount of product can be measured in different ways: e.g. mass (g), volume (cm^3) or concentration ($mol\ dm^{-3}$).
Amount of product formed
Reaction C
Reaction B
Reaction A
Time
More product can be formed by using more reactant.
Flat lines show the reaction has finished.
Time is normally measured in seconds.

Calculating Rates from Graphs

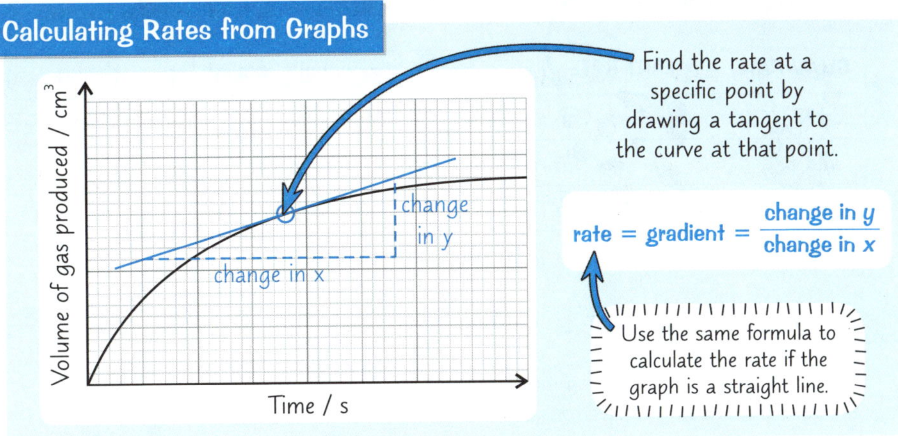

Volume of gas produced / cm^3
Time / s
change in y
change in x
Find the rate at a specific point by drawing a tangent to the curve at that point.
Use the same formula to calculate the rate if the graph is a straight line.

$$\text{rate} = \text{gradient} = \frac{\text{change in } y}{\text{change in } x}$$

Factors Affecting Rates of Reaction

Collision Theory

Reactions happen if particles collide with enough energy.

ACTIVATION ENERGY — minimum amount of energy that particles need to react.

Rate depends on...

Collision frequency — the more collisions between particles, the faster the rate of reaction.

Collision energy — the more collisions with at least the activation energy, the faster the rate of reaction.

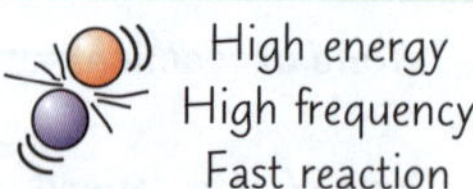

High energy
High frequency
Fast reaction

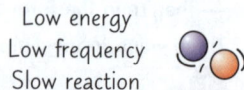

Low energy
Low frequency
Slow reaction

Temperature

Particles move faster and collide more frequently with more energy.

SLOW RATE

Cold

FAST RATE

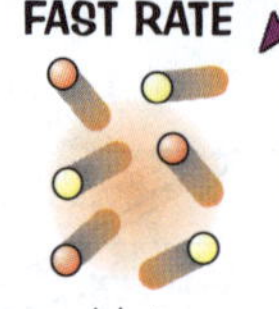

Hot

Pressure or Concentration

Lower concentration = slower rate of revision

More particles in the same volume — more frequent collisions.

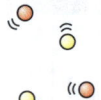

SLOW RATE

Low pressure/ concentration

FAST RATE

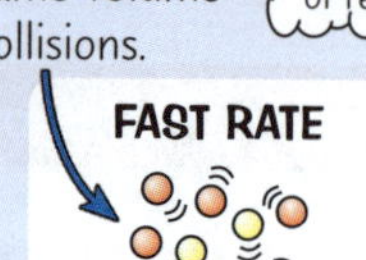

High pressure/ concentration

Surface Area

More area for particles to collide with — more frequent collisions.

SLOW RATE

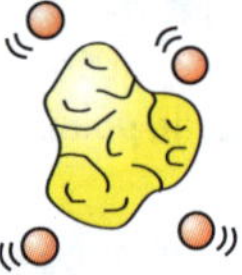

Big pieces

FAST RATE

Small pieces

The smaller the piece of solid, the larger the surface area to volume ratio.

Catalysts

CATALYST — speeds up a reaction without being chemically changed or used up in the reaction, and without changing the products.

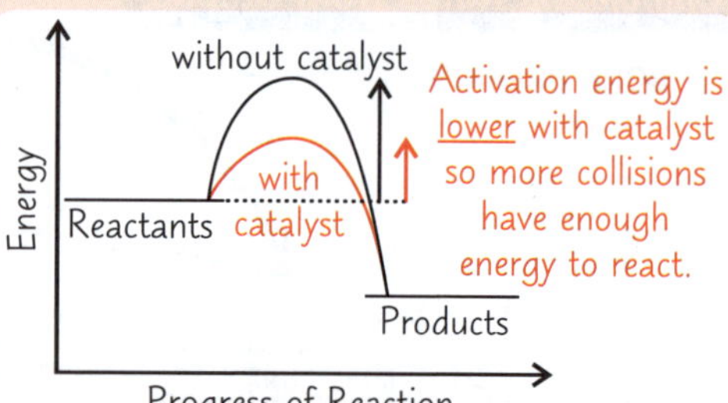

Enzymes are biological catalysts. They can be used to make alcoholic drinks.

Endothermic & Exothermic Reactions

Energy Transfer

ENDOTHERMIC REACTION — takes in heat energy from the surroundings (shown by a fall in temperature).

EXOTHERMIC REACTION — gives out heat energy to the surroundings (shown by a rise in temperature).

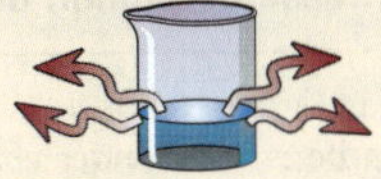

Measuring Temperature Change

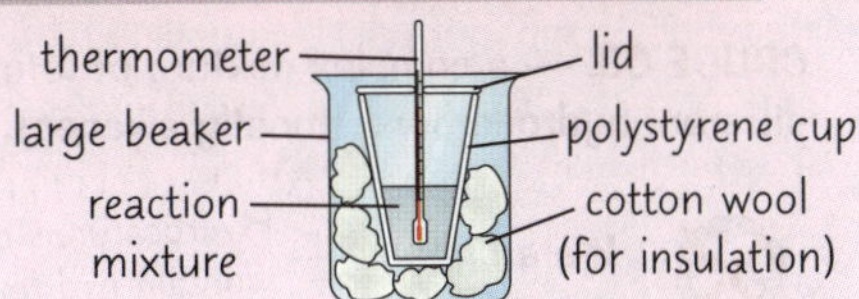

Record initial temperature and maximum/ minimum temperature reached, then calculate temperature change.

You can use this method to investigate:

- **dissolving salts in water**
- **neutralisation, displacement and precipitation reactions.**

Reaction Profiles

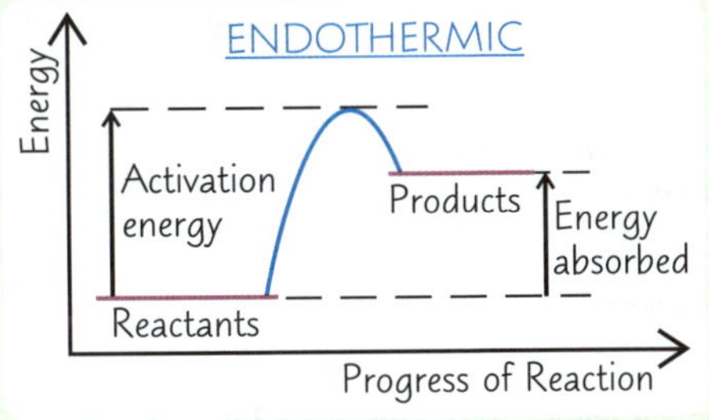

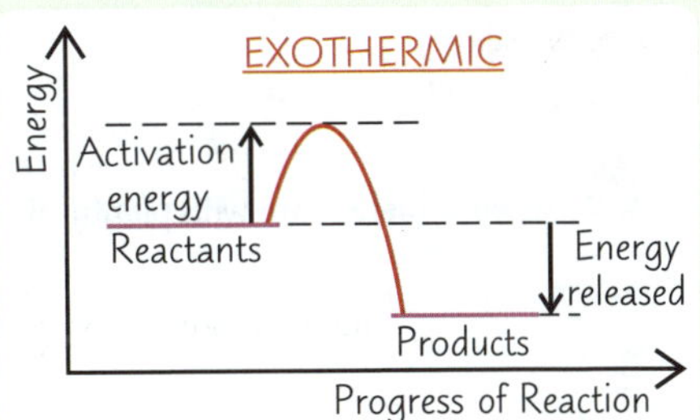

Bond Energies

BOND BREAKING — ENDOTHERMIC

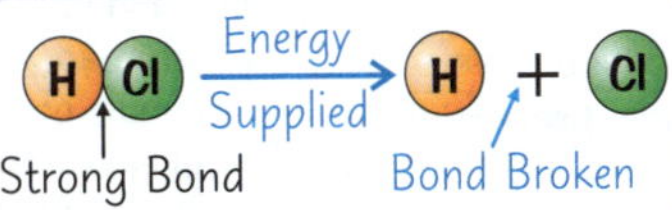

BOND FORMING — EXOTHERMIC

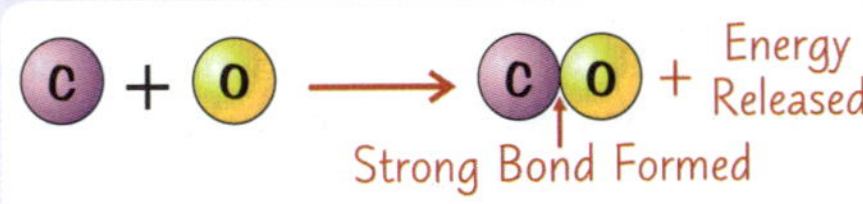

Endothermic reactions: energy used to break bonds is greater than energy released by forming new bonds.

Exothermic reactions: energy released by forming bonds is greater than energy used to break existing bonds.

overall energy change = total energy needed to break bonds − total energy released by forming new bonds

These energies can be calculated from bond energies.

Hydrocarbons

Crude Oil

CRUDE OIL — a complex mixture of lots of different hydrocarbons (mostly alkanes).

Hydrocarbons only contain hydrogen and carbon atoms.

It's a finite resource.

Used as a feedstock to create useful substances in petrochemical industry.

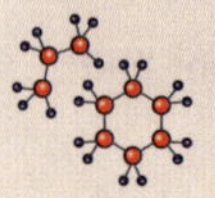

The hydrocarbons have carbon atoms arranged in chains or rings.

Properties of Hydrocarbons

The longer the hydrocarbon chain, the stronger the intermolecular forces — this affects physical properties.

As length of chain increases...
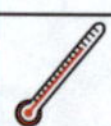 ...boiling point increases.
 ...viscosity increases.
 ...ease of ignition decreases.

Hydrocarbons with longer chains contain more C and H atoms. Each crude oil fraction contains hydrocarbons with similar numbers of C and H atoms.

Combustion

COMPLETE COMBUSTION — a reaction that occurs when a fuel reacts with plenty of oxygen.

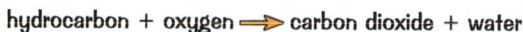

hydrocarbon + oxygen → carbon dioxide + water

Hydrocarbons are used as fuels because combustion releases a lot of energy.

Homologous Series

HOMOLOGOUS SERIES — a family of molecules which have the same general formula and share similar chemical properties.

Alkanes are an example of a homologous series.

In a homologous series:

Molecular formulas of neighbouring compounds differ by a CH_2 unit.

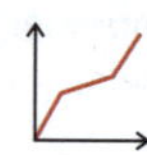

Physical properties vary gradually with length of molecule.

Fractional Distillation and Cracking

Fractional Distillation

FRACTIONAL DISTILLATION — a process used to separate the hydrocarbons in crude oil into fractions according to their boiling points. Each fraction has different uses.

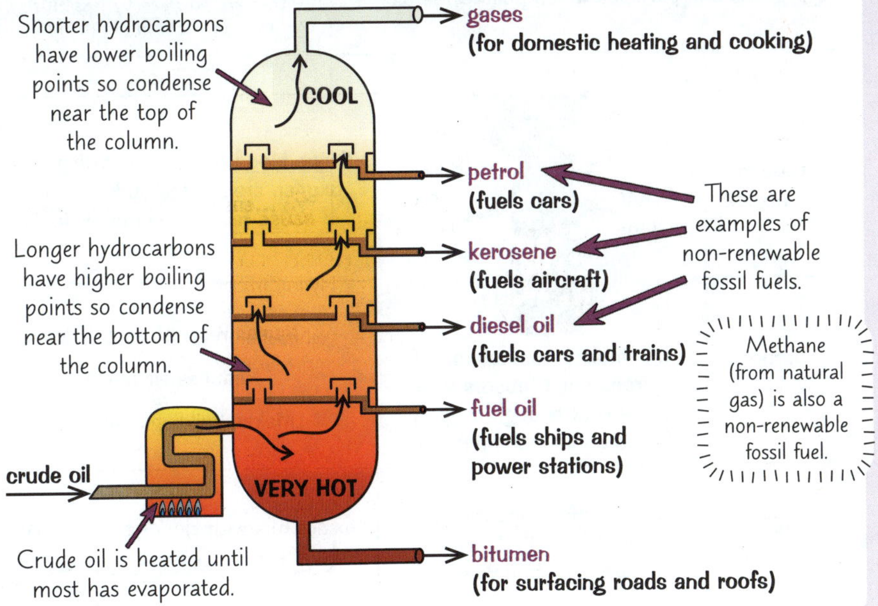

Shorter hydrocarbons have lower boiling points so condense near the top of the column.

COOL

gases
(for domestic heating and cooking)

petrol
(fuels cars)

kerosene
(fuels aircraft)

diesel oil
(fuels cars and trains)

These are examples of non-renewable fossil fuels.

Longer hydrocarbons have higher boiling points so condense near the bottom of the column.

Methane (from natural gas) is also a non-renewable fossil fuel.

fuel oil
(fuels ships and power stations)

crude oil

VERY HOT

Crude oil is heated until most has evaporated.

bitumen
(for surfacing roads and roofs)

Cracking

There is a high demand for fuels with shorter carbon chains.

CRACKING — breaks down long-chain, saturated hydrocarbons (alkanes) into shorter, more useful molecules.

Alkenes are used to make polymers (mostly plastics).

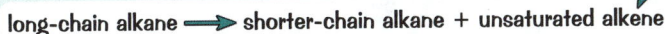

long-chain alkane → shorter-chain alkane + unsaturated alkene

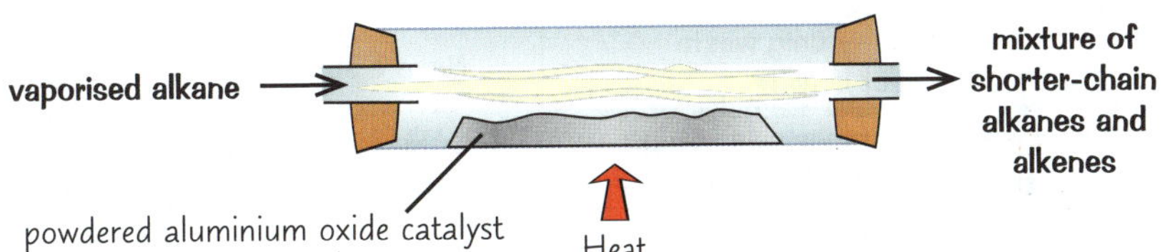

Pollutants and Fuels

Air Pollution

Fossil fuels contain hydrocarbons and sometimes sulfur impurities.

Combustion of these fuels releases gases and particles which pollute the air.

This can happen in appliances that are powered by fossil fuels.

Pollutant	Formation	Effects
Carbon monoxide	carbon monoxide, carbon (soot), water vapour, carbon dioxide Incomplete combustion of hydrocarbons (occurs when there isn't enough oxygen for complete combustion).	Stops blood from transporting enough oxygen around the body — this can cause fainting, coma or death.
Carbon (soot)		Causes respiratory problems Reduces air quality Makes buildings look dirty
Sulfur dioxide	From sulfur impurities in fossil fuels that react during combustion.	Acid rain oxides mix with clouds to form acids NO_x SO_2 damage to trees, statues and buildings lakes become acidic — plants and animals die
Oxides of nitrogen	Reaction between nitrogen and oxygen in the air caused by the heat of burning fuels, e.g. in car engines.	

Hydrogen as a Fuel for Vehicles

Advantages	Disadvantages
Very clean — only waste product is water.	Need a special, expensive engine.
Obtained from a renewable resource (water), so won't run out.	Manufacturing hydrogen is expensive, and often uses energy from fossil fuels.
Can be obtained from the water produced by the cell when used in fuel cells.	Hard to store.

The Atmosphere

Volcanic Gases

Intense volcanic activity released gases.

Early atmosphere probably contained mainly carbon dioxide with some water vapour and small amounts of other gases.

The early atmosphere contained virtually no oxygen gas.

Absorption of Carbon Dioxide

Water vapour condensed to form oceans.

H_2O vapour CO_2

dissolved CO_2

CO_2 gas dissolved in the oceans.

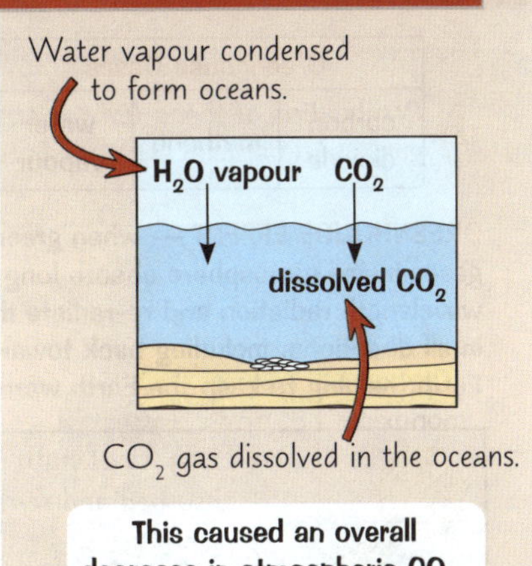

This caused an overall decrease in atmospheric CO_2.

Increase in Oxygen

When green plants evolved, they began to photosynthesise.

MVP

Photosynthesis:

Removes carbon dioxide from the air.

Produces oxygen.

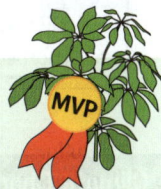

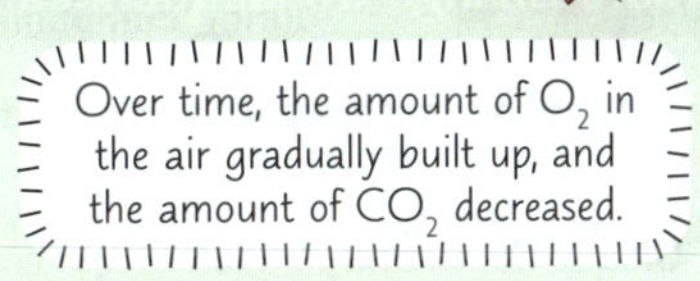

Over time, the amount of O_2 in the air gradually built up, and the amount of CO_2 decreased.

Today's Atmosphere

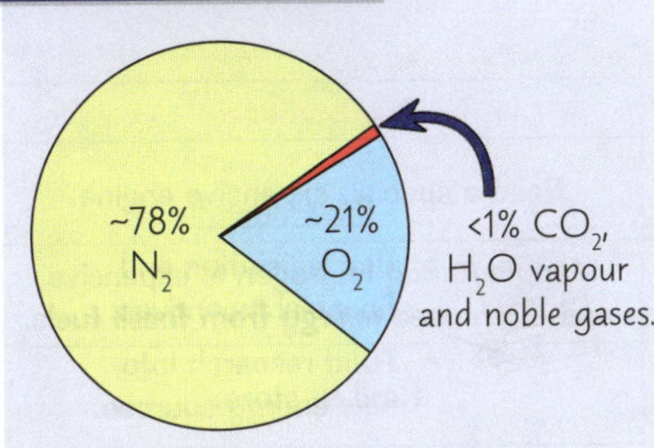

~78% N_2 ~21% O_2 <1% CO_2, H_2O vapour and noble gases.

Test for Oxygen Gas

Oxygen will relight a glowing splint.

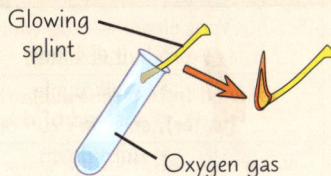

Glowing splint

Oxygen gas

Greenhouse Gases & Climate Change

The Greenhouse Effect

Greenhouse Gases		
carbon dioxide	methane	water vapour

GREENHOUSE EFFECT — when greenhouse gases in the atmosphere absorb long wavelength radiation and re-radiate it in all directions, including back towards Earth, helping to keep the Earth warm.

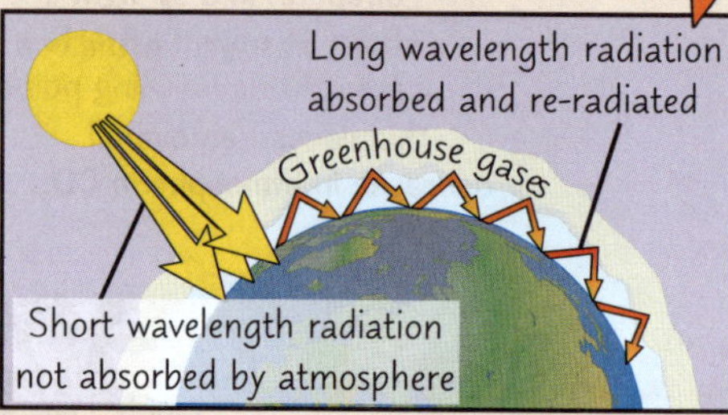

Human Activities

Increased population means more greenhouse gases, because more:

Fossil fuels burnt for energy — more CO_2 released.

Deforestation — less CO_2 removed by photosynthesis.

Farming — more methane produced.

There's strong correlation between increased levels of greenhouse gases and **global warming**.

Global warming is a type of climate change that can cause other types of climate change.

Climate Change Consequences

Two possible consequences of climate change:

1. Flooding due to the melting of the polar ice caps causing sea levels to rise.
2. Changing rainfall patterns.

Historical Climate Data

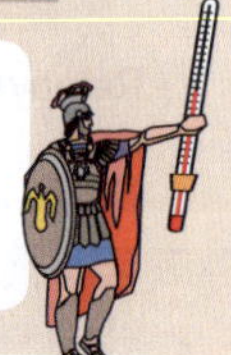

- Less accurate and less representative of global levels than modern data.
- Hard to estimate precisely.

Ways of Reducing CO_2 Emissions

Individuals

- Walk/cycle instead of driving.
- Turn down central heating.

Governments

- Use legislation and financial incentives.
- Fund research into new energy sources.

Scalars, Vectors and Motion

Scalars

SCALAR QUANTITIES — only have magnitude and no direction.

- speed
- distance
- mass
- energy

Vectors

VECTOR QUANTITIES — have a magnitude and a direction.

- force
- velocity
- displacement
- acceleration
- momentum
- weight

Distance and Displacement

DISTANCE (scalar) — how far an object has moved (not including its direction).

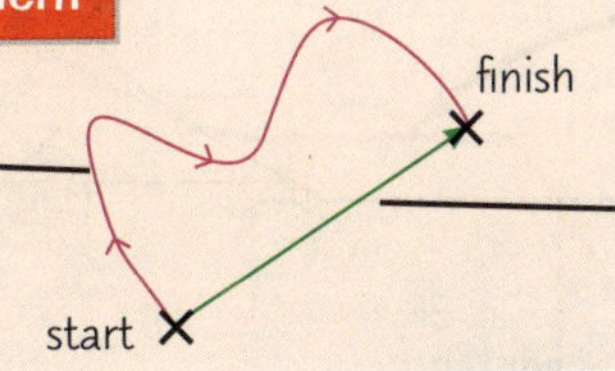

DISPLACEMENT (vector) — the distance and the direction in a straight line from an object's starting point to its finishing point.

Speed and Velocity

SPEED (scalar) — how fast you're going with no regard to direction.

distance travelled (m) = average speed (m/s) × time (s)

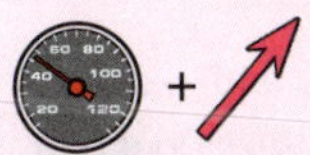

VELOCITY (vector) — speed in a certain direction.

Acceleration

ACCELERATION — the change in velocity in a certain amount of time.

$$a = \frac{(v - u)}{t}$$

- a — acceleration (m/s²)
- $(v - u)$ — change in velocity (m/s) (v is final velocity and u is initial velocity)
- t — time (s)

Acceleration of object due to gravity close to Earth's surface (object in free fall) is roughly 10 m/s².

Typical Speeds

	Typical speed (m/s)
walking	1.4
running	3
cycling	5.5
car (built-up area)	13
car (motorway)	31
train	up to 55
plane	250
wind	5 - 20
sound	340

Objects, sound and wind rarely travel at a constant speed.

Distance/Time and Velocity/Time Graphs

Distance/Time Graphs

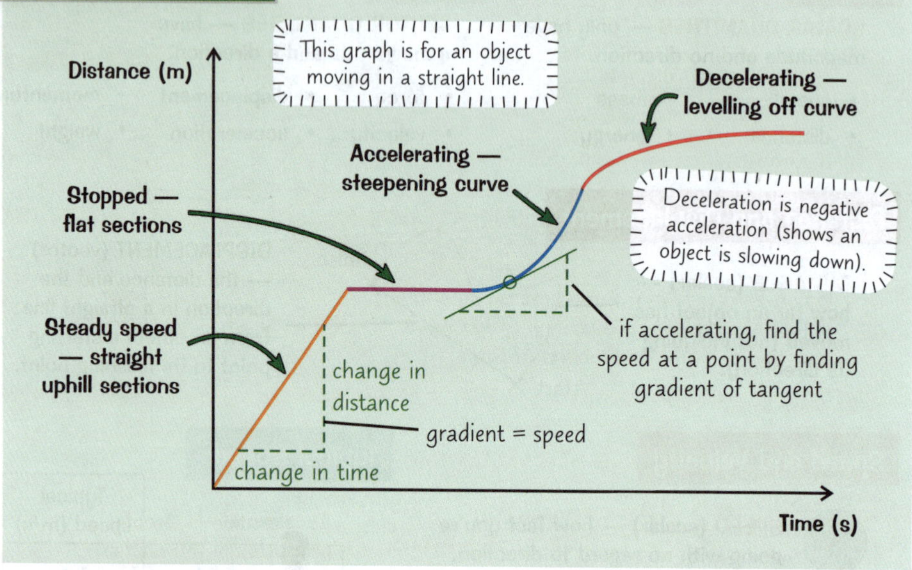

This graph is for an object moving in a straight line.

Distance (m)

Time (s)

Stopped — flat sections

Steady speed — straight uphill sections

Accelerating — steepening curve

Decelerating — levelling off curve

Deceleration is negative acceleration (shows an object is slowing down).

change in distance

change in time

gradient = speed

if accelerating, find the speed at a point by finding gradient of tangent

Velocity/Time Graphs

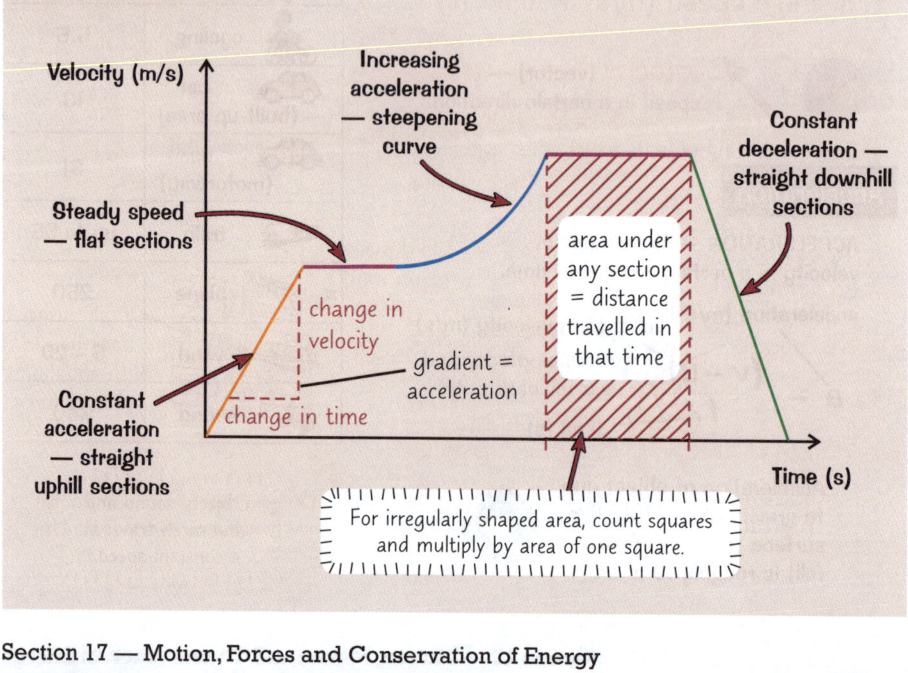

Velocity (m/s)

Time (s)

Steady speed — flat sections

Increasing acceleration — steepening curve

Constant deceleration — straight downhill sections

Constant acceleration — straight uphill sections

change in velocity

change in time

gradient = acceleration

area under any section = distance travelled in that time

For irregularly shaped area, count squares and multiply by area of one square.

Newton's Laws

My word is law.

Newton's First Law

If zero resultant force acts on stationary object, object doesn't move.

If zero resultant force acts on moving object, it continues moving at same velocity (same speed and direction).

If non-zero resultant force acts on object, object accelerates (will change speed, direction or both) in direction of force.

Newton's Second Law

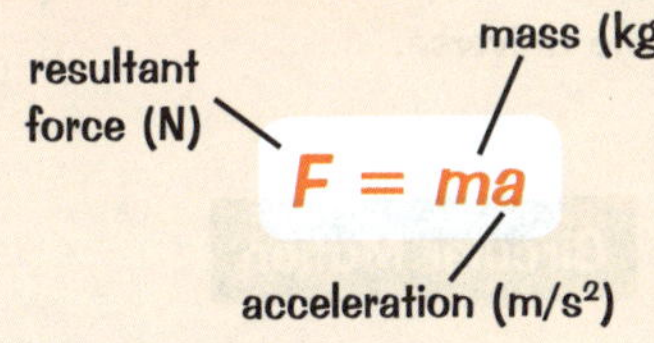

- **Acceleration is directly proportional to resultant force — $F \propto a$.**
- **Acceleration is inversely proportional to mass.**

Newton's Third Law

Two interacting objects exert equal and opposite forces on each other.

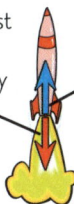

Rocket exhaust gas pushed downwards by rocket.

Causes equal and opposite force as gas pushes back on rocket.

Rocket moves when upwards force is greater than rocket's weight.

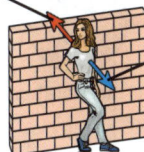

Girl pushes on wall.

Wall pushes back on girl with equal and opposite force.

You don't need to learn these specific examples, but you need to know how to apply Newton's third law to different situations.

Weight, Mass and Circular Motion

Weight, Mass and Gravity

WEIGHT — force that acts on an object due to gravity.

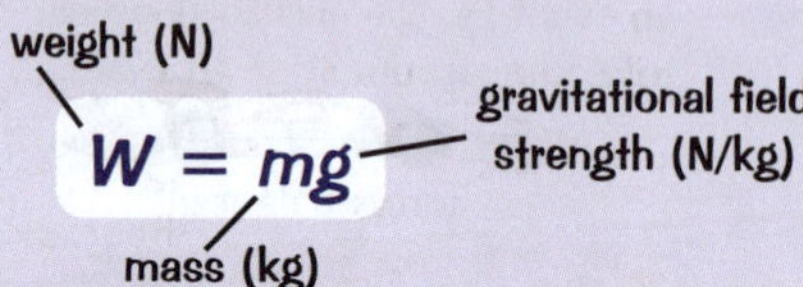

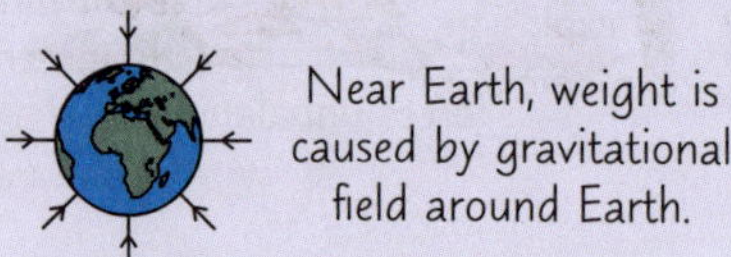

Near Earth, weight is caused by gravitational field around Earth.

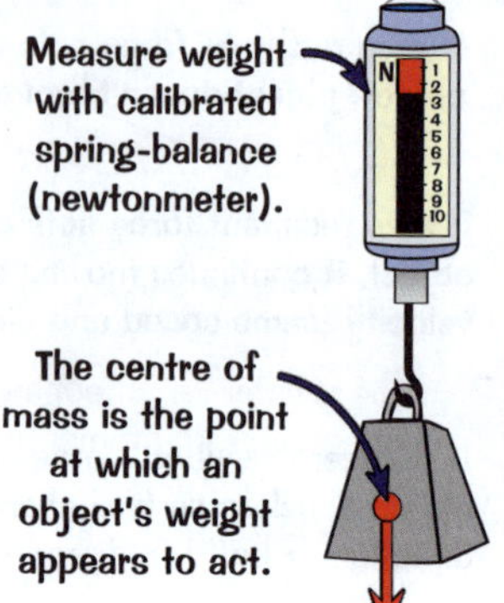

- Object weight depends on strength of gravitational field at object location.
- Object mass has same value anywhere in the Universe.

Mass and Motion

INERTIAL MASS — measure of how hard it is to change an object's velocity. It's the ratio of force over acceleration: $m = F \div a$.

Same force applied to bowling ball and golf ball.

smaller acceleration

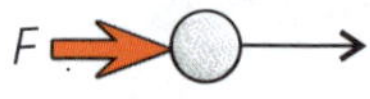

bigger acceleration

Bowling ball has bigger inertial mass, so it's harder to increase its velocity.

Circular Motion

Object in circular motion with constant speed is always changing direction, so object has changing velocity.

Changing velocity means object is accelerating, so there is a resultant force on it.

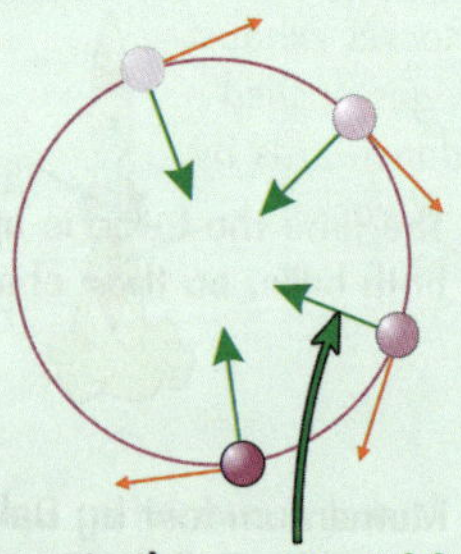

This force is the centripetal force. It always acts towards the centre of the circle.

Momentum

Calculating Momentum

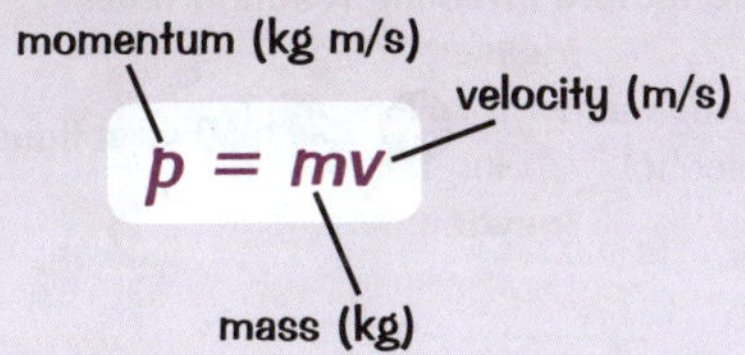

The greater an object's mass, the greater its momentum.

The greater an object's velocity, the greater its momentum.

Conservation of Momentum

CONSERVATION OF MOMENTUM — in a closed system, total momentum before an event (e.g. a collision) equals total momentum after an event.

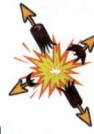

Before explosion, momentum is zero.

After explosion, pieces fly off in different directions so momentum cancels out to zero.

Newton's Third Law and Momentum

For two balls of the same mass:

Ball A approaches with momentum p and collides with Ball B.

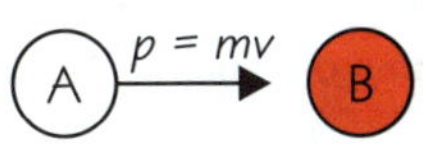

"Yes, it's definitely revision, I promise..."

Ball A and Ball B exert equal and opposite forces on each other due to Newton's Third Law.

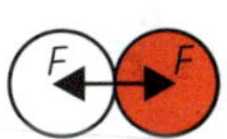

Due to $F = ma$, Ball A decelerates at the same rate that Ball B accelerates.

The time the force is applied is the same for both balls, so their change in speed is the same.

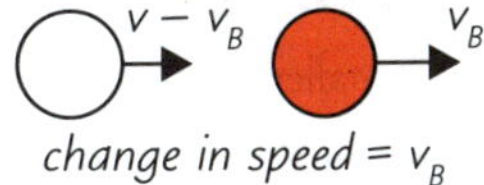

Momentum lost by Ball A equals momentum gained by Ball B. So total momentum before equals total momentum after.

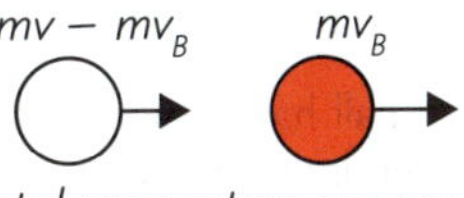

Reaction Times and Stopping Distances

Reaction Times

Typical human reaction time: 0.2 - 0.9 s. Three factors affecting reaction times:

Tiredness

Drugs and alcohol

Distractions

Three Steps to do the Ruler Drop Test

1. Get someone to hold ruler so zero is between your thumb and forefinger.
2. Ruler dropped without warning. Catch it as quickly as possible.
3. Use distance ruler fell to calculate reaction time.

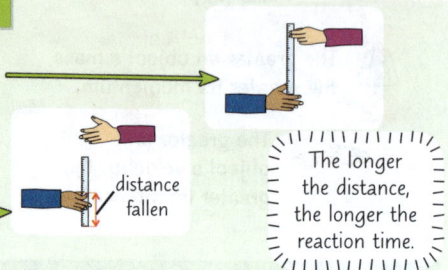

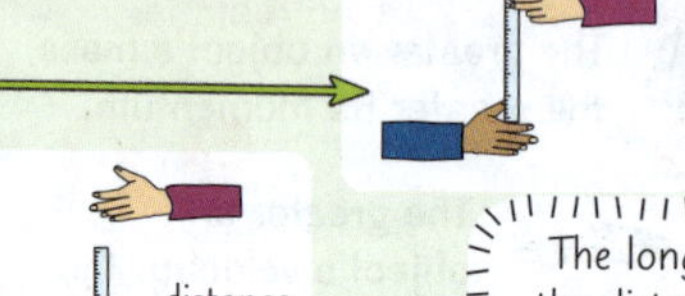

The longer the distance, the longer the reaction time.

Stopping Distance Equation

Stopping distance = Thinking distance + Braking distance

Thinking distance: How far vehicle moves during driver's reaction time.

Braking distance: Distance taken to stop whilst brakes are applied.

Two factors that increase thinking distance:

1. faster vehicle speed
2. long driver reaction times

Four factors that increase braking distance:

1. faster vehicle speed
2. heavier vehicle
3. poor, wet or icy road surface
4. damaged or worn brakes or tyres

Large Decelerations

The faster a vehicle is going, the greater the braking force needed to make it stop in a certain distance. → Larger braking force means larger deceleration ($F = ma$).

If estimating these forces, a good figure for a car's mass is ~ 1000 kg.

Very large deceleration can cause:

brakes to overheat

vehicle to skid

Energy Stores and Transfers

Eight Types of Energy Store

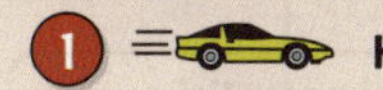
1 Kinetic

2 Gravitational potential

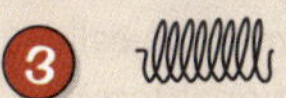
3 Elastic potential

4 Electrostatic

5 Thermal

7 Magnetic

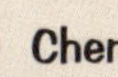
6 Chemical

8 Nuclear

Four Types of Energy Transfer

1 Mechanical (a force doing work)

2 Electrical (work done by moving charges)

3 Heating

4 Radiation (e.g. light or sound)

Kinetic Energy

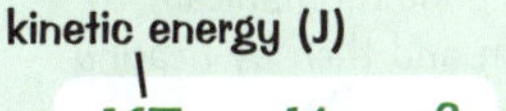

$$KE = \frac{1}{2}mv^2$$

kinetic energy (J), mass (kg), speed (m/s)

Gravitational Potential Energy

$$\Delta GPE = mg\Delta h$$

change in gravitational potential energy (J), mass (kg), gravitational field strength (N/kg), change in vertical height (m)

Systems and Conservation of Energy

SYSTEM — a single object or a group of objects.

CONSERVATION OF ENERGY — energy can be transferred usefully, stored or dissipated but not created or destroyed.

CLOSED SYSTEM — no energy (or matter) is transferred in or out of the system, so there is no net change in total energy.

Clothed system.

Pan and hob = NOT a closed system.
Energy is transferred away to surroundings.

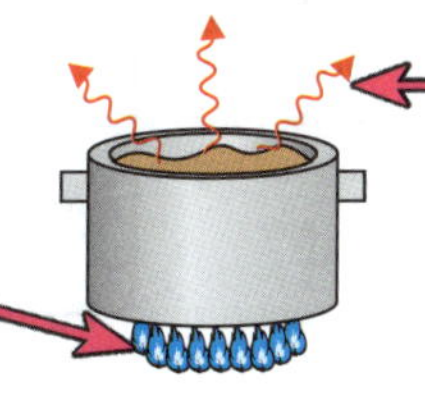

Energy transferred usefully (by heating) to thermal energy store of pan, increasing its temperature.
Some energy dissipated as energy transferred to thermal energy stores of surroundings.

Energy Transfers

Energy Transfer Diagrams for Six Different Systems

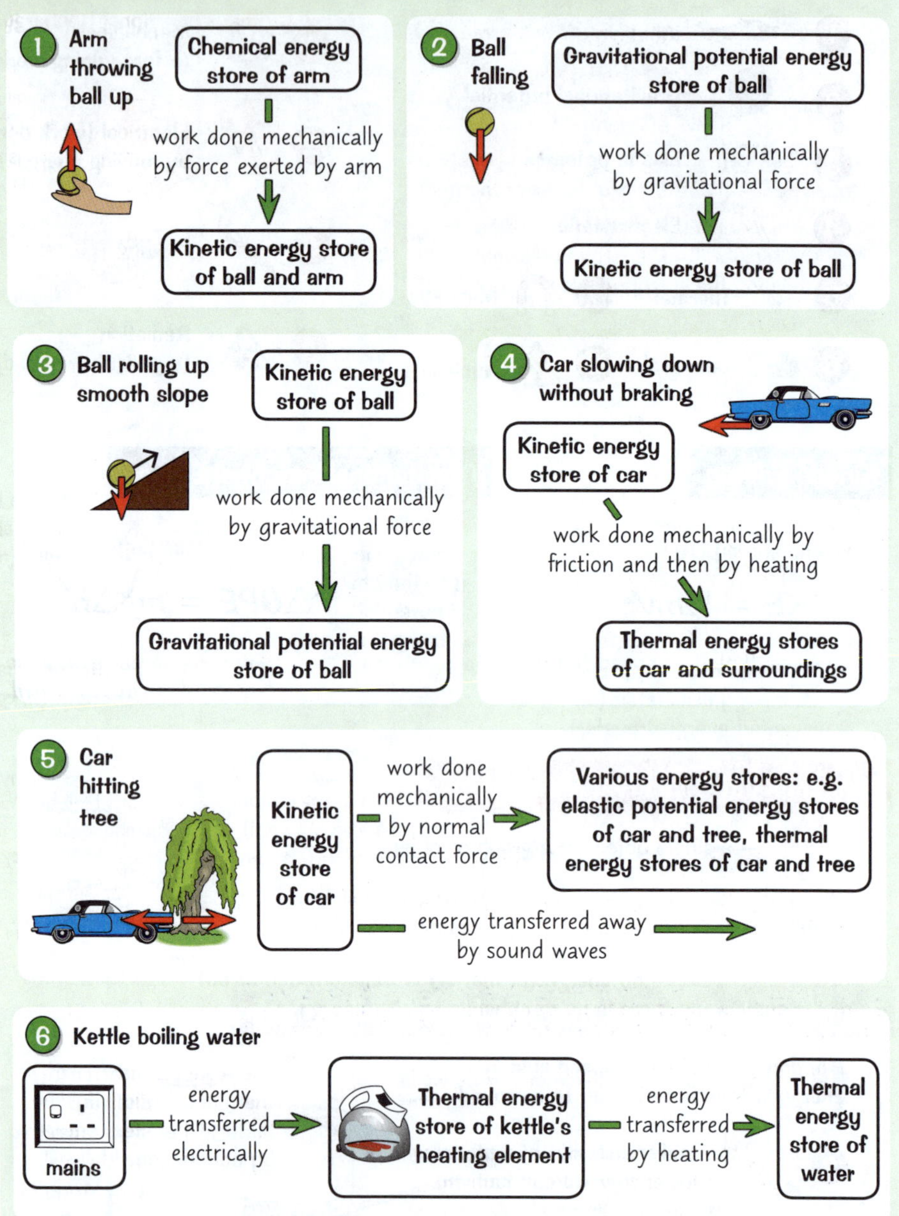

1 Arm throwing ball up
Chemical energy store of arm
work done mechanically by force exerted by arm
Kinetic energy store of ball and arm
2 Ball falling
Gravitational potential energy store of ball
work done mechanically by gravitational force
Kinetic energy store of ball
3 Ball rolling up smooth slope
Kinetic energy store of ball
work done mechanically by gravitational force
Gravitational potential energy store of ball
4 Car slowing down without braking
Kinetic energy store of car
work done mechanically by friction and then by heating
Thermal energy stores of car and surroundings
5 Car hitting tree
Kinetic energy store of car
work done mechanically by normal contact force
Various energy stores: e.g. elastic potential energy stores of car and tree, thermal energy stores of car and tree
energy transferred away by sound waves
6 Kettle boiling water
mains
energy transferred electrically
Thermal energy store of kettle's heating element
energy transferred by heating
Thermal energy store of water

Efficiency and Reducing Energy Loss

Efficiency Equation

$$\text{Efficiency} = \frac{\text{Useful energy transferred}}{\text{Total energy supplied}}$$

No device is 100% efficient.

In all systems, energy is dissipated (wasted) to a store that's not useful (usually thermal).

If a mechanical process causes a rise in temperature, energy is dissipated heating the surroundings.

Efficiency in Diagrams

Arrow widths proportional to energy.

E.g.

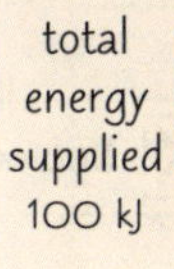
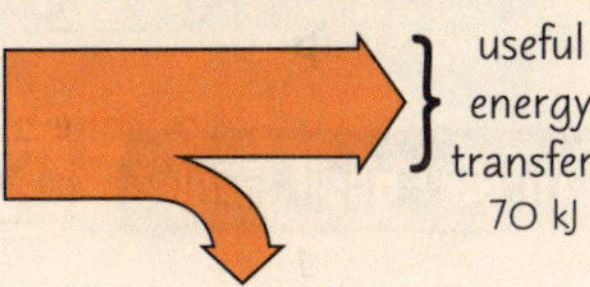

Lubrication and Thermal Insulation

Frictional force acts between moving gears, so energy dissipated (an unwanted energy transfer).

Apply lubricant (e.g. oil).

Frictional force reduced so energy dissipated reduced.

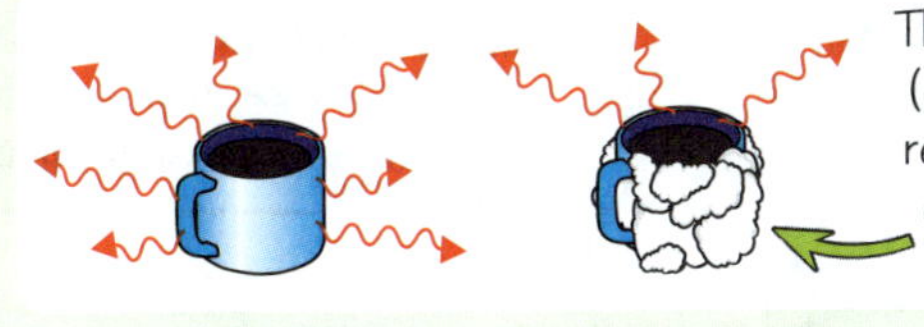

Thermal insulation (e.g. cotton wool) reduces unwanted energy transfers by heating.

Lubrication and thermal insulation increase the efficiency of useful energy transfers.

Two Ways to Decrease How Quickly a Building Cools

1.  Increase thickness of its walls.
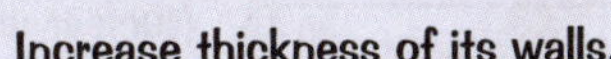
2.  Make walls out of material with lower thermal conductivity.

The higher a material's thermal conductivity, the faster it transfers energy by conduction.

CONDUCTION — where vibrating particles transfer energy to neighbouring particles.

Energy Resources

Non-Renewable and Renewable Energy Resources

NON-RENEWABLE ENERGY RESOURCES — energy resources that will run out one day.

RENEWABLE ENERGY RESOURCES — energy resources that will never run out.

Three Fossil Fuels

☒ Non-renewable

1. **Coal**

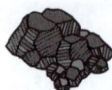

2. **Oil**

   Used to make fuel (petrol and diesel) for cars.

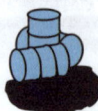

3. **(Natural) Gas**

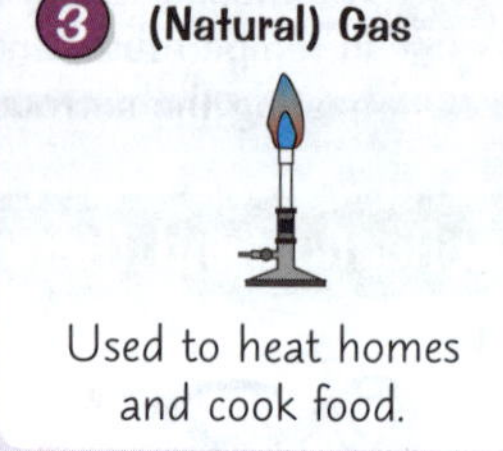

   Used to heat homes and cook food.

All three fossil fuels are burned to generate electricity.

- Burning fossil fuels releases CO_2, contributing to global warming.
- Burning coal and oil releases sulfur dioxide, causing acid rain.

Tidal Power

☑ Renewable

Tide comes in.

↓

Water builds behind the dam.

↓

Water allowed out through turbines.

↓

Electricity generated.

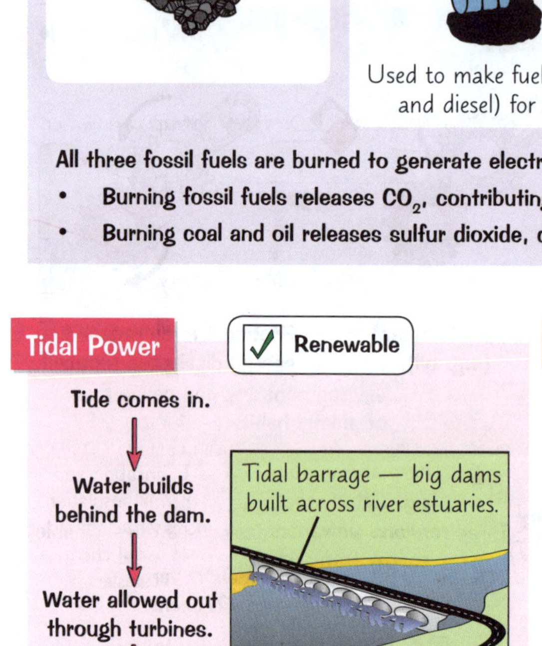

- Produce no pollution when in use.
- Disturb habitats of nearby wildlife and spoil the view.

Nuclear Power

☒ Non-renewable

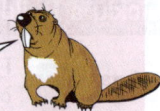

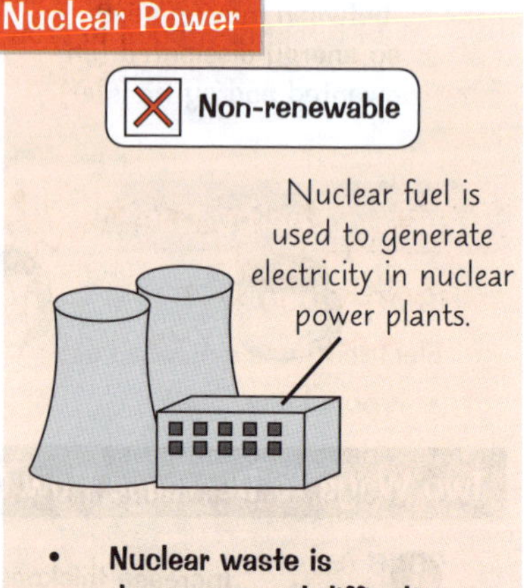

Nuclear fuel is used to generate electricity in nuclear power plants.

- Nuclear waste is dangerous and difficult to dispose of.
- Carries the risk of a major catastrophe.

Energy Resources and Trends in Use

Solar Power

Renewable

Solar cells generate electricity directly from sunlight.

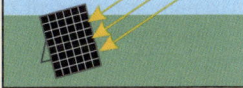

Solar water heaters use the sun to heat water which is then pumped into radiators.

- Produce no pollution when in use.

Wind Power

Renewable

Wind turns wind turbines, generating electricity.

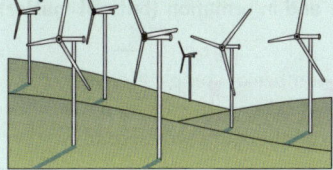

- Produce no pollution when in use.
- Noisy and spoil the view.

Bio-fuels

Renewable

Made from plant products or animal dung.

Bio-fuels are burned to generate electricity, and used as fuel in some cars.

- In some regions, large areas of forest destroyed to grow bio-fuels, so species lose natural habitats.

Hydro-electric Power

Renewable

Big dams built so valley fills up with water.

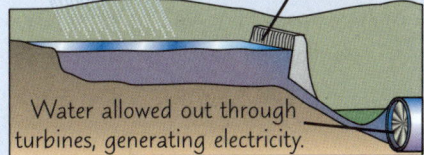

Water allowed out through turbines, generating electricity.

- Produce no pollution when in use.
- Flooding valley has big impact on environment and can cause loss of animal habitats.

Trends in Energy Use

1900 – 2000

Electricity use increased as:

- population grew.
- people began to use electricity for more things.

2000 onwards

Electricity use decreasing as:

- appliances are more efficient.
- people are more careful with amount of energy use.

Three reasons we're increasing use of renewables:

1.  Burning fossil fuels is very damaging to environment.
2.  We need to learn how to get by without non-renewables before they run out.
3. 

Pressure on governments and companies has led them to introduce renewable energy targets.

Changing to renewables is limited by their cost and issues with reliability.

Wave Basics

Wave Properties

When waves travel through a medium, they transfer energy and information (but not matter).

Sound waves move away... ...the air particles don't.

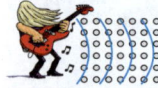

Ripples on water's surface move away... ...the water doesn't.

FREQUENCY — number of complete cycles of the wave passing a certain point each second.

PERIOD — amount of time it takes for one full cycle of a wave.

period = 1 ÷ frequency

AMPLITUDE — maximum displacement of a point on a wave from its rest position.

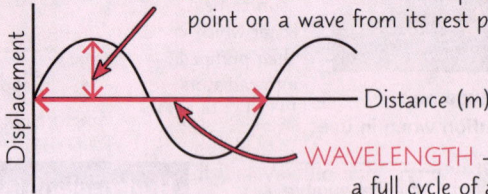

WAVELENGTH — length of a full cycle of a wave.

Displacement

Distance (m)

Transverse Waves

Vibrations perpendicular (at 90°) to direction wave travels.

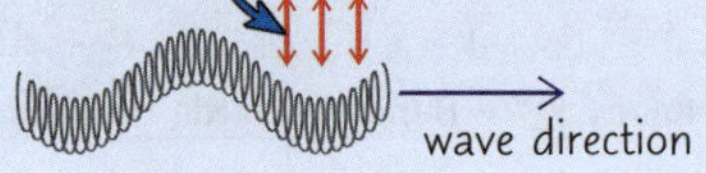

wave direction

Three types of transverse waves:

1. **Ripples in water**
2. **Electromagnetic waves (e.g. light)**
3.  **S-waves**

Longitudinal Waves

Vibrations parallel to direction wave travels.

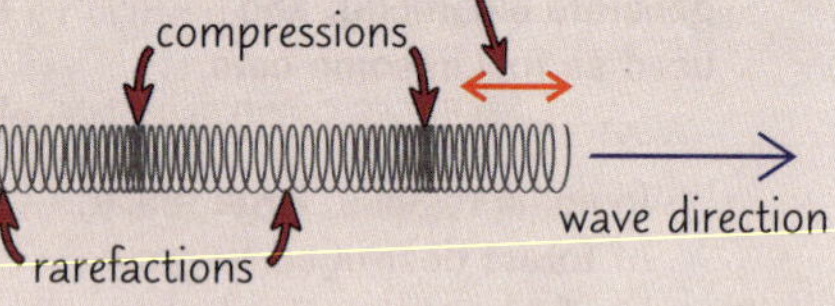

Two types of longitudinal waves:

1. 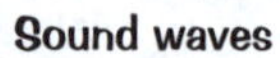 **Sound waves**
2.  **P-waves**

Wave Speed

WAVE SPEED — how quickly a wave moves through space.

Wave velocity is the wave's speed AND direction.

$$v = \frac{x}{t}$$

wave speed (m/s), distance (m), time (s)

$$v = f\lambda$$

wave speed (m/s), frequency (hertz, Hz), wavelength (m)

Wave Behaviour at Boundaries

Waves at Boundaries

When a wave hits a boundary, it can be...

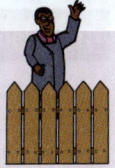

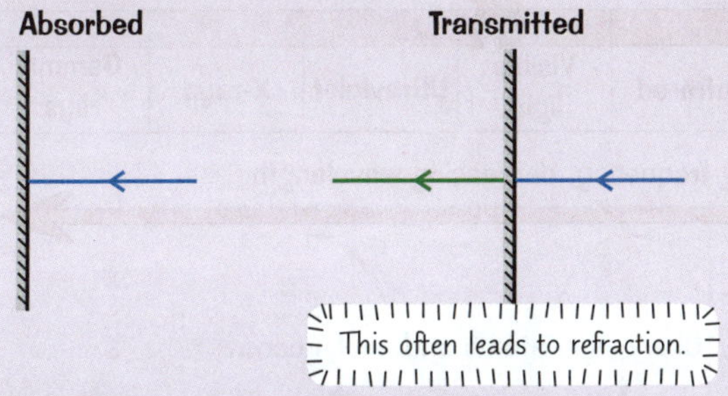

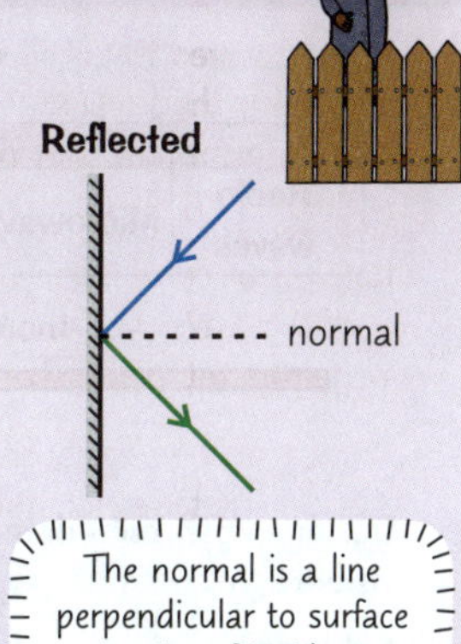

The normal is a line perpendicular to surface at point of incidence.

What happens depends on wavelength of wave and properties of material.

Refraction

REFRACTION — when a wave changes speed and direction as it crosses a boundary between two materials at an angle to the normal.

Wave refracts → slows down → Wavelength decreases. → Bends towards normal.

Wave refracts → speeds up → Wavelength increases. → Bends away from normal.

Frequency never changes during refraction.

Typically, EM waves slow down in denser materials, and speed up in less dense materials.

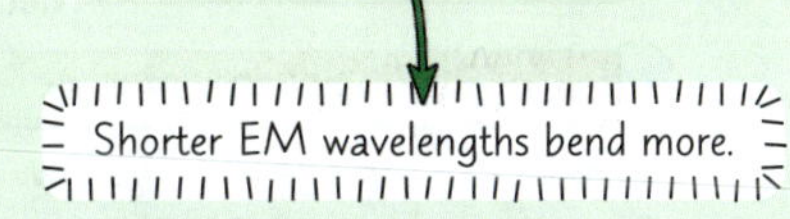

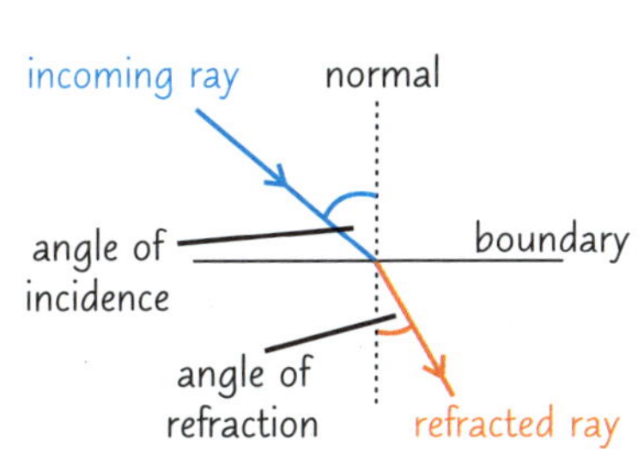

WAVEFRONT — an imaginary line that represents the same point on each wave.

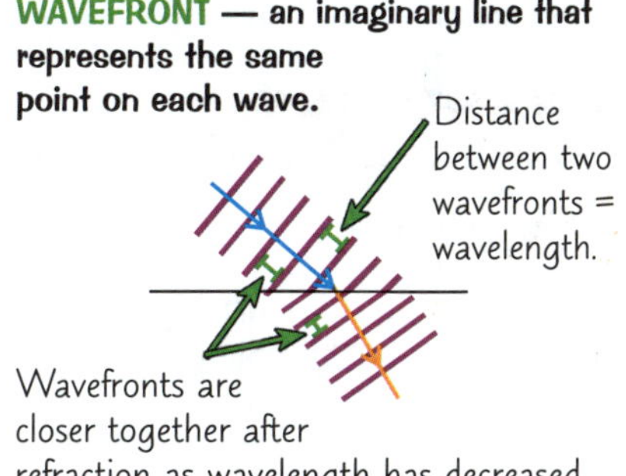

Electromagnetic Waves

The Electromagnetic (EM) Spectrum

The EM spectrum is continuous.

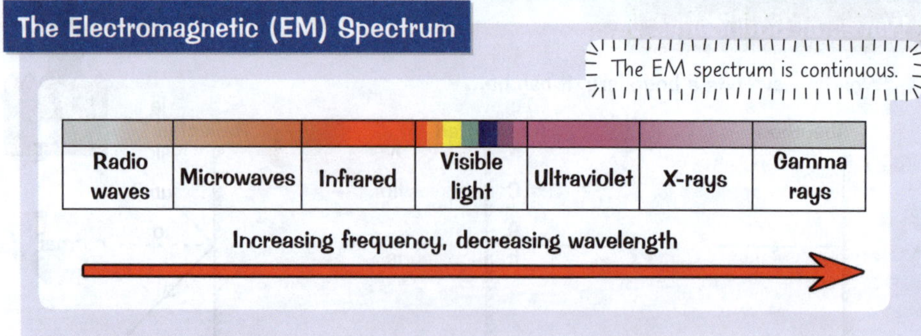
Radio waves
Microwaves
Infrared
Visible light
Ultraviolet
X-rays
Gamma rays
Increasing frequency, decreasing wavelength

Our eyes can only detect visible light.

EM waves:

- **Transfer energy from source to absorber.**
- **Travel at same speed in a vacuum.**

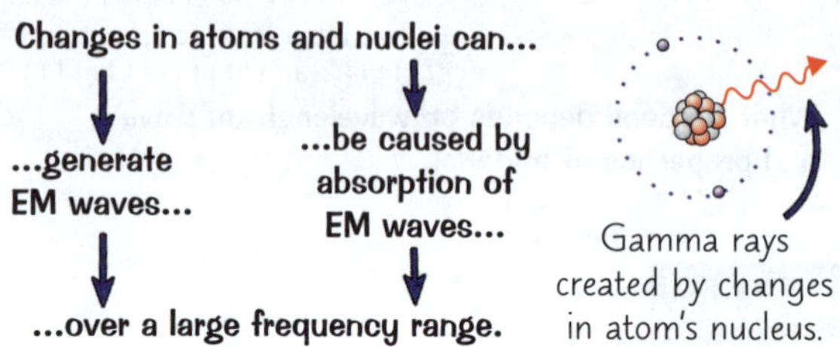
Changes in atoms and nuclei can...
...generate EM waves...
...be caused by absorption of EM waves...
...over a large frequency range.
Gamma rays created by changes in atom's nucleus.

Visible Light

In the visible light spectrum, every colour has a small range of wavelengths.

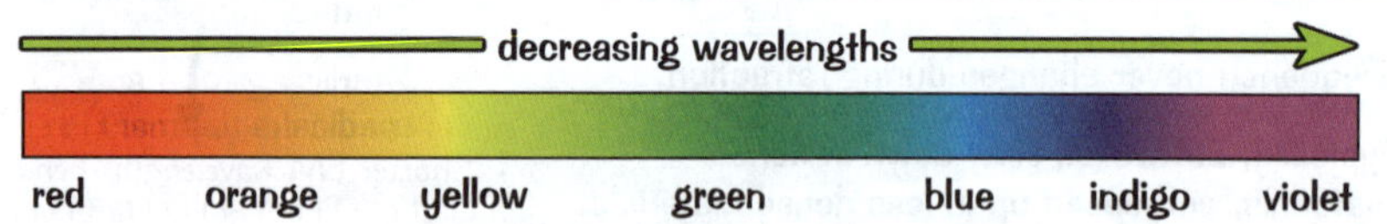
decreasing wavelengths
red
orange
yellow
green
blue
indigo
violet

The colour of a material depends on the wavelengths of light that are reflected, transmitted and absorbed.

Producing Radio Waves

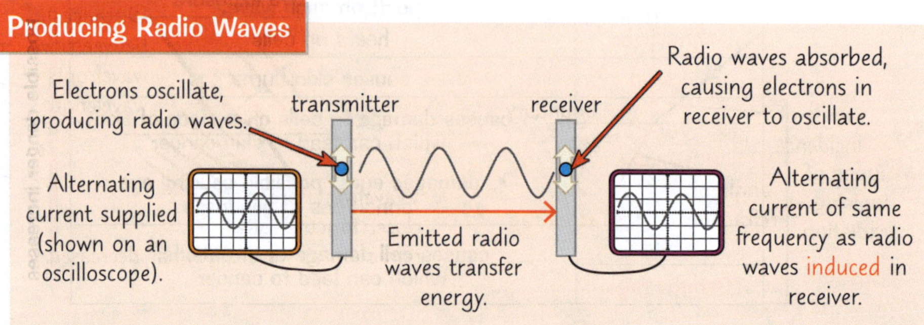
Electrons oscillate, producing radio waves.
transmitter
receiver
Radio waves absorbed, causing electrons in receiver to oscillate.
Alternating current supplied (shown on an oscilloscope).
Emitted radio waves transfer energy.
Alternating current of same frequency as radio waves induced in receiver.

Uses and Dangers of EM Waves

Some Uses of EM Waves

Radio waves

- Broadcasting
- Communications
- Satellite transmissions

Microwaves

- Microwave ovens
- Communications
- Satellite transmissions

Visible light

- Vision
- Illumination
- Photography

Infrared radiation

- Electric heaters
- Cooking
- Thermal imaging
- Optical fibres
- Security systems
- TV remote controls
- Short range communications

UV waves

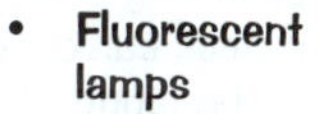

- Fluorescent lamps
- Security marking
- Detecting forged bank notes
- Sterilising water

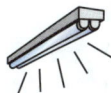

X-rays

- Medical X-rays
- Airport security scanners
- Looking inside objects

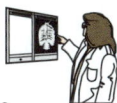

Gamma rays

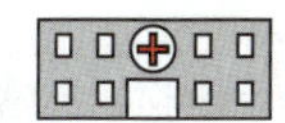

- Detecting and treating cancer
- Sterilising food and medical equipment

Dangers of EM Waves

		Danger of excessive exposure
	Microwaves	heats up cells
	Infrared	causes skin burns
Types of ionising radiation.	Ultraviolet	• causes damage to cells on surface of skin, which can lead to skin cancer • damages eyes, possibly causing eye conditions or blindness
	X-rays	causes cell damage or mutations, which can lead to cancer
	Gamma rays	

Frequency increases, possible danger increases

The Model of the Atom

The History of the Atom

		Developed further after...
	Tiny sphere that can't be broken up.	electron discovery
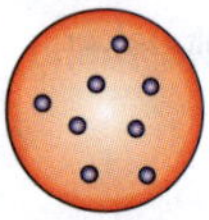	Plum pudding model — sphere of positive charge with negative electrons stuck in it.	alpha scattering experiment
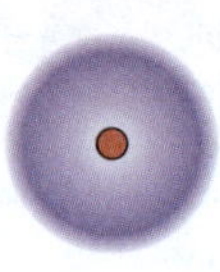	Nuclear model — positively charged nucleus surrounded by cloud of negative electrons.	Niels Bohr's theoretical calculations (that agreed with experimental data).
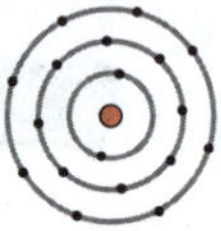	Bohr model — electrons orbit the nucleus at certain distances.	

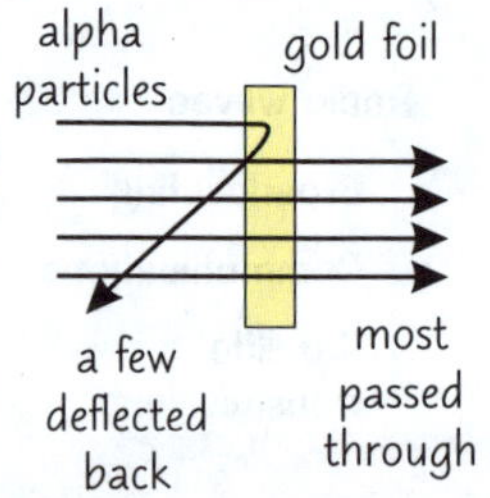

alpha particles
gold foil
a few deflected back
most passed through

Experiment showed:

Most of the mass of an atom is concentrated at a central, tiny nucleus.

Nucleus is positively charged.

The Current Model of the Atom

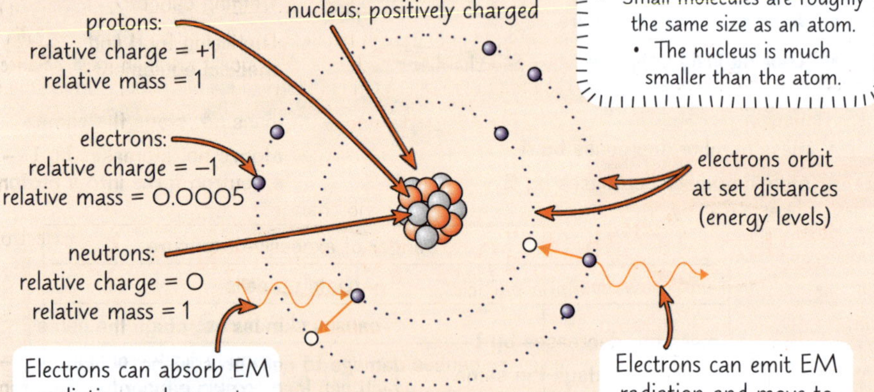

Size of atom ≈ 1×10^{-10} m.
- Small molecules are roughly the same size as an atom.
- The nucleus is much smaller than the atom.

protons:
relative charge = +1
relative mass = 1

electrons:
relative charge = –1
relative mass = 0.0005

neutrons:
relative charge = 0
relative mass = 1

nucleus: positively charged

electrons orbit at set distances (energy levels)

Electrons can absorb EM radiation and move to higher energy levels.

Electrons can emit EM radiation and move to lower energy levels.

An atom's overall electric charge is zero as number of electrons = number of protons.
If an atom loses one or more electrons, it becomes a positively charged ion.

Isotopes and Radioactive Decay

Mass Number and Atomic Number

All atoms of each element have a set number of protons.

ISOTOPES of an element — atoms with the same number of protons but different numbers of neutrons (and so different masses).

MASS NUMBER — total number of protons and neutrons in an atom.

$^{16}_{8}\text{O}$

ATOMIC NUMBER — number of protons in an atom (equal to charge of nucleus).

Radioactive Decay

RADIOACTIVE DECAY — when the nucleus of an unstable isotope decays, giving out radiation to become more stable.

IONISING RADIATION (α, β^-, β^+ and γ) — radiation that knocks electrons off atoms, creating positive ions.

Unstable nuclei can also release neutrons (n) when they decay.

	alpha (α)	beta minus (β^-)	gamma (γ)
Consists of...	2 neutrons and 2 protons (helium nucleus)	fast-moving electron from nucleus	electromagnetic radiation from nucleus
Absorbed by...	Sheet of paper	Sheet of aluminium	Thick sheets of lead
Range in air	Few cm	Few metres	Long distances
Ionising power	Strong	Moderate	Weak

A positron (β^+) has same mass as an electron, but a relative charge of +1. It is ejected from the nucleus in β^+ decay.

Nuclear Equations

Mass and charge on each side of a nuclear equation must balance.

α-decay
- mass number decreases by 4
- atomic number decreases by 2

$$^{238}_{92}\text{U} \longrightarrow {}^{234}_{90}\text{Th} + {}^{4}_{2}\alpha$$

(mass number: −4; atomic number: −2; ${}^{4}_{2}\alpha$ = alpha particle)

neutron emission
- mass no. decreases by 1
- atomic no. stays the same

γ-decay
- mass no. and atomic no. stay the same

When particles in nucleus rearrange due to decay, energy lost as gamma.

β⁻-decay
- mass no. stays the same
- atomic no. increases by 1 — a neutron turns into a proton

$$^{14}_{6}\text{C} \longrightarrow {}^{14}_{7}\text{N} + {}^{0}_{-1}\beta$$

(mass number: no change; atomic number: +1; ${}^{0}_{-1}\beta$ = electron)

β⁺-decay
- mass no. stays the same
- atomic no. decreases by 1 — a proton turns into a neutron

$$^{18}_{9}\text{F} \longrightarrow {}^{18}_{8}\text{O} + {}^{0}_{1}\beta$$

(mass number: no change; atomic number: −1; ${}^{0}_{1}\beta$ = positron)

You don't need to know these exact equations, just how mass and atomic numbers change during decays.

Radiation and Half-life

Activity

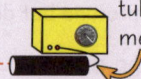

Radioactive decays can be detected by photographic film.

Radioactive decay is **random**.
Can't say if or when a nucleus will decay.

ACTIVITY — the rate at which a source decays, measured in **becquerels (Bq)**.

A Geiger-Muller tube and counter measures activity.

Background Radiation

BACKGROUND RADIATION — low-level radiation that's always around us.

Two types of sources:

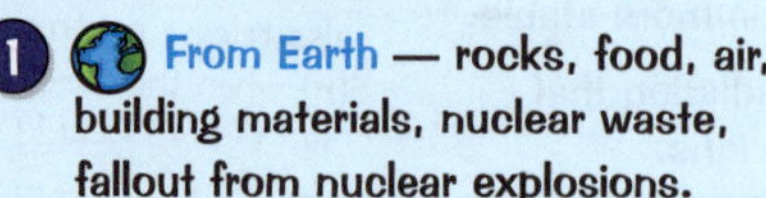

1. **From Earth** — rocks, food, air, building materials, nuclear waste, fallout from nuclear explosions.

2. **From space** — cosmic rays.

Half-life

HALF-LIFE — time taken for the number of nuclei of an isotope in a sample to halve.

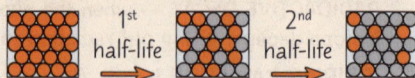

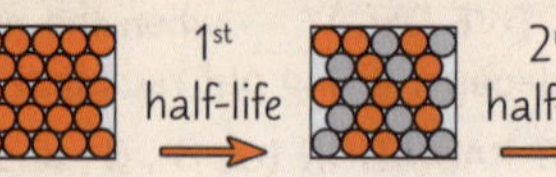

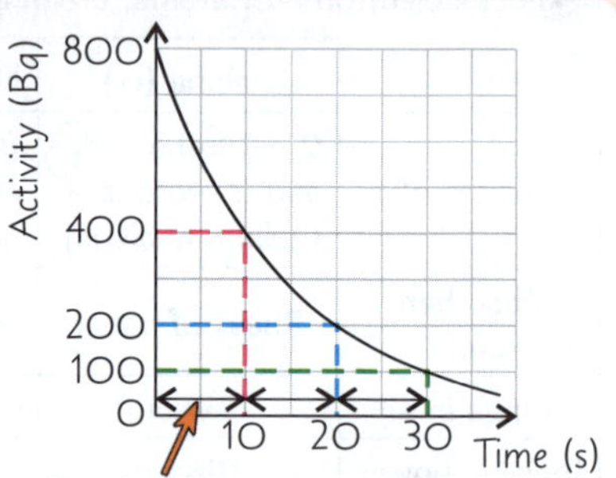

One half-life is the time taken for the activity of a sample to halve.

Contamination and Irradiation

RADIOACTIVE CONTAMINATION — getting unwanted radioactive atoms onto or into an object.

IRRADIATION — the exposure of an object to ionising radiation (doesn't make the object radioactive).

Risk of Radiation

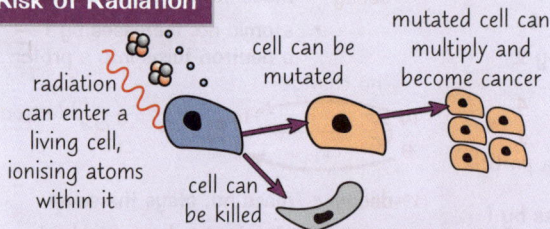

radiation can enter a living cell, ionising atoms within it

cell can be mutated

mutated cell can multiply and become cancer

cell can be killed

Inside body:
- α is most dangerous
- γ is least dangerous

Outside body:
- γ is most dangerous
- α is least dangerous

Three precautions to reduce exposure:

1. **Keep sources in lead-lined boxes.**

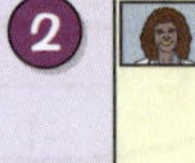

2. **Stand behind barriers or be in a different room to the source.**

3. **Wear protective clothing and use tongs to handle sources.**

People exposed to radiation (e.g. hospital staff and patients) should have their exposure limited.

Work Done, Power and Forces

Most of the stuff on pages 81-83 can also be assessed as part of this section (and so can be tested on papers 5 and 6).

Work Done

Work done = energy transferred.

When a force moves an object from one point to another, work is done on the object and energy is transferred.

work done (J) (1 joule = 1 newton metre) — force (N)

$$E = Fd$$

distance moved in the direction of the force (m)

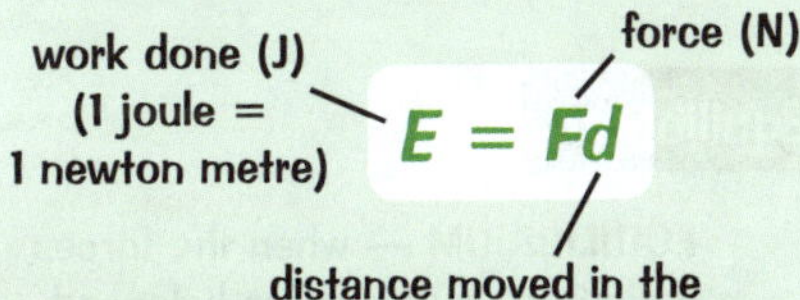

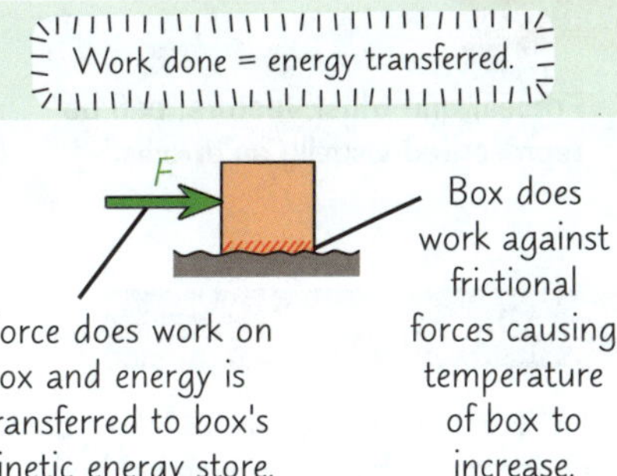

Power

POWER — rate of energy transfer (or rate of doing work).

One watt (W) = one joule of energy transferred per second (J/s).

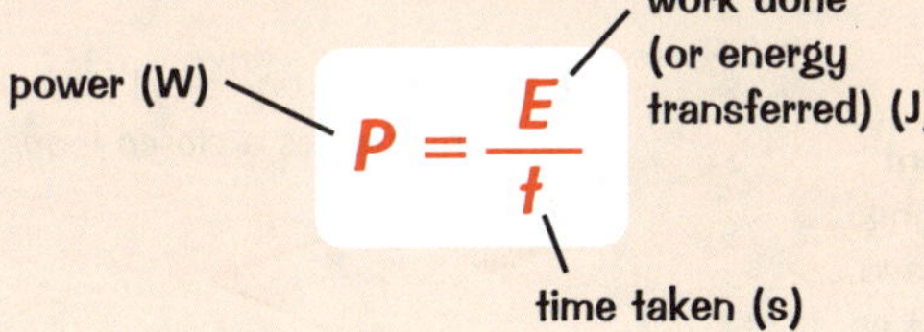

2 W motor transfers more energy per second than 1 W motor, so lifts mass faster.

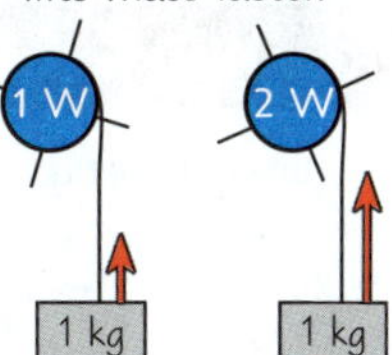

Force Basics

FORCE — a push or a pull on an object caused by it interacting with something.

When two objects interact, they exert an equal but opposite force on each other. This pair of forces is an interaction pair.

Two types of forces:

1. **Contact forces: objects have to be touching.**

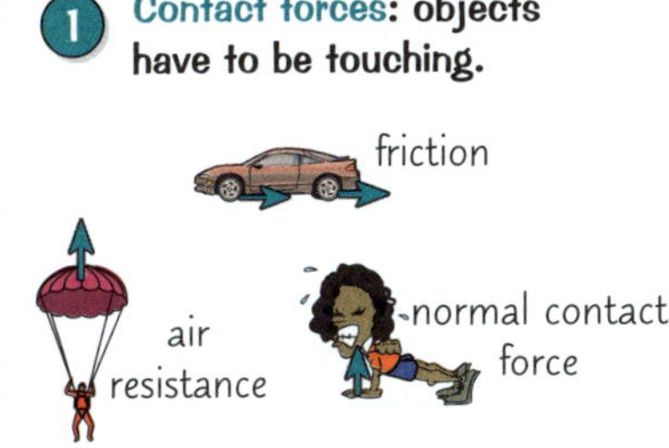

2. **Non-contact forces: objects don't need to be touching.**

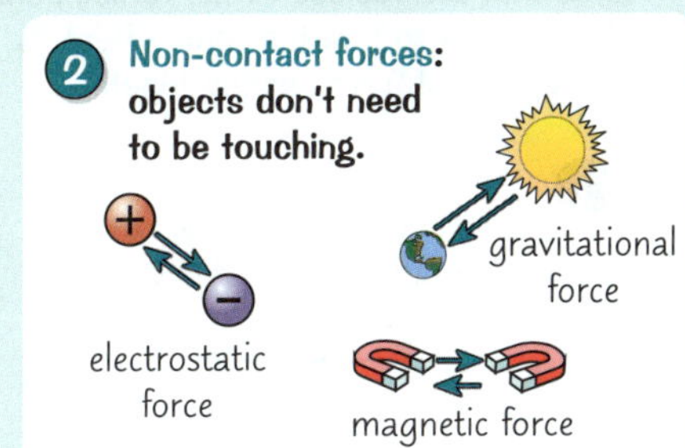

Forces

The stuff on scalars and vectors on page 75 can also be assessed in this section.

Vectors

Forces, and other vectors, can be represented visually as arrows.

Direction of arrow shows direction of quantity.
Length of arrow shows magnitude.

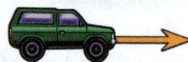

Free Body Force Diagrams

FREE BODY FORCE DIAGRAM — shows all forces acting on an isolated body.

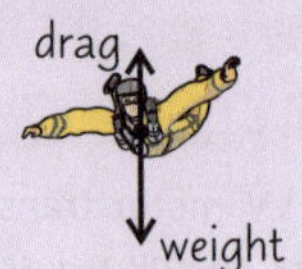

Arrows show relative magnitudes and directions of forces acting.

Resolving Forces

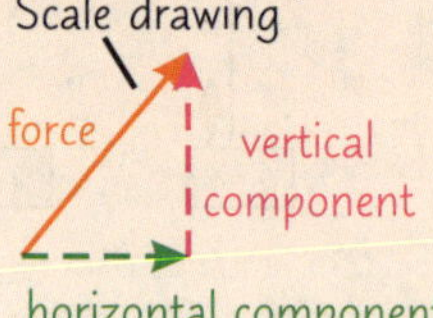

Component forces acting together have same effect as the single force.

Equilibrium

EQUILIBRIUM — when the forces acting on an object are balanced and the resultant force is zero.

Object in equilibrium

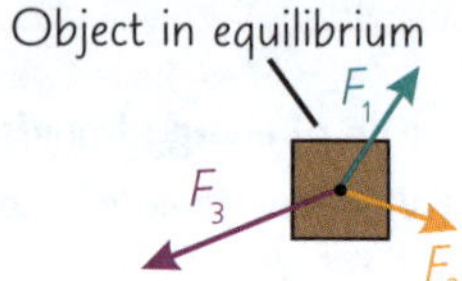

Drawing forces tip-to-tail in scale drawing creates a closed loop.

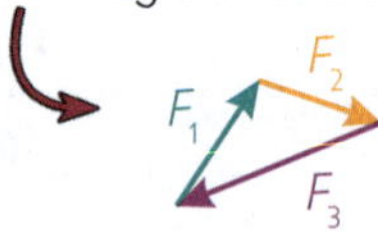

Two Ways to Calculate Resultant Force

RESULTANT (NET) FORCE — a single force that can replace all the forces acting on an object to give the same effect as all the original forces acting together.

1. Add forces pointing in same direction. Subtract forces pointing in opposite directions.

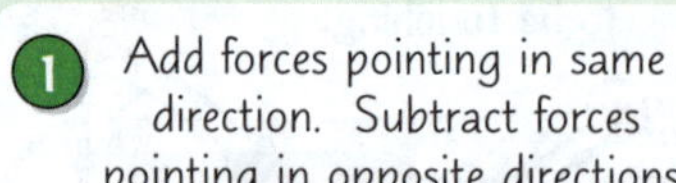
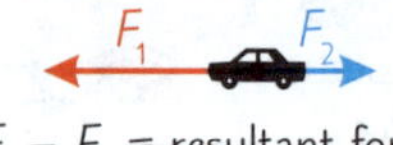

$F_1 - F_2$ = resultant force

2. Draw forces to scale and tip-to-tail.

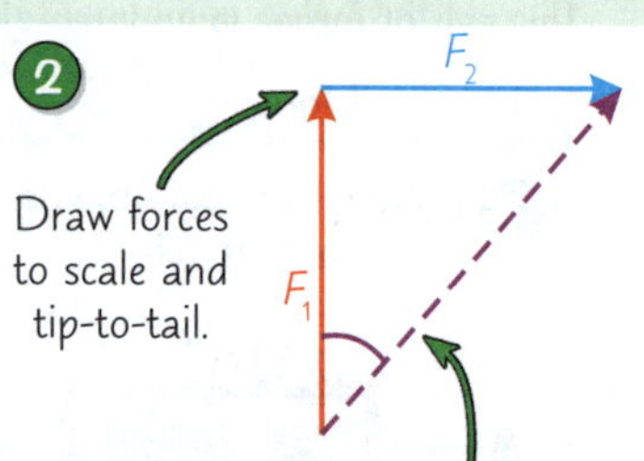

Measure length of resultant force to find its magnitude, and angle to find its direction.

Current and Circuits

Some of the stuff in 'The Current Model of the Atom' box on page 90 can also be assessed as part of this section.

Current

ELECTRIC CURRENT — the rate of flow of charge.

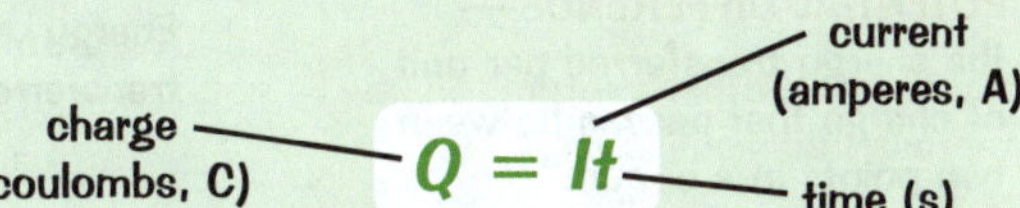

In metals, current is caused by a flow of electrons.

Current in Circuits

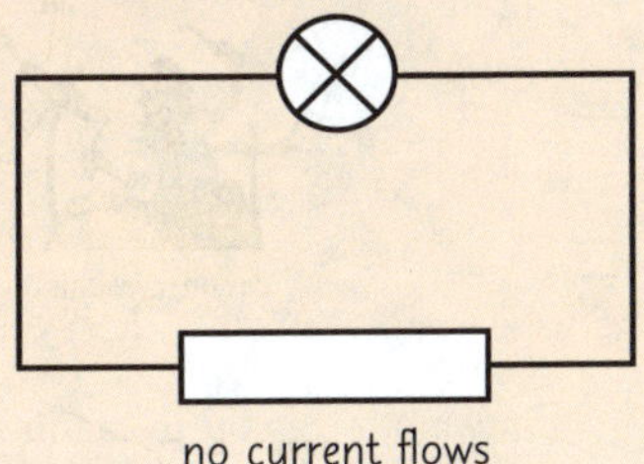

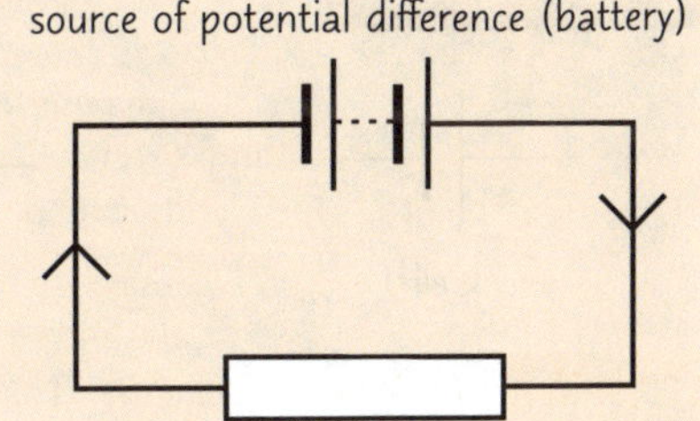

Current through Components

potential difference (volts, V) — $V = IR$ — **current (amperes, A)**, **resistance (ohms, Ω)**

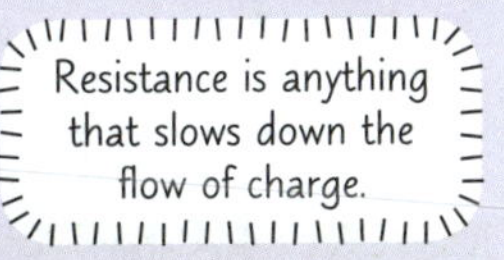

Resistance is anything that slows down the flow of charge.

Current through a component depends on the component's resistance and the potential difference (p.d.) across the component.

The greater the resistance, the smaller the current (at a fixed p.d.).

Use a variable resistor to change the current in a circuit:

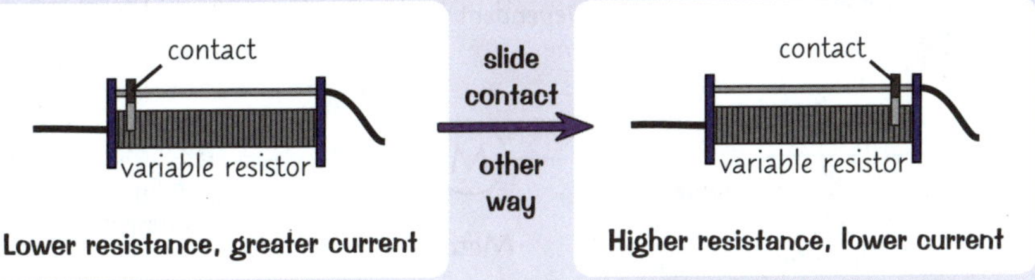

Potential Difference & Circuit Symbols

Potential Difference

POTENTIAL DIFFERENCE — the energy transferred per unit of charge that passes between two points in a circuit.

Potential difference can also be called voltage.

Energy, Charge and P.d. Equation

$$E = QV$$

- E — Energy transferred (J)
- Q — charge moved (C)
- V — potential difference (V)

1 volt (V) = 1 joule per coulomb (J/C)

Circuit Symbols

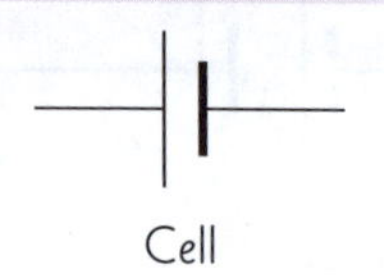
Cell

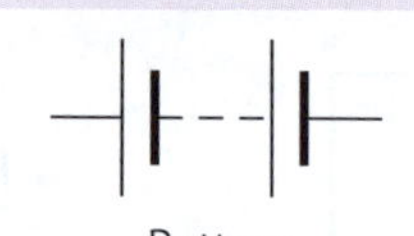
Battery

circuit cymbals

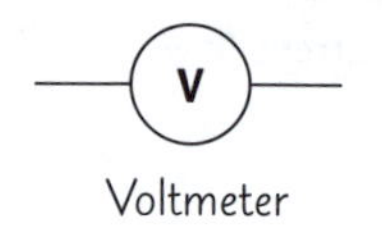
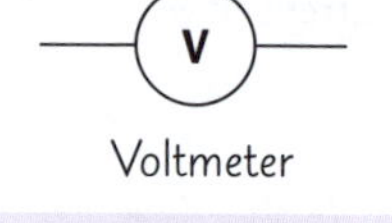

Voltmeter

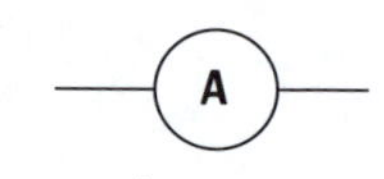

Ammeter

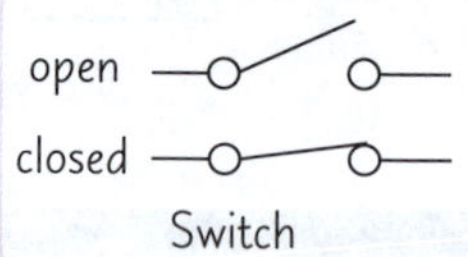

Switch

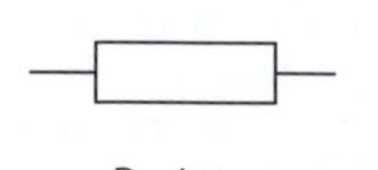
Resistor

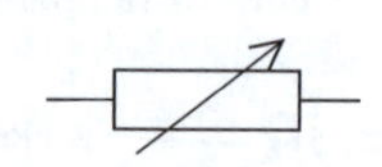
Variable resistor

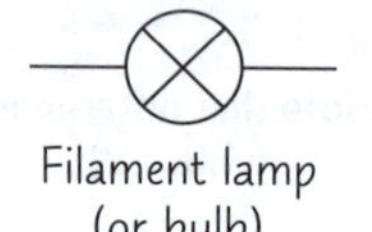
Filament lamp (or bulb)

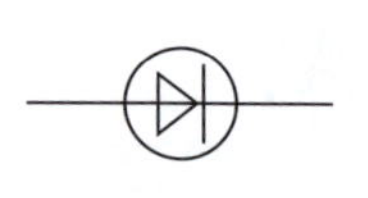
Diode

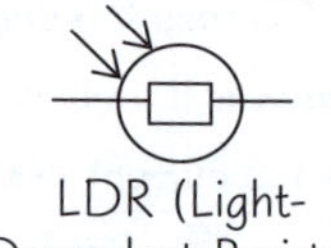
LDR (Light-Dependent Resistor)

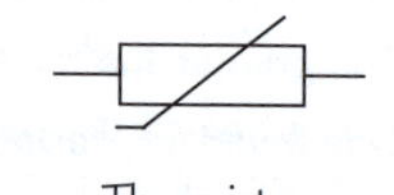
Thermistor

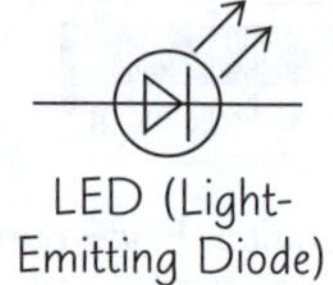
LED (Light-Emitting Diode)

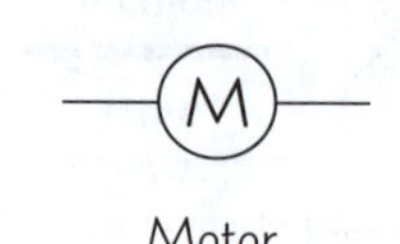

Motor

Components are connected by straight lines — they represent the wires.

Components of Circuits

Three Different Current-Potential Difference Graphs

1 A fixed resistor at constant temperature

Current is directly proportional to potential difference...

... so resistance doesn't change.

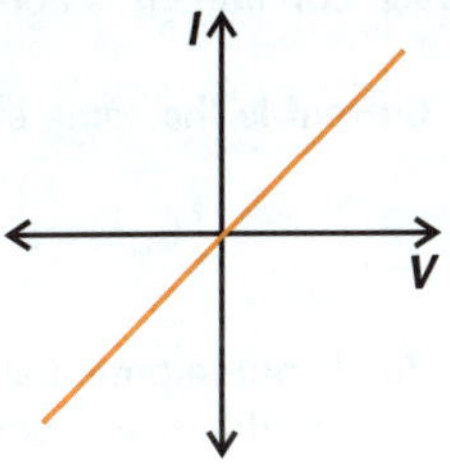

This graph is linear.

I

V

Components with changing **resistance** (when current through them varies):

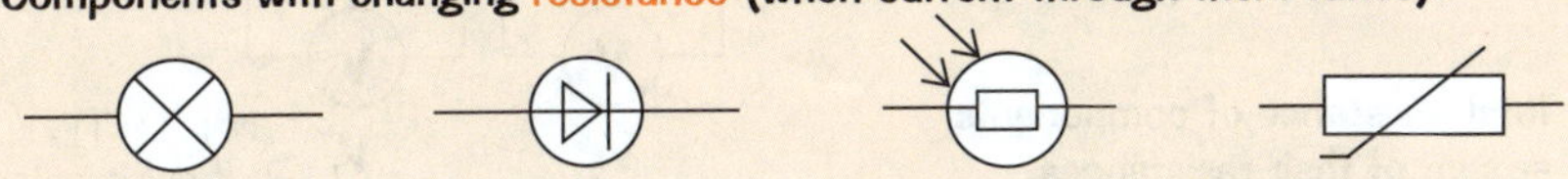

2 Filament lamp

Current increases...

... so temperature of filament increases...

... so resistance increases.

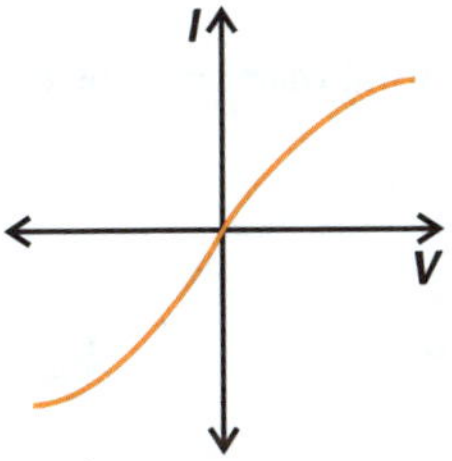

3 Diode

High resistance in one direction...

... so current only flows in the other direction.

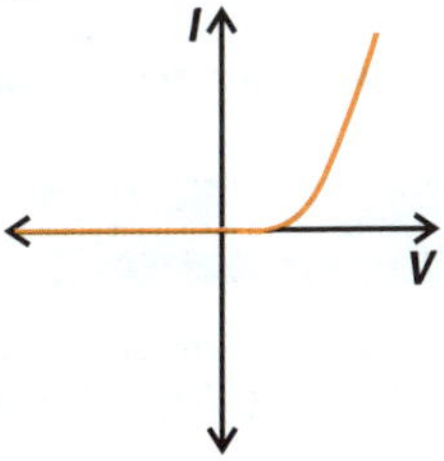

These graphs are non-linear.

LDRs and Thermistors

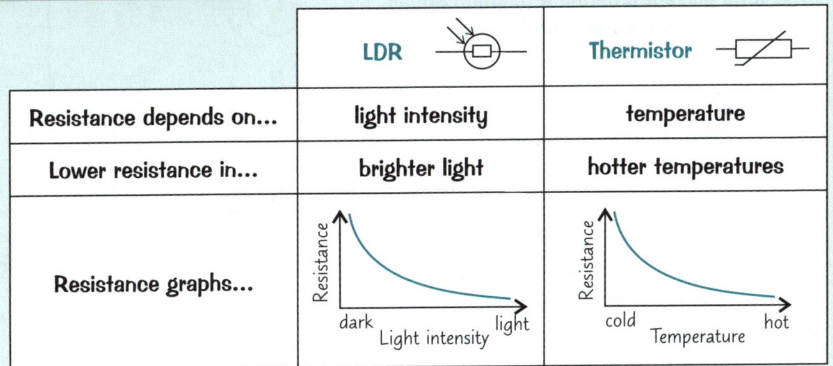

	LDR	Thermistor
Resistance depends on...	light intensity	temperature
Lower resistance in...	brighter light	hotter temperatures
Resistance graphs...		

Series and Parallel Circuits

Series Circuits

Serious Sir Kitten

Each component is connected in a line, end-to-end with power source.

Current is the same everywhere.

$$I_1 = I_2$$

Total source potential difference is shared between components.

$$V_{total} = V_1 + V_2$$

Total resistance of components = sum of their resistances.

$$R_{total} = R_1 + R_2$$

V_{total}, I_2, A, A, I_1, R_2, R_1, V, V, V_2, V_1

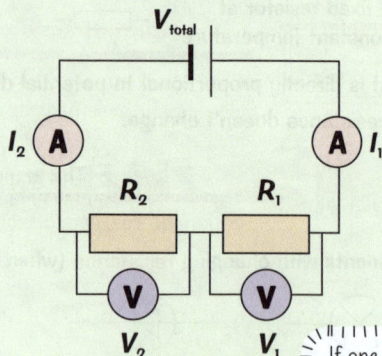

If one component breaks, no current flows in circuit.

Adding a resistor in series increases the total resistance of the circuit.

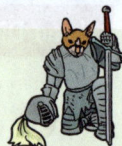

Parallel Circuits

Each component is separately connected on a different branch of the circuit.

Total current flowing around a circuit = sum of the currents through each branch.

$$I_{total} = I_1 + I_2$$

The total current entering a junction equals the total current leaving the junction.

Potential difference across each branch is the same as the source potential difference.

$$V_1 = V_2 = V_{total}$$

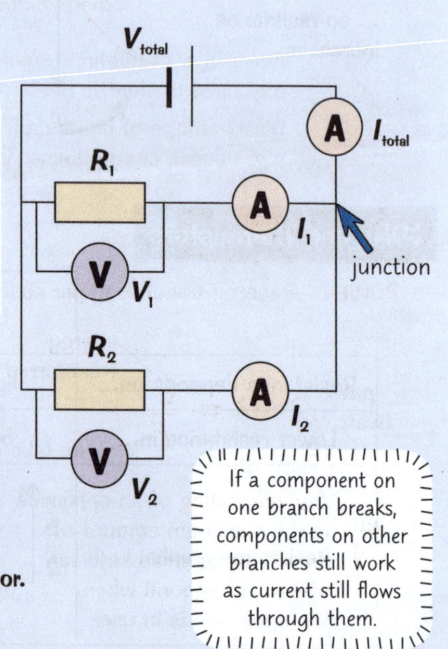

The total resistance of resistors in parallel is less than the resistance of the smallest resistor.

Adding a resistor in parallel decreases the total resistance of the circuit.

Energy and Power in Circuits

Energy Transfers

When charge flows, work is done (and so energy is transferred).

Energy transferred electrically

to thermal energy store of the heating element inside the kettle.

Energy transferred electrically

to kinetic energy store of the fan's motor.

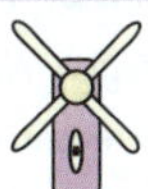

Dissipated Energy in Circuits

Some energy is dissipated to thermal energy stores when a current does work against resistance. This has a heating effect.

Current flows through a resistor → Electrons collide with, and transfer energy to, the lattice of ions in the resistor → Ions vibrate more, so energy in thermal energy store increases → The resistor heats up

Advantage of heating effect — e.g. used in electric heaters, toasters, etc.

Disadvantage of heating effect — e.g. causes energy losses in circuits.

Low resistance wires used to reduce energy losses in circuits.

Energy and Power

POWER — energy transferred per second.

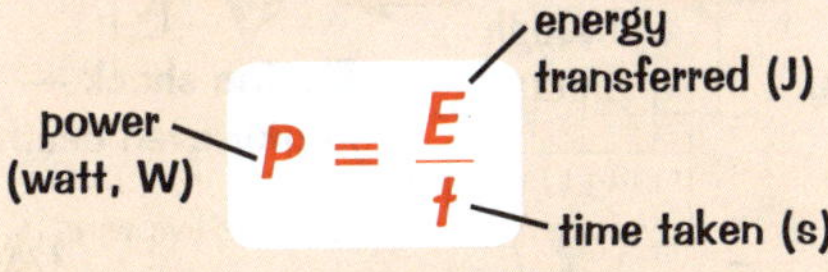

A power rating of an appliance is the maximum amount of energy transferred between stores per second when the appliance is in use.

Calculating Power

The higher the current through or potential difference across a device, the greater its power.

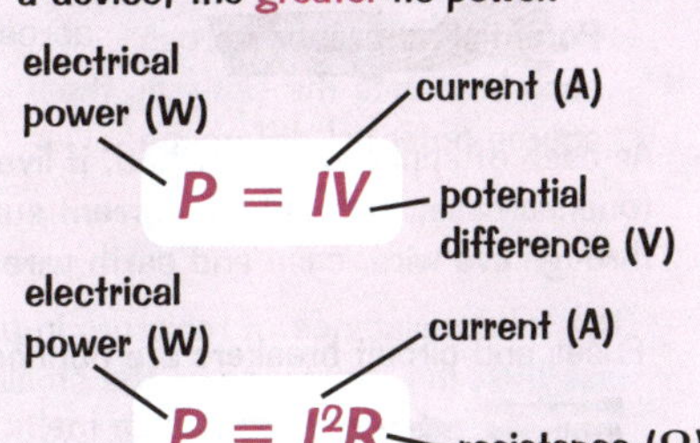

Electricity at Home

Two Types of Electricity Supply

1. **ALTERNATING CURRENT** (a.c.) — current where movement of charge constantly changes direction.
   Produced by an alternating voltage, where the positive and negative ends of the potential difference keep alternating.
   Used in UK mains supply.
2. **DIRECT CURRENT** (d.c.) — current where movement of charge is only in one direction.
   Produced by a direct voltage, where the potential difference is only positive or negative, not both.
   Supplied by cells and batteries.

Three Facts about UK Mains Supply

1. a.c. supply
2. frequency of 50 Hz
3. voltage around 230 V

Three-core Cables

	live wire	neutral wire	earth wire
Function	Provides alternating potential difference from mains supply.	Completes the circuit.	Safety — stops appliance casing becoming live.

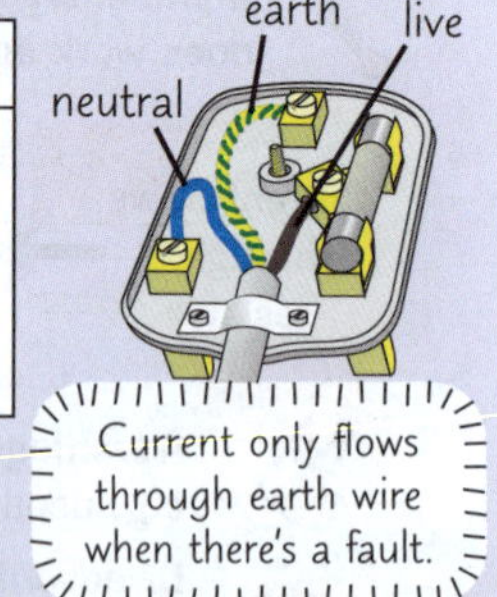
earth
live
neutral

- Potential difference between live wire and neutral or earth wires = 230 V.
- Potential difference between neutral and earth wire = 0 V.

Current only flows through earth wire when there's a fault.

Electric Shocks and Safety

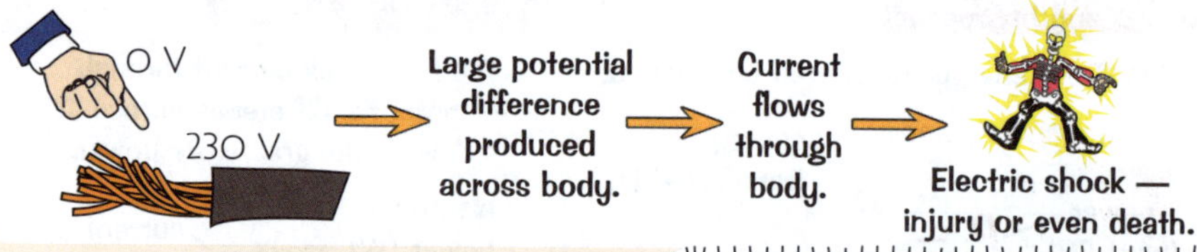
0 V
230 V
Large potential difference produced across body.
Current flows through body.
Electric shock — injury or even death.

As case of appliance is earthed, if live wire touches case, then LARGE current surges through live wire, case and earth wire.

Any connection between the live wire and the earth can be dangerous — e.g. it could cause a fire.

Fuses and circuit breakers are connected to live wire of a device, so if current surges...

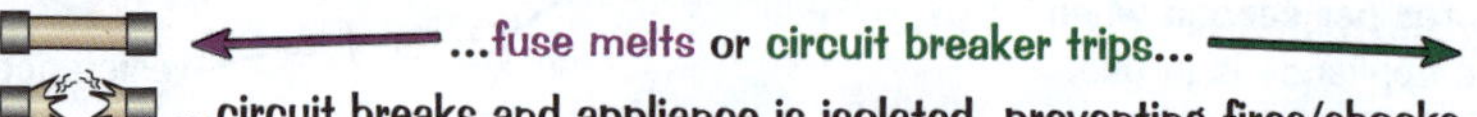
...fuse melts or circuit breaker trips...
...circuit breaks and appliance is isolated, preventing fires/shocks.

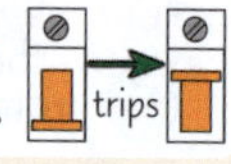
trips

Magnets

Magnetic Fields

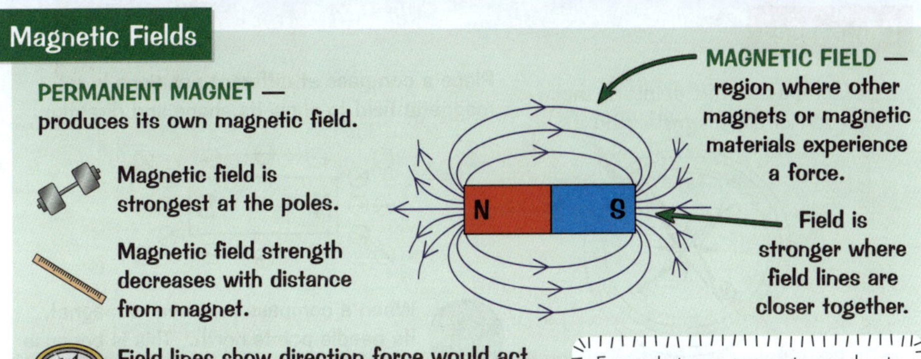

PERMANENT MAGNET — produces its own magnetic field.

Magnetic field is strongest at the poles.

Magnetic field strength decreases with distance from magnet.

Field lines show direction force would act on a north pole, if placed at that point.

MAGNETIC FIELD — region where other magnets or magnetic materials experience a force.

Field is stronger where field lines are closer together.

Forces between magnets are due to their magnetic fields interacting.

Magnetic Repulsion

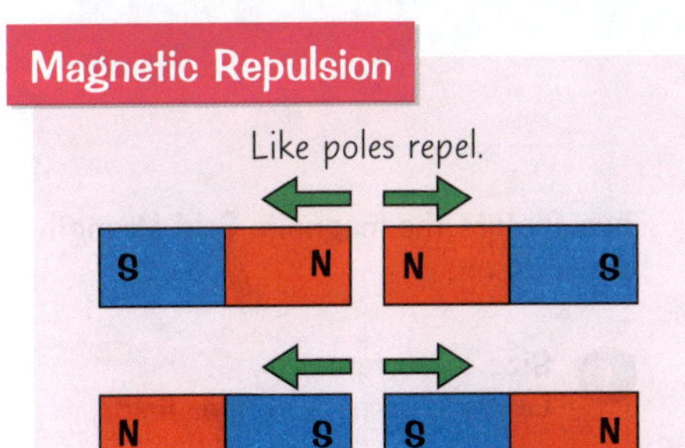

Magnetic Attraction

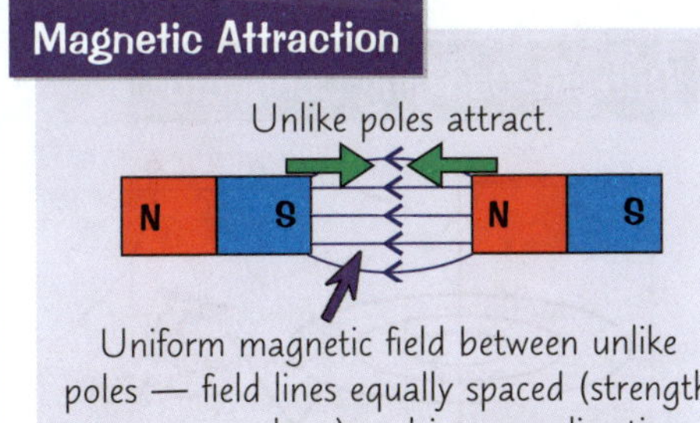

Uniform magnetic field between unlike poles — field lines equally spaced (strength same everywhere) and in same direction.

Induced Magnets and Magnetic Materials

INDUCED MAGNET — a magnetic material that only produces a magnetic field when it's in another magnetic field.

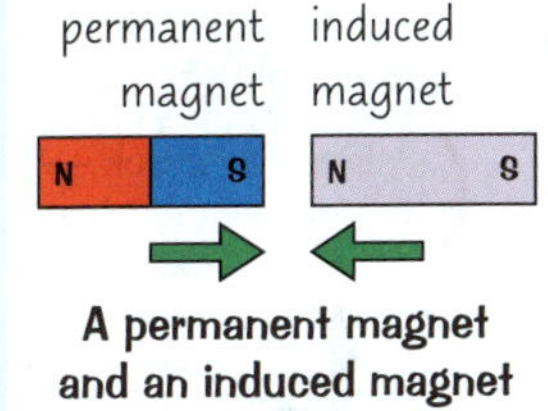

A permanent magnet and an induced magnet are always attracted to each other.

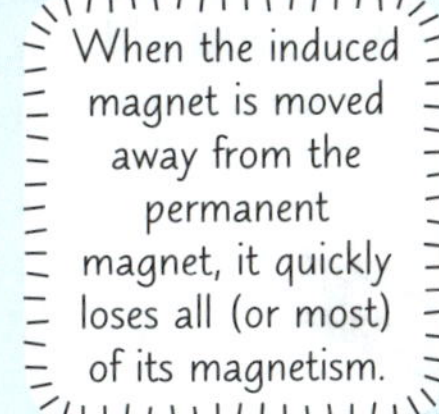

When the induced magnet is moved away from the permanent magnet, it quickly loses all (or most) of its magnetism.

Four magnetic materials:

 1 iron  2 steel 3 nickel  4 cobalt

Uses of Magnets

Fridge doors

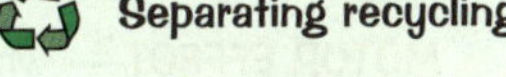

Separating recycling

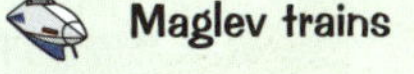

Maglev trains

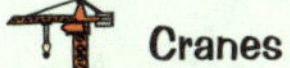

Cranes

Compasses and the Motor Effect

Compasses

Compass needle points in the direction of the magnetic field it's in.

A compass needle is a small bar magnet.

Place a compass at different positions in a magnetic field to show its shape and direction.

When a compass isn't near a magnet, its needle points north. This is because Earth produces its own magnetic field (Earth's core is magnetic).

Current-Carrying Conductor

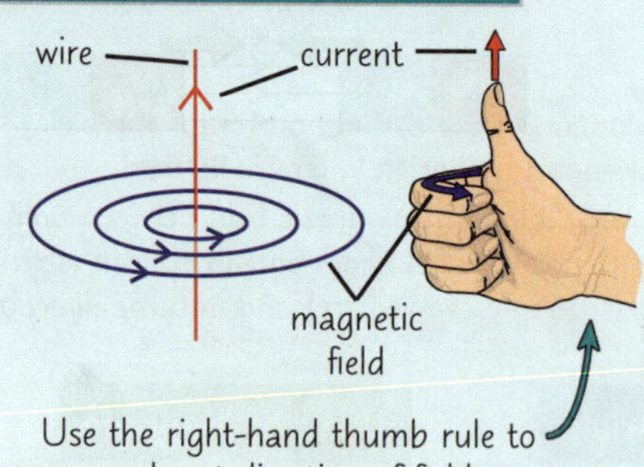

Use the right-hand thumb rule to work out direction of field.

Two factors the magnetic field strength depends on:

1. **Size of current. Larger current, stronger field.**
2. **Distance from the conductor. Closer = stronger field.**

Force on a Conductor

MOTOR EFFECT — when a magnet and a current-carrying conductor exert an equal and opposite force on each other.

Fleming's left-hand rule.

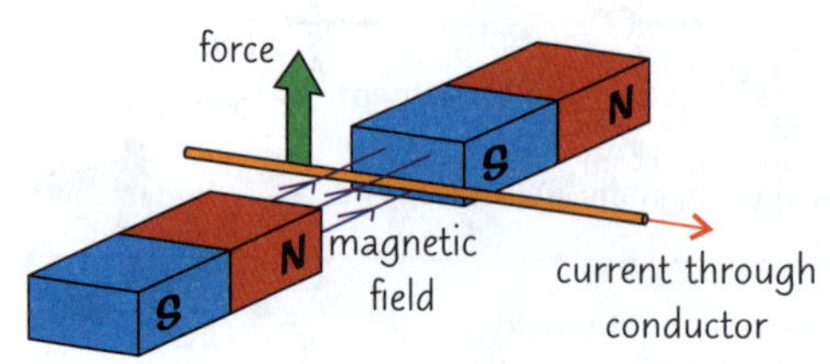

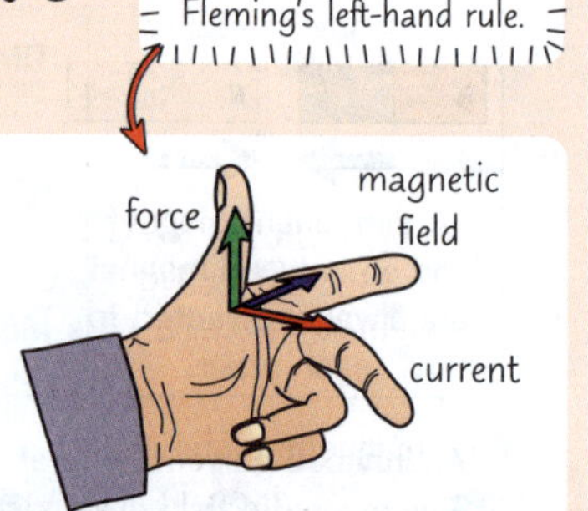

Solenoids and Induced P.d.

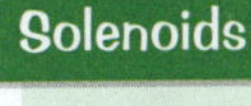

Solenoids

SOLENOID — a long cylindrical coil of wire.

A solenoid is an example of an electromagnet.

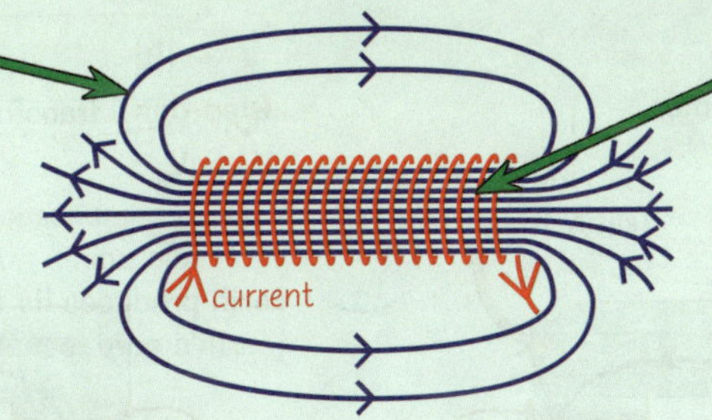

Outside solenoid, magnetic fields cancel to form weaker field, which is same shape as a bar magnet's field.
Inside solenoid, magnetic fields of each turn of wire add together to form strong and almost uniform field.
current

Electromagnetic Induction

ELECTROMAGNETIC INDUCTION — the induction of a p.d. (and current if there's a complete circuit) in a wire which is experiencing a change in magnetic field.

	1	2
Two ways to induce a potential difference...	Move the wire.	Move the magnet.
To swap the direction of the potential difference...	**Move the wire in the opposite direction. or Start with both magnets the other way round.**	**Move the magnet in the opposite direction. or Start with the magnet the other way round.**
To increase the size of the induced potential difference...	**Increase the speed of the movement. or Increase the magnetic field strength.**	For a coil, can also increase turns per unit length.

An induced current generates its own magnetic field.
This magnetic field always acts against the change that made it.

Transformers and the National Grid

Transformers

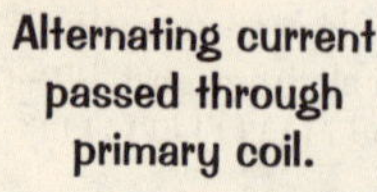

Alternating current passed through primary coil.

Changing magnetic field induced in iron core.

Alternating current induced in secondary coil.

Step-up transformer

$V_P < V_S$

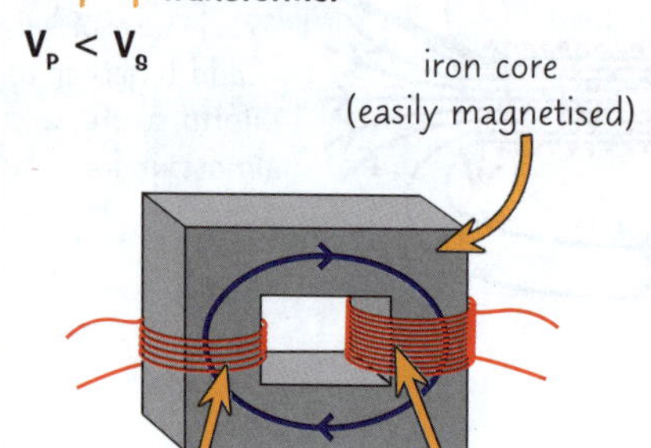
iron core
(easily magnetised)
primary coil
(fewer turns)
secondary coil
(more turns)

Step-down transformer

$V_P > V_S$

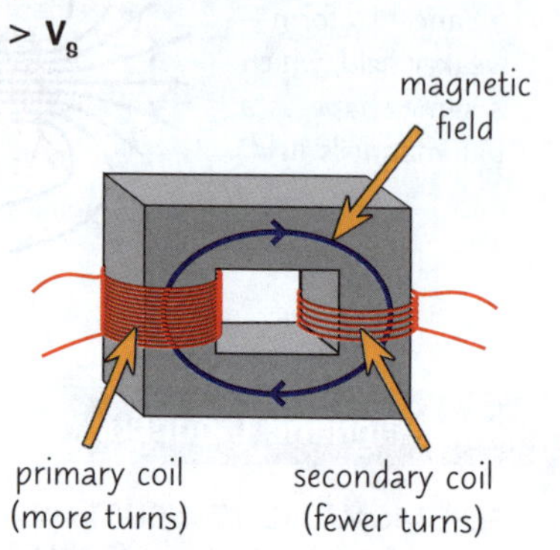
magnetic
field
primary coil
(more turns)
secondary coil
(fewer turns)

If transformer is 100% efficient: input power = output power.

The National Grid

NATIONAL GRID — a system of cables and transformers that connect power stations to consumers.

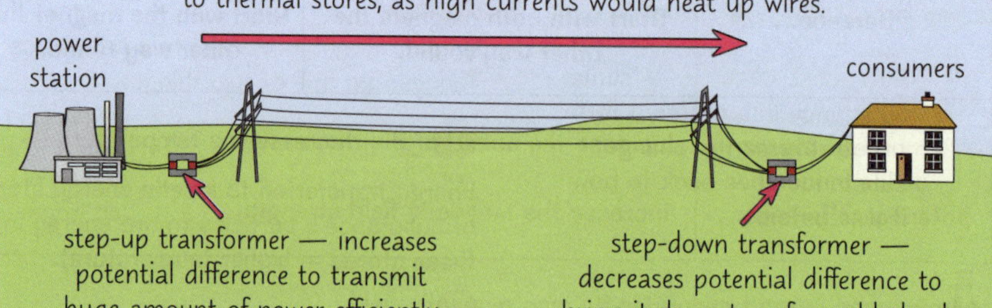
Electrical power transferred at a high potential difference and a low current. This is more efficient as it reduces energy losses to thermal stores, as high currents would heat up wires.
power
station
consumers
step-up transformer — increases potential difference to transmit huge amount of power efficiently
step-down transformer — decreases potential difference to bring it down to safe, usable levels

Density and The Particle Model

Density

DENSITY — mass per unit volume.

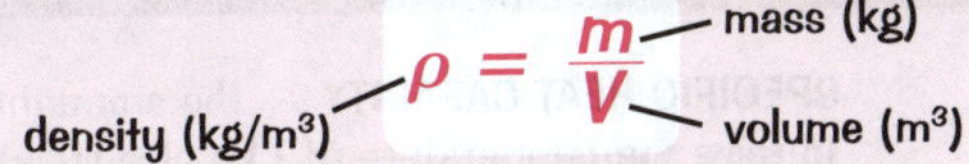

States of Matter

Density decreases (Solid → Liquid → Gas)

	Particle arrangement	Forces between particles	Distance between particles	Particle motion
SOLID	Regular, fixed	Strong	Very small	Vibration only
LIQUID	Irregular	Weak	Small	Slow
GAS	Irregular	Very weak	Large	Fast

Changes of State

Changes of state are physical changes. Mass is always conserved.

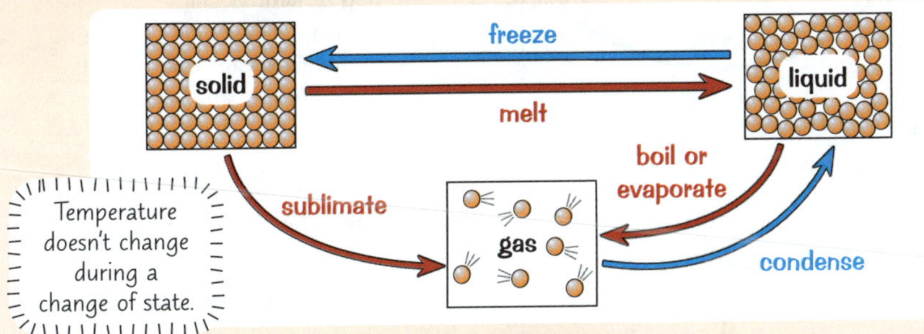

Temperature doesn't change during a change of state.

Physical and Chemical Changes

PHYSICAL CHANGE — same substance in a different form. If you reverse the change, substance goes back to how it was before.

CHEMICAL CHANGE — new substance created.

Heating

Heating transfers energy to a substance. This can do one of two things:

1.  Increase the temperature — Energy transferred to kinetic energy stores of substance's particles (more energy in these stores = higher temperature).
2.   Change the state — Energy used to break bonds.

Heating, Temperature and Pressure

Specific Heat Capacity and Specific Latent Heat

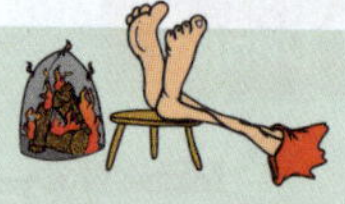
Specific feet capacity

SPECIFIC HEAT CAPACITY — the amount of energy needed to raise the temperature of 1 kg of a substance by 1 °C.

SPECIFIC LATENT HEAT — the amount of energy needed to change 1 kg of a substance from one state to another, without changing its temperature.

SPECIFIC LATENT HEAT OF FUSION — the specific latent heat of changing between a solid and a liquid.

SPECIFIC LATENT HEAT OF VAPORISATION — the specific latent heat of changing between a liquid and a gas.

Absolute Zero

Converting between kelvin and Celsius:

This is MINUS 273.

ABSOLUTE ZERO — 0 K, or –273 °C. The temperature at which particles have as little energy as possible in their kinetic energy stores — they're almost still.

Absolute zero is the coldest possible temperature.

Gas Pressure

Gas particles are constantly moving randomly.

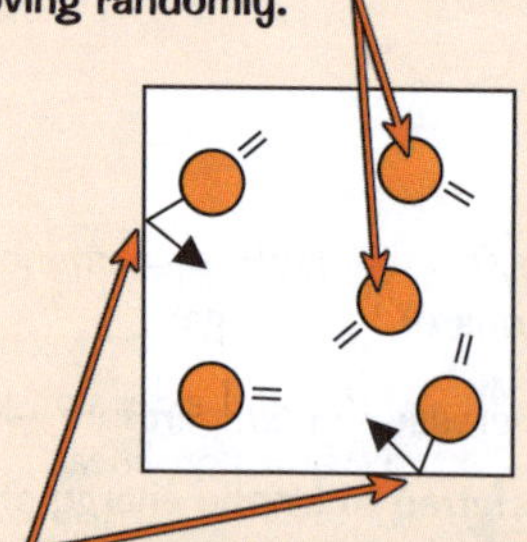

When particles collide with a surface...

... they exert a force, and so a pressure.

A Gas at Constant Volume

Temperature increases

Particles get faster and collide with the container with more force and more often.

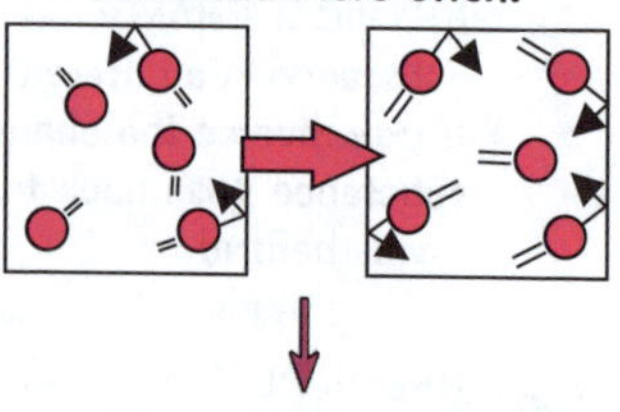

Pressure increases

Elasticity

Changing Shape

More than one force has to act on a stationary object to change its shape.

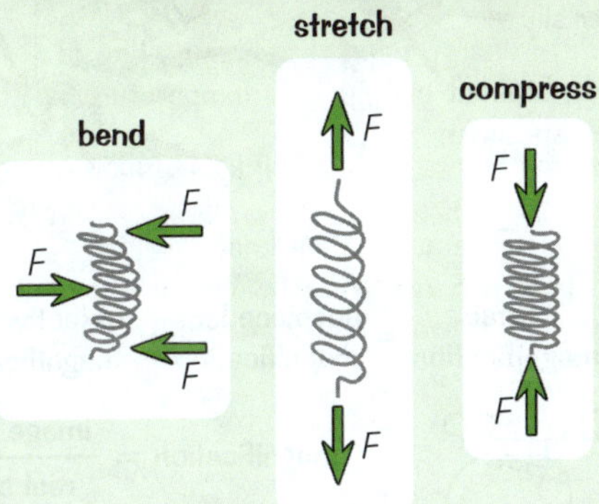

Two Types of Distortion

1. **ELASTIC** — object goes back to its original shape and length after forces have been removed.

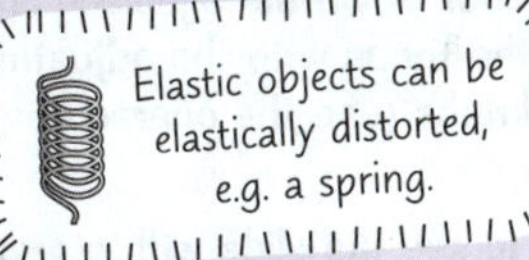

Elastic objects can be elastically distorted, e.g. a spring.

2. **INELASTIC** — object doesn't go back to its original shape and length after forces have been removed.

Force-Extension Relationship for an Elastic Object

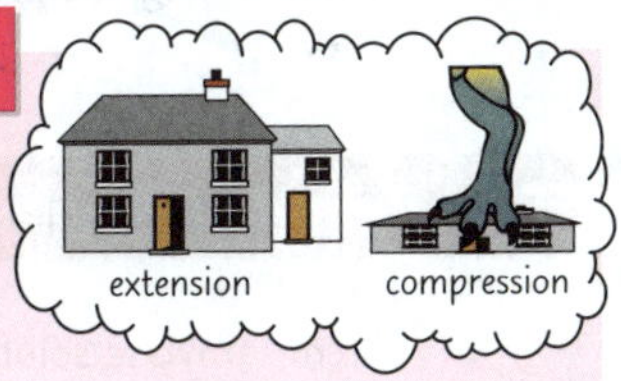

extension

compression

$$F = kx$$

force (N)

spring constant (N/m)

extension or compression (m)

limit of proportionality

Force

Extension

There is a linear relationship between the extension of a stretched spring and the load or force applied.

Force gets too big — relationship between force and extension is now non-linear.

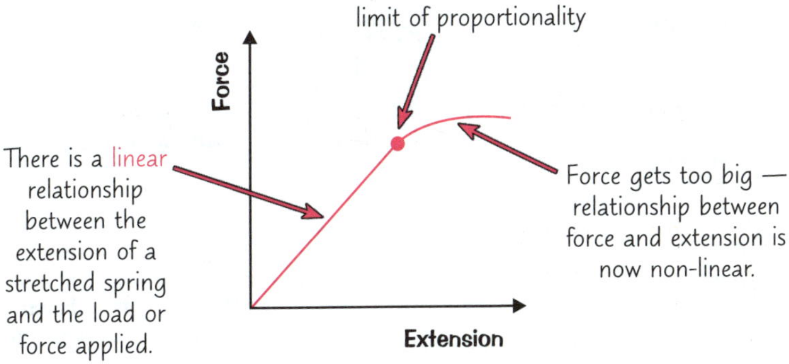

Biology Core Practicals 1

Microscopy

Start with the lowest-powered lens then move the stage up with the coarse adjustment knob.

Look down the eyepiece and adjust the focus with the adjustment knobs (use the coarse one first).

To see the slide with a greater magnification, swap to a higher-powered lens and refocus.

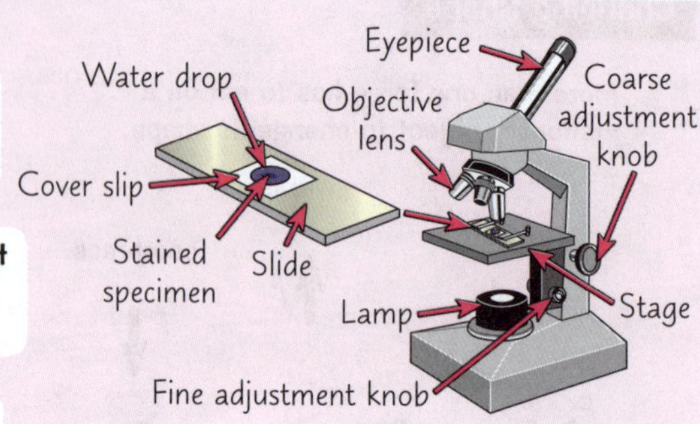

total magnification = eyepiece lens magnification × objective lens magnification

Drawing your observations:

- use a sharp pencil
- draw unbroken lines
- label important features
- include a magnification scale.

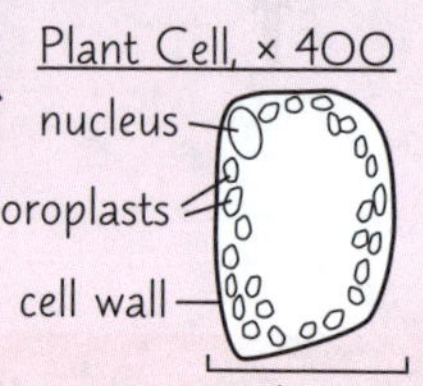

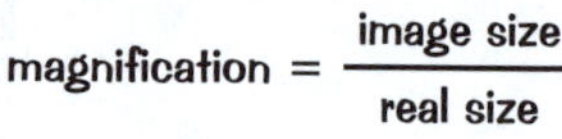

$$\text{magnification} = \frac{\text{image size}}{\text{real size}}$$

Use standard form to write really small numbers. E.g. $0.0045 = 4.5 \times 10^{-3}$

Effect of pH on Amylase Activity

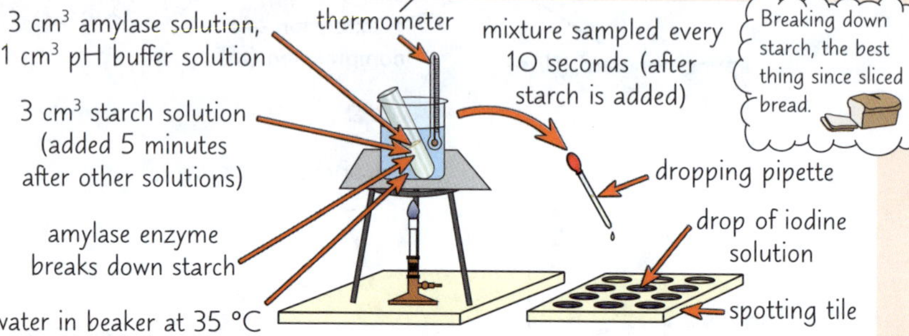

repeat with different pH buffers

record time when iodine solution remains browny-orange after sample is added

pH	time (s)	rate (s^{-1})
5	80	12.5
6	30	33.3
7	50	20.0
8	90	11.1

Independent Variable	Dependent Variable
pH of solution	time taken for amylase to break down starch

$$\text{Rate of reaction } (s^{-1}) = \frac{1000}{\text{time (s)}}$$

time (s) — for reaction to happen

Biology Core Practicals 2

Osmosis

Four steps to investigate osmosis in potatoes:

1. Cut a potato into identical cylinders.
2. Divide the cylinders into groups of three and measure the mass of each group.
3. Prepare beakers containing different concentrations of sucrose solution and one of pure water. Put one group of cylinders in each beaker.

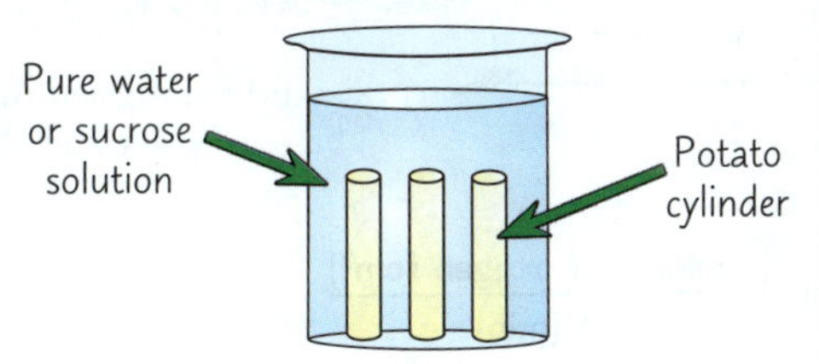
Pure water or sucrose solution
Potato cylinder

4. Leave for at least 40 minutes, then take out the cylinders and dry them gently with a paper towel. Measure the mass of each group again.

$$\text{\% change in mass} = \frac{\text{final mass} - \text{initial mass}}{\text{initial mass}} \times 100$$

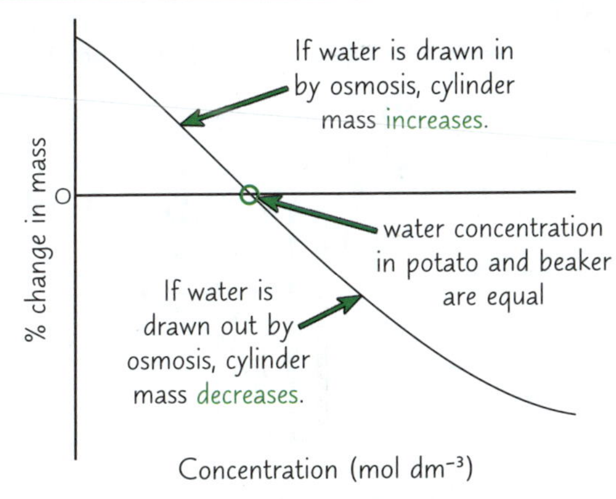
If water is drawn in by osmosis, cylinder mass increases.
0
% change in mass
water concentration in potato and beaker are equal
If water is drawn out by osmosis, cylinder mass decreases.
Concentration (mol dm⁻³)

Independent Variable	Dependent Variable
concentration of sucrose solution	potato cylinder mass

Biology Core Practicals 3

Effect of Light Intensity on Photosynthesis Rate

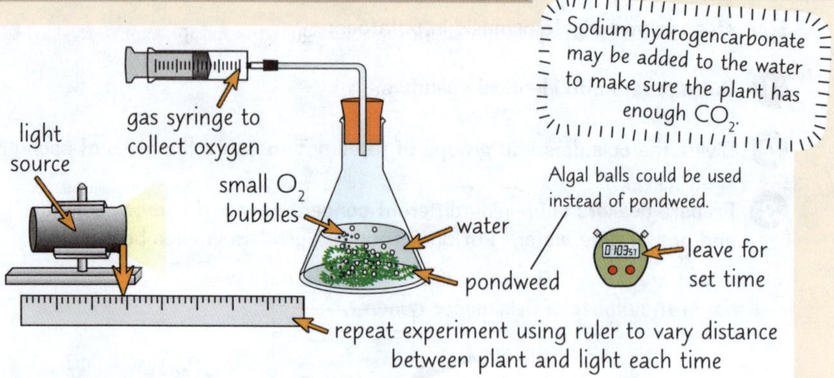

$$\text{Rate (cm}^3\text{ min}^{-1}) = \frac{\text{volume of oxygen (cm}^3)}{\text{time (min)}}$$

Higher light intensity → **Faster rate of photosynthesis** → **Faster rate of O_2 production**

Independent Variable	Dependent Variable
distance from light	volume of O_2

Rate of Respiration

A respirometer can be used to investigate the effect of temperature on respiration rate:

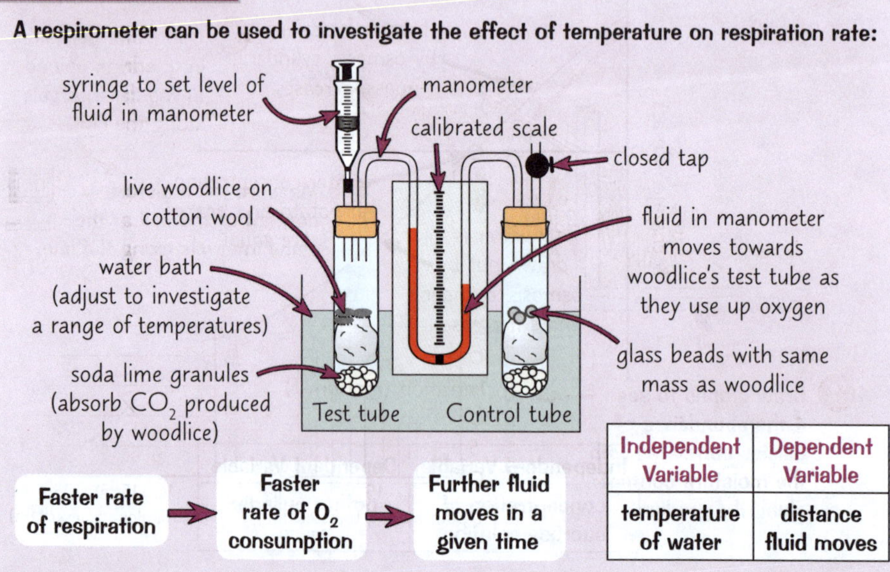

Faster rate of respiration → **Faster rate of O_2 consumption** → **Further fluid moves in a given time**

Independent Variable	Dependent Variable
temperature of water	distance fluid moves

Biology Core Practicals 4

Distribution and Abundance of Organisms

Four steps to estimate population size of small organisms using quadrats:

1. Place a 1 m^2 quadrat at random in a field.

2. Count all the daisies within it.

Watch out for wild quad-rats.

3. Repeat steps 1 and 2 several times and work out the mean number of daisies per quadrat.

$$\text{mean} = \frac{\text{total number of organisms}}{\text{number of quadrats}}$$

E.g. 154 daisies in 7 quadrats means there are 22 daisies per m^2.

4. Multiply the size of the entire area by the number of organisms per m^2.

E.g. if the field has an area of 800 m^2, the population size estimate is 17 600 daisies.

Four steps to find how organisms are distributed along a gradient using a belt transect — e.g. distribution of daisies as you move from a wet environment to a drier one:

1. Mark out a line using a tape measure.
2. Count the daisies in quadrats placed at regular intervals along the line.
3. Measure the moisture content of the soil at the same intervals along the line.

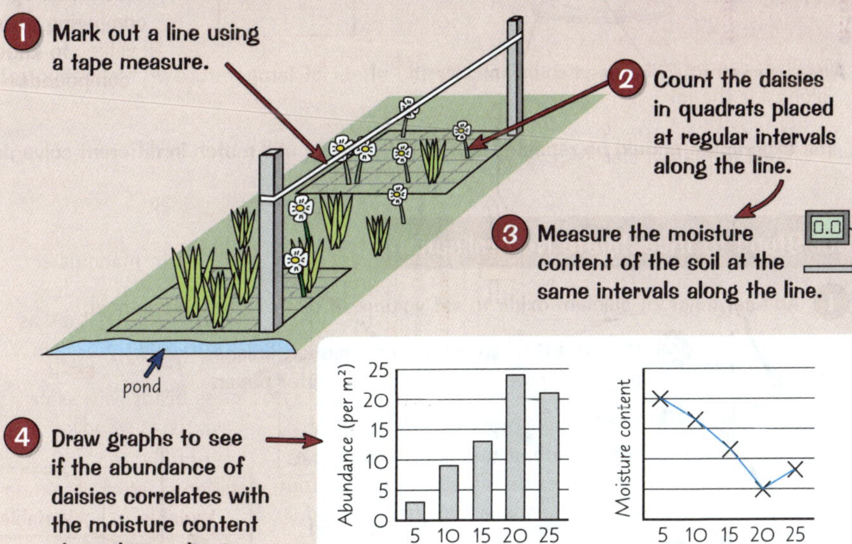

4. Draw graphs to see if the abundance of daisies correlates with the moisture content along the gradient.

Chemistry Core Practicals 1

Two Techniques for Investigating Composition of Inks

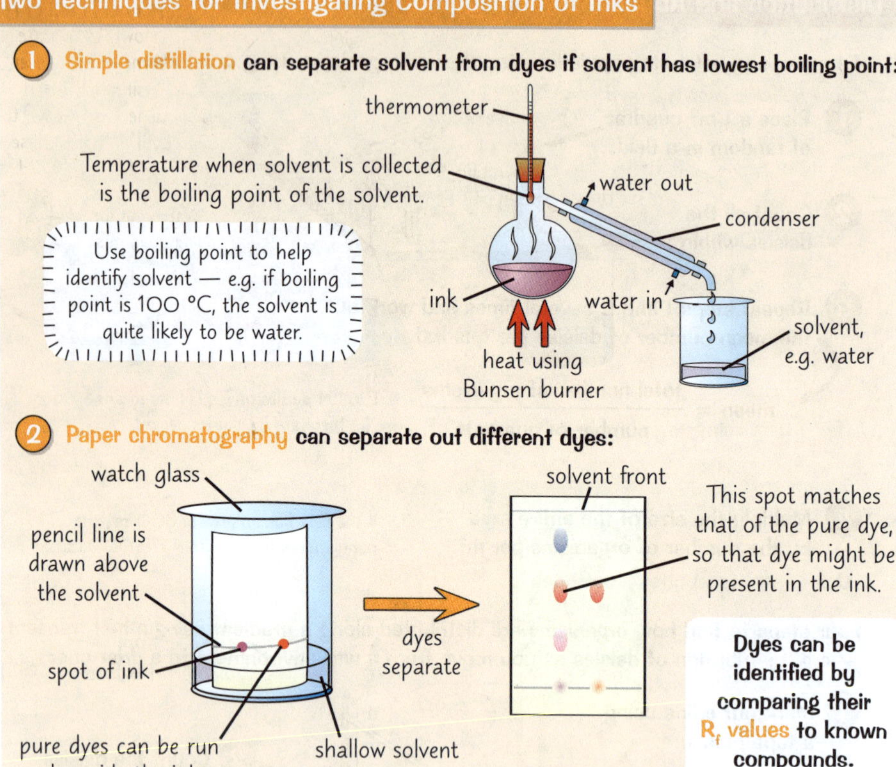
1 Simple distillation can separate solvent from dyes if solvent has lowest boiling point:
thermometer
Temperature when solvent is collected is the boiling point of the solvent.
water out
condenser
Use boiling point to help identify solvent — e.g. if boiling point is 100 °C, the solvent is quite likely to be water.
ink
water in
heat using Bunsen burner
solvent, e.g. water
2 Paper chromatography can separate out different dyes:
watch glass
pencil line is drawn above the solvent
spot of ink
pure dyes can be run alongside the ink
shallow solvent
dyes separate
solvent front
This spot matches that of the pure dye, so that dye might be present in the ink.
Dyes can be identified by comparing their R_f values to known compounds.

The experiment should be repeated to see if the spots still match in different solvents.

Four Steps to Investigate Neutralisation

1. **Add set mass of calcium oxide to set volume of dilute hydrochloric acid.**
2. **Record pH of solution after reaction finishes using pH probe or universal indicator paper.**
3. **Keep adding set mass of calcium oxide and measuring pH until some calcium oxide remains at the bottom — this means all acid has reacted.**
4. **Plot a graph to show how pH changes with mass of base added:**

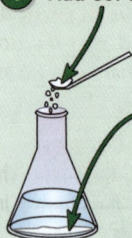

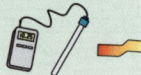

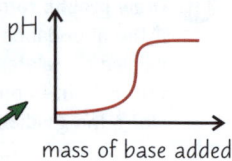

pH
mass of base added

Chemistry Core Practicals 2

Making Copper Sulfate

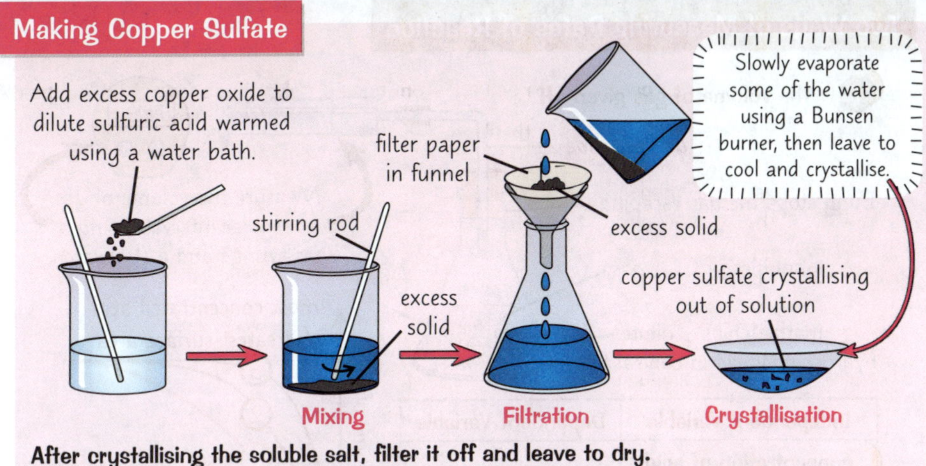
Add excess copper oxide to dilute sulfuric acid warmed using a water bath.
stirring rod
excess solid
Mixing
filter paper in funnel
excess solid
Filtration
Slowly evaporate some of the water using a Bunsen burner, then leave to cool and crystallise.
copper sulfate crystallising out of solution
Crystallisation

After crystallising the soluble salt, filter it off and leave to dry.

Electrolysis of Copper Sulfate Solution

Using inert (graphite) electrodes:

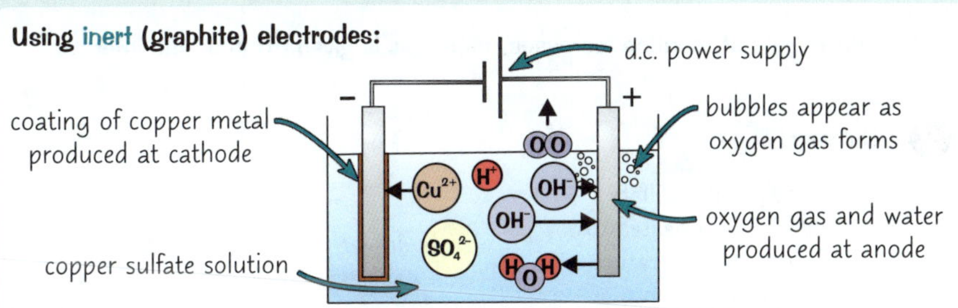
d.c. power supply
coating of copper metal produced at cathode
copper sulfate solution
bubbles appear as oxygen gas forms
oxygen gas and water produced at anode
Cu2+
H+
OH-
SO4 2-
O O
H O H

Using copper electrodes:

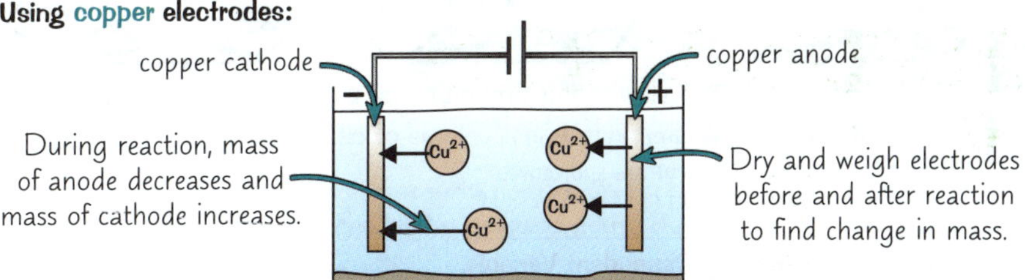
copper cathode
copper anode
During reaction, mass of anode decreases and mass of cathode increases.
Dry and weigh electrodes before and after reaction to find change in mass.
Cu2+

Independent Variable	Dependent Variable
current	change in mass of electrodes

The greater the current, the faster the rate of electrolysis, so the change in mass of the electrodes is greater.

Chemistry Core Practicals 3

Two Ways of Measuring Rates of Reaction

1 The volume of gas given off

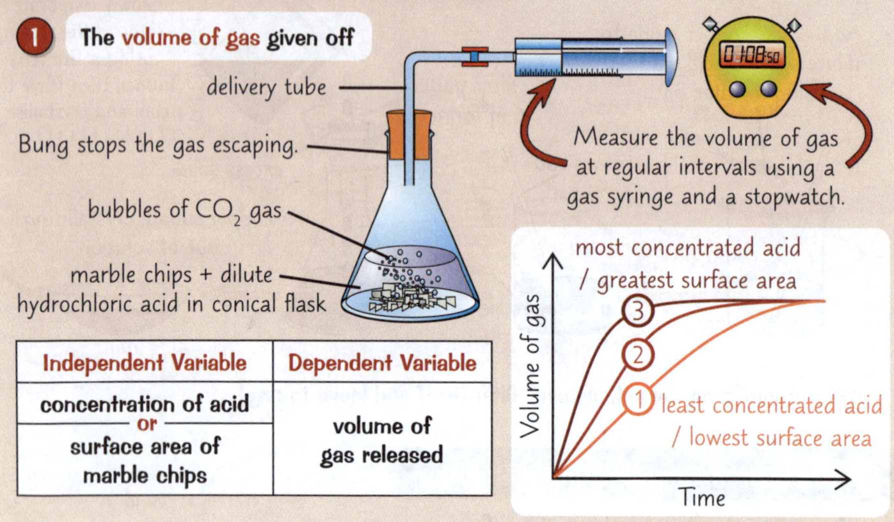

Independent Variable	Dependent Variable
concentration of acid **or** surface area of marble chips	volume of gas released

When rate of reaction increases, more gas is given off in a time interval.

2 Colour change

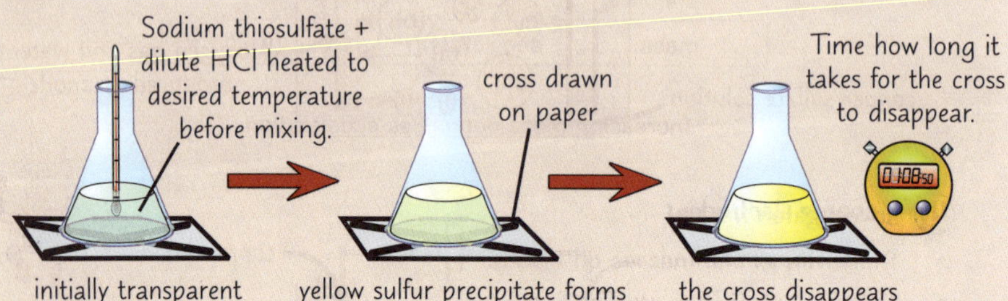

The results of this experiment are subjective.

Independent Variable	Dependent Variable
temperature	time (for cross to disappear)

When rate of reaction increases, the cross disappears faster.

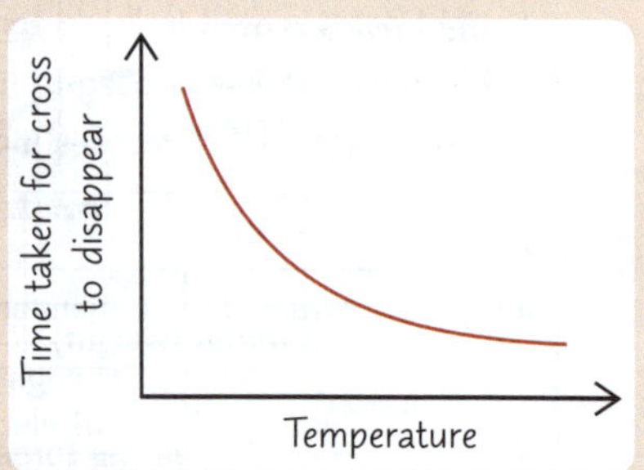

Physics Core Practicals 1

Two Experiments that Test $F = ma$

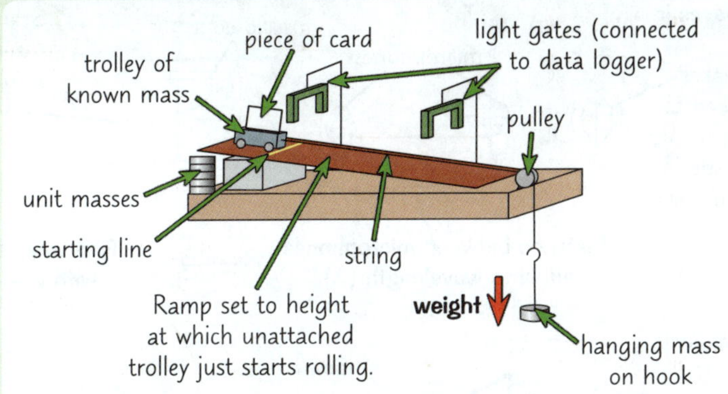

1 Investigate effect of mass

- **Add unit mass to trolley.**
- **Release trolley from starting line.
  Light gates record trolley's acceleration.**
- **Add another mass to trolley and repeat until all masses added.**

Each light gate measures speed and time when trolley passes through. Acceleration is found from change in speed ÷ time taken.

Independent Variable	Dependent Variable	Control Variable
mass	acceleration	force (weight)

Increasing mass decreases acceleration.

2 Investigate effect of force

- **Start with all unit masses on trolley.**
- **Release trolley from starting line.
  Light gates record trolley's acceleration.**
- **Move a mass from trolley to hook and repeat measurement.**
- **Keep going until all masses moved.**

Safety Tip #314 — be careful with hooks...

Independent Variable	Dependent Variable	Control Variable
force (weight)	acceleration	mass

Increasing force applied increases acceleration.

Physics Core Practicals 2

Measuring Properties of Three Different Waves

1 Waves in air.

Speaker attached to signal generator set to specific frequency (f).

microphones

oscilloscope

Start with both microphones next to speaker. Move one microphone until waves line up.

Distance between microphones equal to wavelength (λ). ⟶ Find wave speed with $v = f\lambda$.

2 Waves in a ripple tank.

dipper connected to signal generator

lamp

water

Shadow lines cast by waves. Distance between each shadow line = one wavelength.

screen

ruler

To find frequency (f) — time how long it takes ten shadow lines to pass a point. $f = 10 \div$ time taken.

To find average wavelength (λ) — measure distance between shadow lines that are ten wavelengths apart and divide by ten.

If you're struggling to measure this precisely, take a photo of screen and ruler.

Find wave speed with $v = f\lambda$.

3 Waves in a solid.

clamps

elastic bands

metal rod

Microphone connected to computer to find peak (loudest) frequency.

length

Tap the rod with the hammer to produce a wave.

Peak (loudest) frequency (f) is created by the wave whose wavelength (λ) is twice the length of the rod. ⟶ Find wave speed with $v = f\lambda$.

Core Practicals

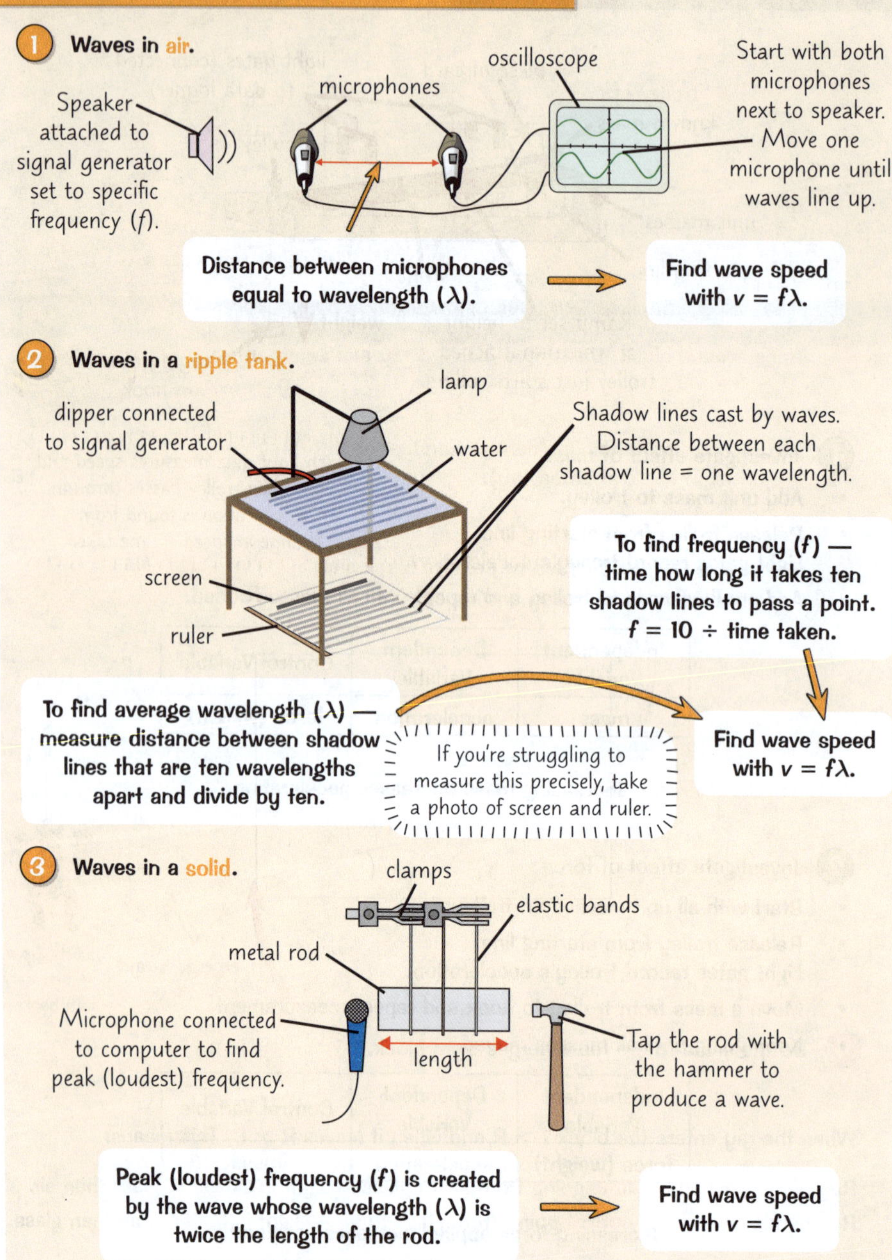

Physics Core Practicals 3

Four Steps to Investigate Refraction

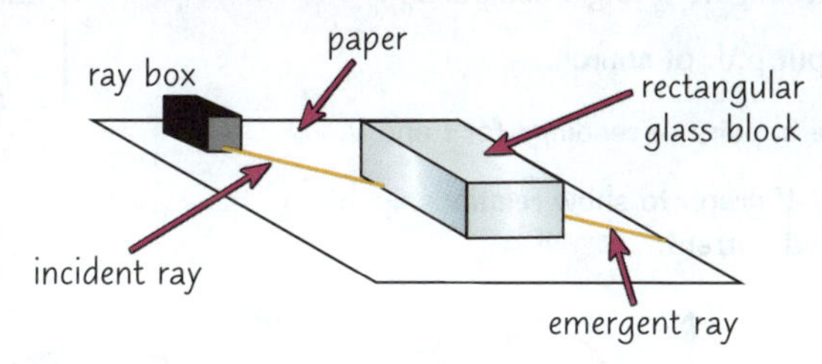

1. Trace around block, then trace incident ray and emergent ray.

Incident Ray: he's here to help.

2. Remove block and join incident ray and emergent ray with straight line (refracted ray).

3. Draw normal where incident ray enters block and measure angle of incidence, *I*, and angle of refraction, *R*.

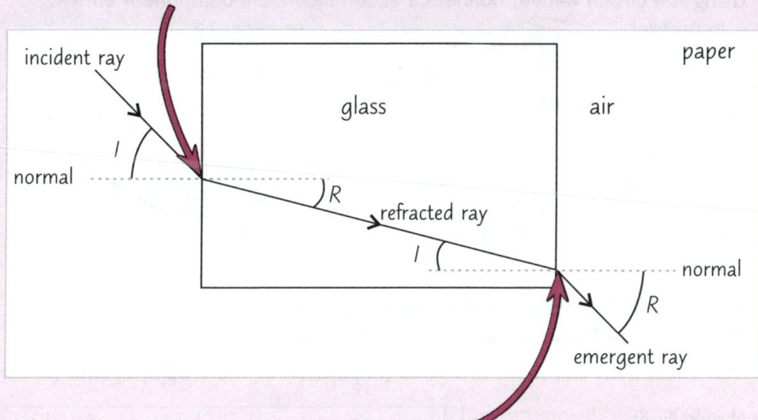

4. Do the same where ray emerges from block.

When the ray enters the block I > R and when it leaves R > I. This means:

Ray bends towards normal going from air to glass — light is slower in glass than air.
Ray bends away from normal going from glass to air — light is faster in air than glass.

Physics Core Practicals 4

Investigating Components and Circuits

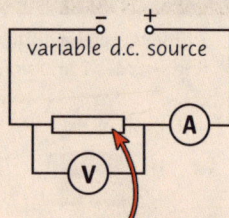

variable d.c. source

Component being investigated — e.g. resistor or filament lamp.

Two steps to investigate a single component:

1. **Vary output p.d. of source.**
2. **Take several pairs of readings for *I* and *V*.**

Plot values on *I-V* graph to show relationship between p.d. and current:

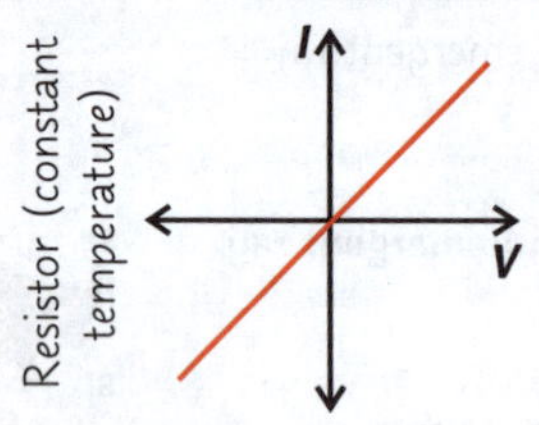

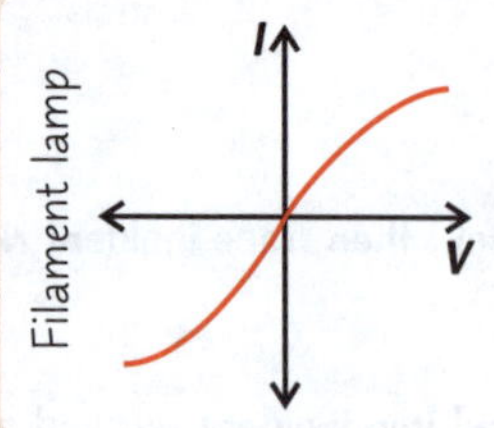

Make sure the circuit doesn't get too hot — disconnect it for a while if it starts to warm up.

Use $V = IR$ to work out the resistance for each pair of measurements to see how it changes along with *I* and *V*.

Investigating series and parallel circuits:

- **Using the circuit above, connect a second identical component either...**
  ...in parallel...

Each branch has a component, an ammeter and a voltmeter.

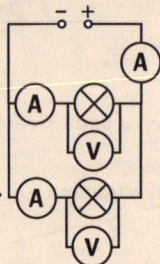

...or in series:

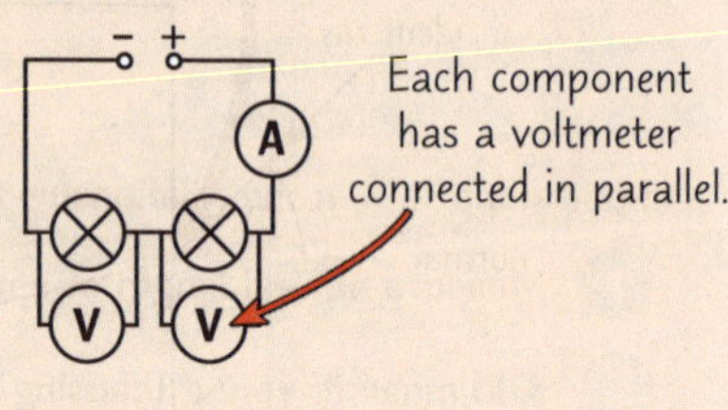

- **Follow steps 1-2 above for the new circuit — see how *I* and *V* change for each component and the circuit as a whole.**
- **You could then add more branches (in parallel) or more components (in series).**

You should find:

	Series	Parallel
Increase source p.d.	Total current through circuit also increases.	
P.d. across each component	Source p.d. shared between components.	Same as source p.d.
Total current through circuit	Same everywhere, decreases as components added.	Equals sum of current in branches, increases as components added.

Physics Core Practicals 5

Determining Density of Solids and Liquids

To measure density of a solid or liquid, find its mass and volume, then use: $\text{density (kg/m}^3\text{)} = \dfrac{\text{mass (kg)}}{\text{volume (m}^3\text{)}}$

Regular solid

Use balance to find mass.

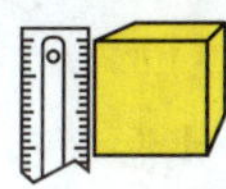

Measure object. Calculate volume using relevant formula for shape.

Irregular solid

mass of object = m_1

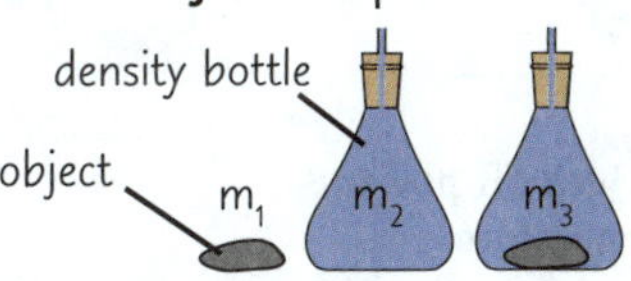

To find volume:

mass of displaced water = $m_1 + m_2 - m_3$

volume of displaced water = mass of displaced water ÷ density of water (known)

volume of object = volume of displaced water

Liquid

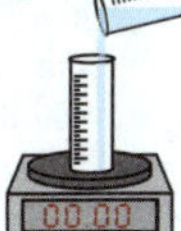

Pour liquid into measuring cylinder on balance set to 0.

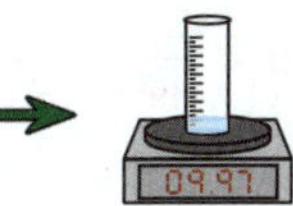

Record mass shown on balance and volume shown on cylinder.

1 ml = 1 cm^3

Investigating Springs

Four steps to find the relationship between force and extension:

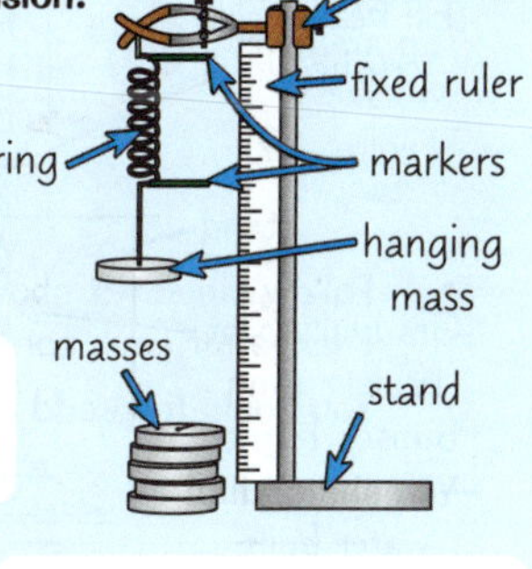

 Measure natural length of spring with ruler.

 Add mass to spring (causing it to extend).

 Calculate force and extension:

Force = weight of masses = mg
(m is total mass on spring, g is gravitational field strength)

Extension = new length – natural length

Independent Variable	force applied to spring
Dependent Variable	extension

 Add another mass and repeat readings. Plot a graph when you have at least 6 pairs of readings.

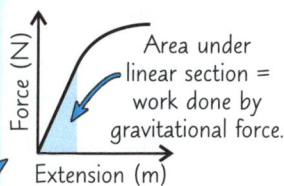

Force (N)
Extension (m)
Area under linear section = work done by gravitational force.

Physics Core Practicals 6

Four Steps to Find the Specific Heat Capacity of Water

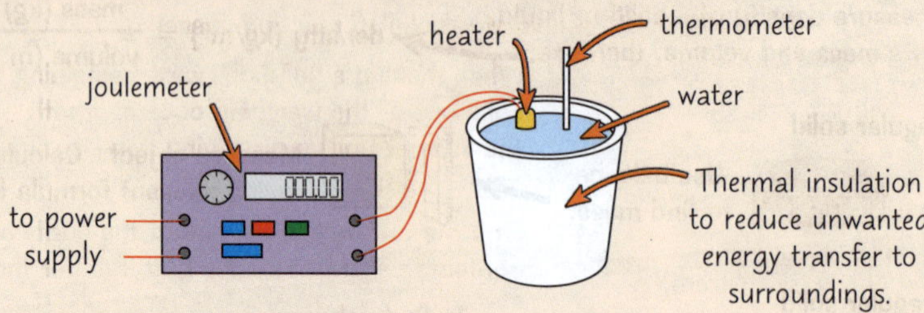
heater
thermometer
joulemeter
water
to power
supply
Thermal insulation to reduce unwanted energy transfer to surroundings.

1. Fill the container with a known mass of water.
2. Measure temperature and turn on power.
3. When temperature has increased e.g. 10 °C, turn off power. Record energy from joulemeter and final temperature.
4. Use your measurements to calculate specific heat capacity:

$$\text{Specific heat capacity} = \frac{\text{energy supplied}}{\text{mass of water} \times \text{temperature change}}$$

You'll be given this equation — you don't have to memorise it.

Investigating Melting Ice

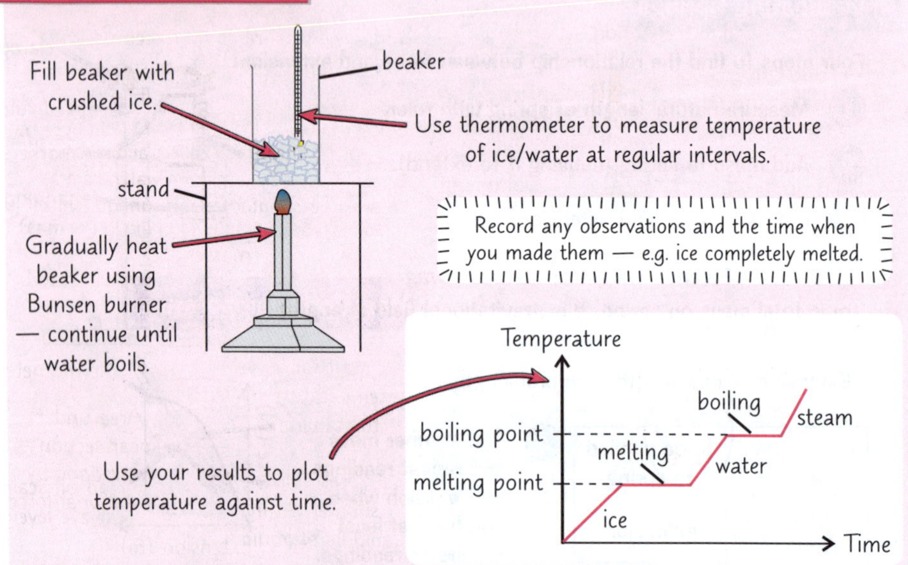
Fill beaker with crushed ice.
beaker
Use thermometer to measure temperature of ice/water at regular intervals.
stand
Gradually heat beaker using Bunsen burner — continue until water boils.
Record any observations and the time when you made them — e.g. ice completely melted.
Use your results to plot temperature against time.
Temperature
boiling point
melting point
boiling
steam
melting
water
ice
Time

Measuring

Measuring Mass

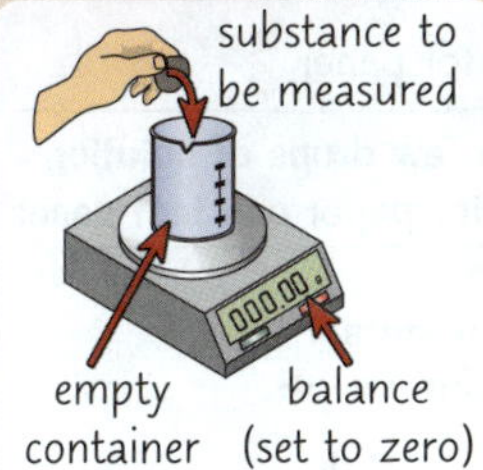

Transferring solid to reaction vessel:

When making a solution, wash remaining solid out of the weighing container with the solvent you're dissolving it in.

or

Find the difference in mass of the container and its contents before and after you transfer the solid.

Measuring Volume

Liquid — three methods

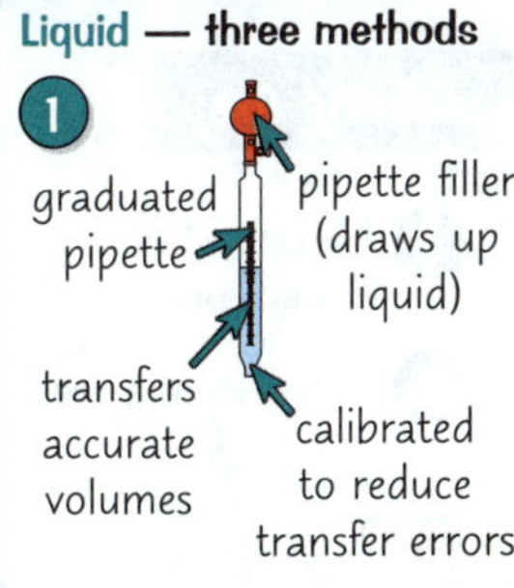

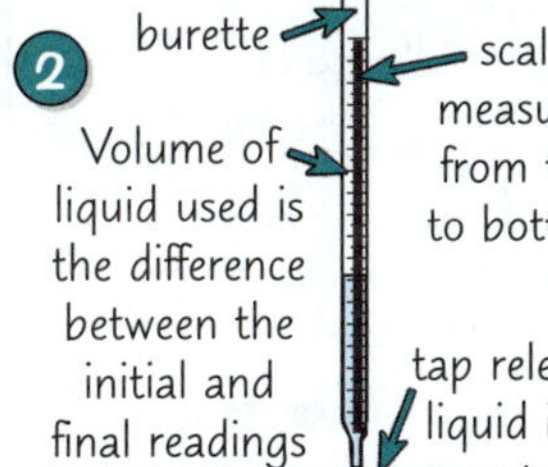

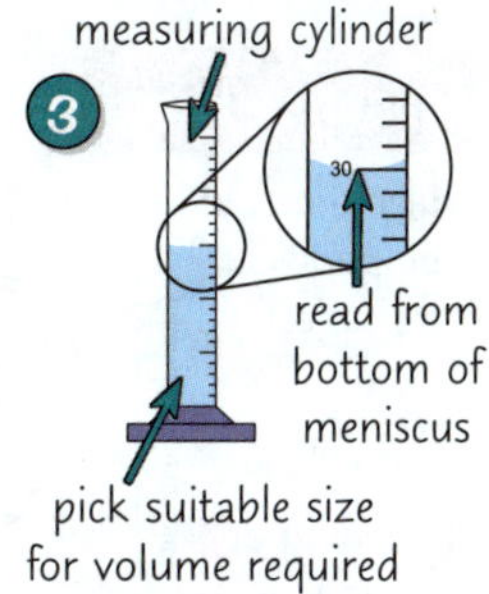

Gas produced in a reaction

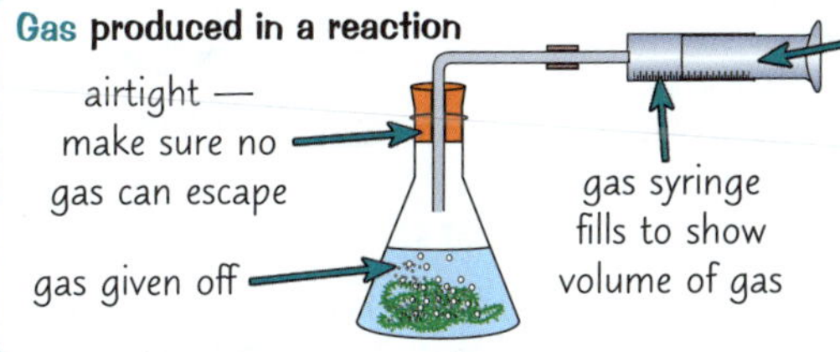

You can also collect and measure gas by displacing water from a filled, upturned measuring cylinder.

Measuring Time

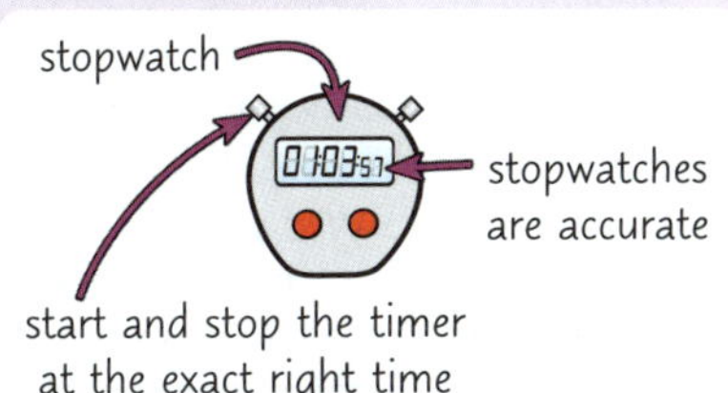

Measuring Temperature

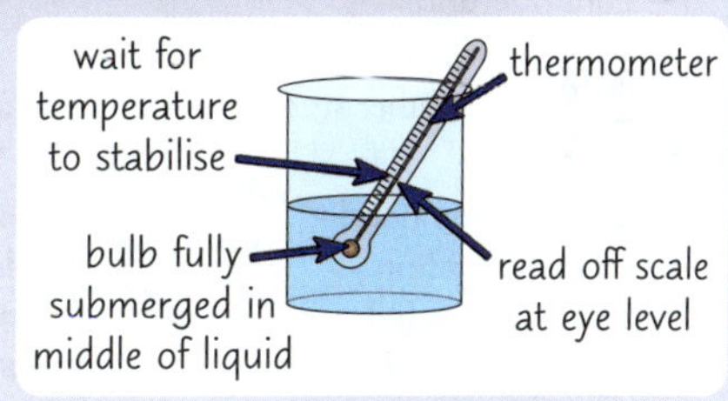

Measuring and Ethics

Measuring pH

Indicator solution	Indicator paper 
Changes colour of whole solution	• For testing a few drops of solution • Damp indicator paper can test gases

UNIVERSAL INDICATOR — mixture of indicators that changes colour gradually as pH changes.

Litmus:

Blue litmus paper turns red in acid.

Red litmus paper turns blue in alkali.

pH probes and **pH meters** give a numerical value for pH.

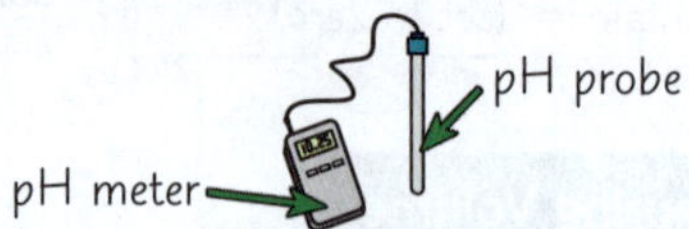

Measuring Length

ruler should be parallel to object

take reading at eye level

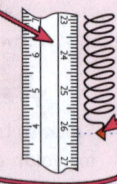

use a marker to make sure you always measure from the same point

Micrometers can measure small distances accurately. Metre rulers and measuring tapes are good for large distances.

If it's tricky to measure length of just one of something (e.g. wavelength of one water wave), measure length of e.g. ten of them and divide to find length of one.

Measuring Area

1. Measure the dimensions.
2. Calculate the area.

- Rectangle: length × height
- Circle: πr^2 (r = radius)
- Triangle: ½ × base × height

Measuring Angles

align angle vertex with protractor's centre point

measure the angle at this line

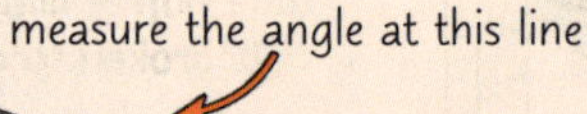

line up baseline of protractor with one angle line

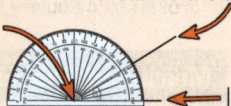

Draw angles with a sharp pencil to reduce errors.

Ethics

Other students shouldn't be forced or pressured into participating in experiments.

Any organisms used in an investigation need to be treated safely and ethically.

Animals kept in the lab should be cared for in a humane way.

Wild animals captured for study should be returned to their original habitat.

Working with Electronics

Voltmeters

Connect a voltmeter in parallel with a device to measure the potential difference across it.

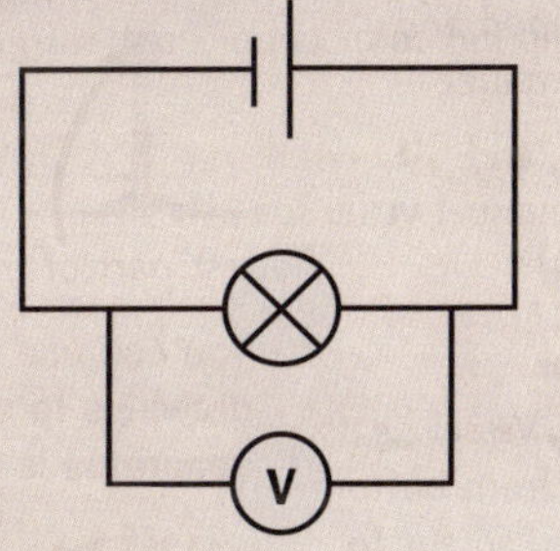

Ammeters

Connect an ammeter in series with a device to measure the current through it.

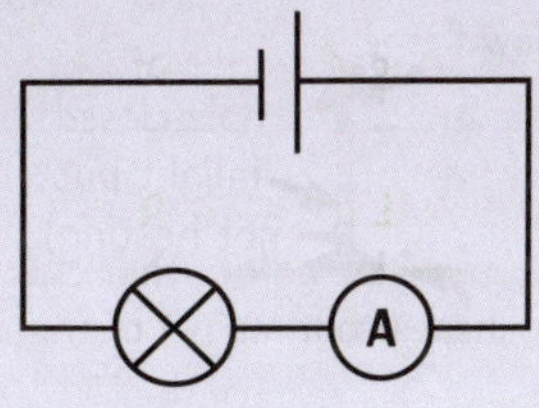

Make sure you use an ammeter or voltmeter with an appropriate scale, e.g. mA, mV.

Multimeters

Multimeters are devices that can measure current, resistance or potential difference.

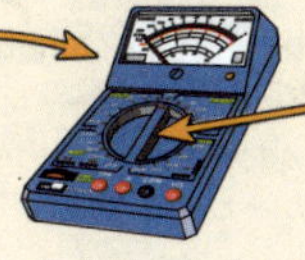

Connect them correctly and turn the dial to select the quantity you want to measure.

Light Gates

Light beam is shone from one side of light gate to detector on other side.

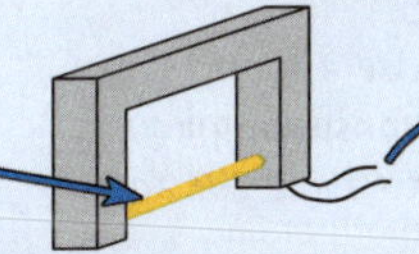

Detector sends information to computer. Computer measures time that light beam is broken by object.

Two quantities measured using light gates:

Speed

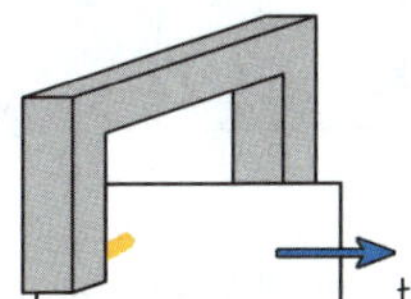

Use object length and time that light beam is broken to calculate speed of object.

object passes through light gate

Acceleration

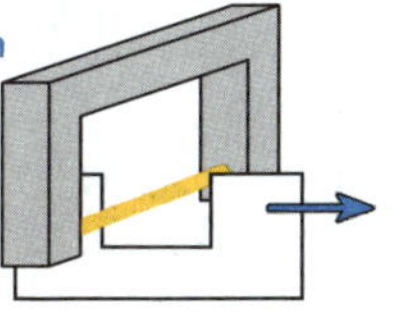

Calculate speed of each part of the object and use this to calculate acceleration.

shape of object means light beam is interrupted twice

Heating and Safety

Heating

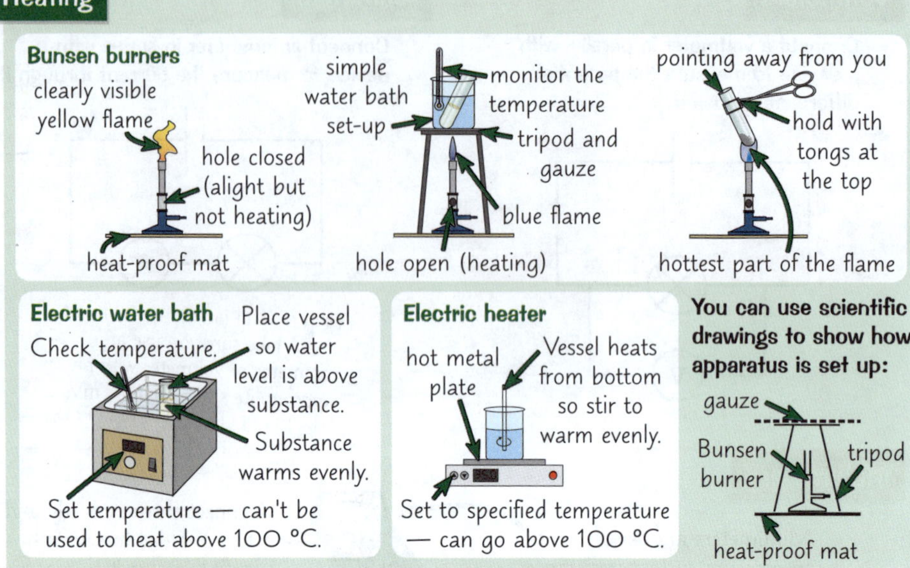
Bunsen burners
clearly visible yellow flame
hole closed (alight but not heating)
heat-proof mat
simple water bath set-up
monitor the temperature
tripod and gauze
blue flame
hole open (heating)
pointing away from you
hold with tongs at the top
hottest part of the flame
Electric water bath
Check temperature.
Place vessel so water level is above substance.
Substance warms evenly.
Set temperature — can't be used to heat above 100 °C.
Electric heater
hot metal plate
Vessel heats from bottom so stir to warm evenly.
Set to specified temperature — can go above 100 °C.
You can use scientific drawings to show how apparatus is set up:
gauze
Bunsen burner
tripod
heat-proof mat

Safety Precautions

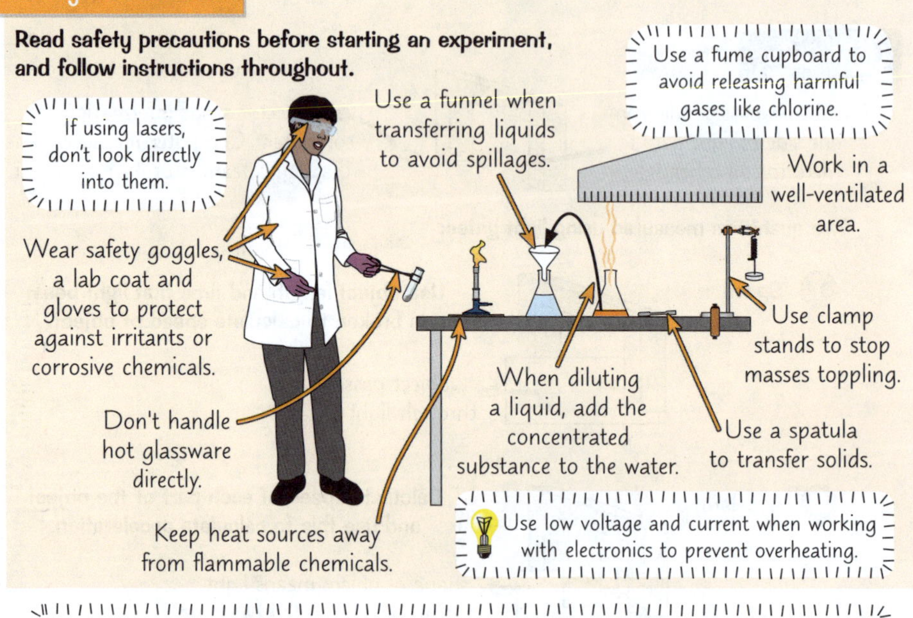
Read safety precautions before starting an experiment, and follow instructions throughout.
If using lasers, don't look directly into them.
Wear safety goggles, a lab coat and gloves to protect against irritants or corrosive chemicals.
Don't handle hot glassware directly.
Keep heat sources away from flammable chemicals.
Use a funnel when transferring liquids to avoid spillages.
Use a fume cupboard to avoid releasing harmful gases like chlorine.
Work in a well-ventilated area.
Use clamp stands to stop masses toppling.
When diluting a liquid, add the concentrated substance to the water.
Use a spatula to transfer solids.
Use low voltage and current when working with electronics to prevent overheating.

Wow! That's the last page of ALL the facts you need to know. Great job making it this far!